Dedication

To the Cabin Kids: Antonia, Gabriella, Zoey, Aryeh, and Tziporah.
And to my grandfather, John Cress.

HOW TO RENT
A PUBLIC CABIN
IN
SOUTHCENTRAL
ALASKA

Access and adventures for hikers,
kayakers, anglers, and more

ANDROMEDA ROMANO-LAX

WILDERNESS PRESS
BERKELEY

FIRST EDITION May 1999

Copyright © 1999, by Andromeda Romano-Lax
All rights reserved

Cover photo by Andromeda Romano-Lax
Original maps by Andromeda Romano-Lax and edited by Jaan Hitt
Design by Jaan Hitt
Cover design by Jaan Hitt

Excerpt from *Going to Extremes* by Joe McGinniss, originally published by Penguin Books, was reprinted with permission from Sterling Lord Literistic, Inc.

"Beyond the Backyard: The Elkutna Traverse" by Peter Porco, was reprinted with permission from "We Alaskans"/ the *Anchorage Daily News*, where it first appeared.

Library of Congress Card Number 99-26307
ISBN 0-89997-227-6

Manufactured in the United States of America

Published by **Wilderness Press**
1200 5th St.
Berkeley, CA 94710
Phone (800) 443-7227
mail@wildernesspress.com

Visit our web site at **www.wildernesspress.com**
Contact us for a free catalog

Front cover photo: *Eagle River Nature Center Cabin*
Back cover photos: *Hook Point Cabin (top); Bald Lake Cabin (bottom)*
Frontispiece: *Upper Paradise Lake Cabin setting*

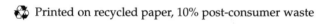 Printed on recycled paper, 10% post-consumer waste

Library of Congress Cataloging-in-Publication Data

Romano-Lax, Andromeda, 1971-
    How to rent a public in southcentral Alaska : access and adventure for hikers, kayakers, anglers and more / Andromeda Romano-Lax. -- 1st ed.
        p.   cm. -- (How to--)
    Includes bibliographical references and index.
    ISBN 0-89997-227-6 (alk. paper)
    1. Camp sites, facilities, etc.--Alaska Guidebooks. 2. Vacation homes--Alaska Guidebooks. 3. Alaska Guidebooks.   I. Title.
II. Title: Rent a public in southcentral Alaska   III. Series: How to-- (Berkeley, Calif.)
GV191.42.A4R66 1999
917.9804'51--DC21   99-26307
                                                                              CIP

TABLE OF CONTENTS

PART II   CABIN-TO-CABIN ON THE KENAI

Popular Peninsula Bays, Lakes, and Trails (Including Seward and Homer)

PART III   THE LONELY COAST
Remote Coastal Cabins From Kodiak To Cordova

ACKNOWLEDGEMENTS

A huge thanks to my sponsor, Lyle Hancock at Folding Kayak Adventures, a Seattle company that provides fantastic service and equipment. (For our adventures, we used a family-sized Feathercraft Klondike, with three seats.)

This book couldn't have been written without the hospitality and friendship of Karen, Stewart and Zoey Ferguson; and Jeff, Christine, Gaby and Antonia Brune. Thanks for the beds, the meals, and the endurance. We know what a mess is left in our wake.

A round of applause for the Alaska Marine Highway System, especially Linda Mickle. I'm also grateful to the companies that supported the research for this book with discounts or other forms of support: Lazy Otter Charters (Whittier), Andrew Airways (Kodiak), and Scenic Mountain Air (Moose Pass). Thanks for a speedy "unplanned charter" and understated professionalism from Trail Ridge Air (Anchorage). A final thanks to a wonderful Cordova establishment, the Northern Nights Inn.

A personal, heartfelt thanks to all the members of the Romano/Zarzana/Lax clan, and especially to those who helped maintain intermittent sanity in our house after Tziporah was born and during the period this book was being written: Catherine Romano, Evelyn Lax, Honoree Romano, and Eliza Romano. Thanks also to Caroline Winnett, who understands the challenges of balancing work and family (in or out of a kayak), to Paul Backhurst for sensitive editing, and to the entire Wilderness Press gang for professional assistance and personal support.

Additional thanks go to Roger MacCampbell, Wayne Biessel, Kevin Murphy, and John Wilber (Alaska State Parks); Cliff Larson, Dana Smyke, and Steve Hennig (U.S. Forest Service); Rick Johnston (Kenai National Wildlife Refuge); George Andrews (National Park Service);Asta Spurgis (Eagle River Nature Center); Craig Medred and Chris Barth (Anchorage Daily News); and Mark Miraglia, Kirk Towner, and Wayne Todd (Mountaineering Club of Alaska). Thanks to fellow travelers and wordsmiths Dean Littlepage, Richard Larson, Ellen Bielawski, Nancy Deschu, William Ashton, and Jim Adams. Gracias, again, to contributors Bill Sherwonit, Peter Porco, Marybeth Holleman, Jeff Brune, and Sherry Simpson. And a belated (and ongoing) thanks to "We Alaskans" editor George Bryson, whose support of my freelancing has made this and other long-term writing projects possible.

Thank you, Aryeh, for being strong and brave; and thank you, Tziporah, for being tolerant and well-tempered. Finally, my eternal gratitude goes to my husband, Brian, who fell into a rushing river, crushed his ribs, inhaled countless bugs, and in 10,000 other ways went beyond the call of duty during research trips for this book: Yes, we'll keep visiting cabins, but no, we won't have to take as many notes.

Hiking, skiing, and snowshoeing in the backcountry, and kayaking on open water entail unavoidable risk that every explorer assumes and must be aware of and respect. The fact that an excursion is described in this book is not a representation that it will be safe for you. Outtings vary greatly in difficulty and in the degree of conditioning and agility one needs to enjoy them safely. Some routes may have changed or conditions may have deteriorated since the descriptions were written. Also trail conditions can change even from day to day, owing to weather and other factors. A trail that is safe on a dry day or for a highly conditioned, agile, properly equipped explorer may be completely unsafe for someone else or unsafe under adverse weather conditions. Just as important, you should always be aware of your own limitations and of conditions existing when and where you are exploring.

You can minimize your risks on the trail by being knowledgeable, prepared and alert. There is not space in this book for a general treatise on safety in the mountains, but there are a number of good books and public courses on the subject and you should take advantage of them to increase your knowledge. If conditions are dangerous, or if you're not prepared to deal with them safely, choose a different excursion! It's better to have wasted a drive than to be the subject of a mountain rescue.

These warnings are not intended to scare you off the trails or off the water. Millions of people have safe and enjoyable wilderness adventures every year. However, one element of the beauty, freedom and excitement of the wilderness is the presence of risks that do not confront us at home. When you venture into the wilds you assume those risks. They can be met safely, but only if you exercise your own independent judgement and common sense.

The author and the publisher of this book disclaim any liability or loss resulting from the use of this book.

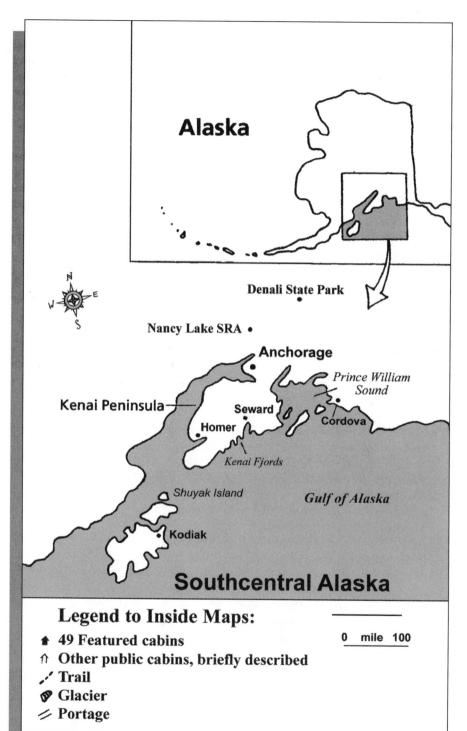

Alaska

Denali State Park

Nancy Lake SRA •

Anchorage

Prince William Sound

Kenai Peninsula —

Seward

Homer

Cordova

Kenai Fjords

Shuyak Island

Gulf of Alaska

Kodiak

Southcentral Alaska

Legend to Inside Maps:

0   mile   100

⬧ **49 Featured cabins**

⇧ **Other public cabins, briefly described**

/⁴ **Trail**

🪨 **Glacier**

⫽ **Portage**

INTRODUCTION

Cabin, my cabin

There was a time I slept in a tent or under the stars. Then I moved to Alaska.

My apologies to outdoors purists, but above the 55th parallel I have come to appreciate shelter. The many reasons constitute a litany that will be repeated throughout this book: bugs, bears, endless sun (or none at all), piercing cold, and rain, rain, rain. Where I was raised, in the Midwest, you laid your sleeping bag on the ground to feel a little closer to the wilderness — a wilderness that was, for the most part, entirely imagined. In Alaska, you close the door to keep real wilderness from taking you in its jaws and never letting go.

Okay, I'm exaggerating... but only a little. There's a place for camping in this superlative state, too. But there's a darn good reason that public cabin construction is booming. Even private organizations are getting in on the act. Friends of Eagle River Nature Center opened a cabin in Chugach State Park in 1998. More volunteer-built cabins on public lands are slated to open over the next few years. The total number of public cabins in Southcentral Alaska — 105 at this writing — will continue to climb.

I fantasized for years about building and owning the perfect cabin, tucked into the woods, overlooking a glassy lake or slim crescent of wave-battered beach. Then I realized three things. I'd never find a setting as perfect as the ones already found in Alaska's federal forests and state and national parks (and by extension, already owned by me, the taxpayer). I'd never build one as cheaply as I can rent. And I'd rather spend less time hammering, and more time biking, hiking, sea kayaking, fishing, and exploring the great lands in which Alaska's public cabins are situated.

When people used to talk about Southcentral Alaska's public cabins, they were referring to the 42 Forest Service cabins, most of which were built in the late 1960s and the 1970s. (At $2 a night when the fee system was first implemented, the cabins were popular even then.) But a renaissance is underway. The newest and most attractive cabins in the state are being built or renovated by Alaska State Parks. About half of the 49 featured cabins in this book weren't available to the public ten years ago. Since 1988, the number of cabins at Nancy Lake State Recreation Area, near Willow, has increased from five to 13. Just in the last few years, gorgeous new coastal cabins — lighter, brighter and more lovingly crafted than many of the old public-use cabins — have been constructed near Homer, Seward, and Valdez with funds from the Exxon Valdez oil-spill settlement.

The new coastal cabins are one example of an environmental tragedy being parlayed into a recreational opportunity, but there's a second element to the irony. Most of the newest public cabins are constructed of spruce — an attractive use for the light-colored wood now in abundance, due to harvesting of spruce bark beetle-killed trees in this region.

If you're from outside of Alaska (or simply "Outside," as we say here), you've stumbled upon one of our state's greatest bargains and best-kept secrets. Some of these recently constructed State Park cabins have been discovered by local enthusiasts and are booked weeks or months in advance. Others are so new that they've barely been visited as of this writing. The newest cabins still smell of freshly milled wood. Their honey-colored log walls glow. The pages of their visitor logs wait, blank and fresh, for tales of fish caught, whales spotted, peaks summited, sunset paddles enjoyed.

For $25 to $50 a night — one-third to one-half the cost of a typical Alaska hotel or B&B — today's cabins allow recreationists to extend their reach not only farther into the wilderness but farther into the year as well. With roof, walls, and wood or oil stove waiting at day's end, cabin-to-cabin traverses or week-long single-cabin retreats become possible, even in the depths of winter. Some of my favorite trips — like a January ski trip to the cabin at Exit Glacier near Seward, when the mercury measured ten below zero — wouldn't have been possible without the public-cabin system. Other trips simply wouldn't have been as enjoyable.

Many Alaskans' idea of the perfect vacation is to be dropped off at a remote cabin with enough food and diversion to last until their permit expires — usually three or seven days, maximum. With a plane, boat, or snowmachine to do the hauling, people transport their own gourmet-cooking supplies, kids and pets, kayaks and snowshoes, enough fishing tackle to outfit an offshore fleet, and games and books. They move in.

Schrode Lake and Cabin

They practically homestead. Who cares that there is no plumbing? People create their own sense of luxury. The most common visitor-log comment, second to wildlife sighted, is the story of a perfect cabin meal, crafted with diligence and enjoyed all the more for its rustic setting.

Some of the older structures are simple, even crude. But the surroundings are priceless. Most public cabins are located on pristine lakes and streams, in scenic alpine valleys, or on the shores of island-studded lagoons. Instead of a mint on your pillow, there are unnamed peaks (or famous ones, like Denali) out your window. Instead of maid service, there are visits by moose and Steller's jays and salmon that thrash their way practically to your door.

Few private developers could afford to build on such prime pieces of real estate. If they did, chances are they'd build with the masses in mind, eliminating the most valuable aspect of remotely situated public cabins: privacy. Increasingly, newer cabins are being built in clusters of two or three, but usually there is just one — and absolutely nothing else for miles around. Unlike a campground, which must be shared, an Alaska public cabin can be hogged. Once you have a permit in hand, no one will else may rightfully occupy your cabin, even if you are a party of one and the cabin is large enough to hold eight. This makes Alaska cabins different from some public-use cabins, shelters, and lodges in other states.

This book was written to help you take advantage of a great deal, to find your own perfect refuge or retreat, to have successful outdoor experiences in a wild (and often wet) land where the occasional roof over your head and wood stove blazing at your back are greatly appreciated. It's written not just as a where-to, how-to guidebook, but as an adventure book, spliced with essays and sidebars that, hopefully, will inspire you to get planning and packing.

I am indebted to the contributors who added their essays to this project. Reading them, you'll get not only a mental image of cabin areas, but a sense of place from authors who know Alaska well. These writers spare chamber-of-commerce-style gloss in favor of honest reporting and reflection. Peter Porco admits some trepidation in skiing the Eklutna Traverse, a backyard jaunt for people who spend a lot of time on glaciers, and a terrifying hut-to-hut expedition for the rest of us. Bill Sherwonit describes a fantastic wildlife-watching trip in the Kenai Fjords, but he doesn't forget to mention the biting flies, the wind, and the waves. In time for the Exxon Valdez disaster's 10th anniversary, Marybeth Holleman writes about the lingering traces (and lasting psychic effects) of the oil spill as observed from Green Island, site of a Forest Service cabin. Short pieces by Jeff Brune and Sherry Simpson, and a brief book excerpt from Joe McGinniss, add humor — always appreciated, sometimes desperately needed — to the subject of cabin trips.

Alaska's public cabins are valuable resources in and of themselves. But what they offer, in addition to basic shelter, is possibility: the chance to enjoy once-in-lifetime experiences, buoyed by the promise of warmth and safety at night's end.

Like kayaking in the land of Kodiak bears. Hiking historic gold rush trails. Fishing for days on end, without tangling lines and jostling with crowds. Introducing family and friends to a weekend without

Prince William Sound from Paulson Bay

watches or phones. Whale-watching. Beachcombing. Discovering silence. Learning how to split wood. Or just learning how to be alone in one of the most beautiful places in the world.

How to use this book and other sources of cabin information

Things change. All guidebooks begin with that warning, but I beseech you to pay attention this time around. I was astounded how quickly information became outdated during the year this book was being written. New cabins are being added every summer. At a slower rate, some cabins are no longer being offered for rent. The U.S. Forest Service has changed its reservation system and rental rates several times in recent years, most recently in October 1998. Charter operations come and go. Prices climb.

During this renaissance period in the short history of Alaska public cabins, most changes are for the better: furnishings added, trails improved, new wood stoves installed, and accessibility improved. In this book, I have described the cabins in detail, but don't be surprised if a few details have been modified over time.

There are some things I haven't described — such as whether a particular saw, axe, or lantern is still available at a cabin, because theft is common and you simply can't bet on moveable objects being there the next time around. To be safe, you must plan your trip as if you're going backpacking, bringing all that you need to survive a night outdoors (see also "What to expect inside the cabins" and "What to bring..." below).

In researching this book, my fellow contributors and I personally visited all of the book's 49 featured cabins. (Brian Lax and I visited 39; Brian and Stewart Ferguson visited another eight; and two other contributors, Bill Sherwonit and Marybeth Holleman, visited and wrote about one each.) Among these highlighted cabins are all of the more accessible and most of the more popular structures available to the public in Southcentral Alaska, a triangle-shaped region bordered by Kodiak Island in the west, Denali State Park on the north, and Cordova on the east. You can find cabin listings by consulting the "Table of Contents," the "Index," or by flipping through the guide for its handy, regional tabs.

The cabin listings are arranged as follows. Each cabin's name is followed by the park or forest where the cabin is found (for example, Shuyak Island State Park), followed by the land manager or organization that rents out the cabin (in this example, Alaska State Parks). Next, I've provided a "Snapshot" description, plus details like "View and surroundings" to let you know what you'll see outside your cabin window, and "Recreation" to let you know popular activities for each cabin area.

Under "Map," I've named the commercial Trails Illustrated™

map (where applicable) and relevant USGS quadrangle map (at scale 1:63,360) for each cabin. You'll need at least one of them to find your way to and around a cabin area — especially if you get lost or decide to wander farther afield, away from the main cabin-access trail. This book provides sketched maps of cabin locations, and most land agencies will include similar locator maps (excellent in some cases, poorly photocopied or crudely drawn in others) with your proof of reservation, but a USGS or Trails Illustrated™ map is still essential.

The Trails Illustrated™/National Geographic maps (see Appendix 2 for ordering information) are part of an excellent, frequently updated series that covers most of the the Kenai Peninsula, Western and Eastern Prince William Sound, and Kenai Fjords/Seward area, with a new map covering Kachemak Bay State Park to be published in 1999. These maps, at a scale of 1:105,600, cover more territory than the USGS maps, so you'll need only one for most trips. The Trails Illustrated™ maps are also waterproof and tearproof. Most of the State Park, Forest Service, and National Park cabins are marked on these maps. At this scale, however, you sacrifice some topographical details (closest to the cabins, the cabin symbols themselves sit like elephants, covering a one-quarter square-mile section of map).

The USGS maps cover some areas that Trails Illustrated™ maps don't — like Shuyak Island State Park and areas north of the Kenai Peninsula. They also have finer topographical detail. Often, however, they were surveyed in the 1970s and are now 20 or more years out-of-date. In most cases, only the older Forest Service cabins appear on the USGS maps. Most State Park and National Park cabins, and many newer trails and even roads don't appear on the USGS maps.

All but one or two Kenai National Wildlife Refuge cabins don't appear on any map. These require some work. Start with a USGS quadrangle. By consulting the appropriate township, range, and section specified under "Map Location" in the Refuge cabin listings, you can narrow cabin locations to a one-quarter-square-mile area, but precise coordinates aren't given and often, the cabins themselves are hidden from view.

In all cases, be prepared to do some orienteering with map and compass, especially in snowy or foggy conditions, or if you wander off-trail. While most cabins located on hiking trails or along the coast are easily spotted, be prepared to find your way using landmarks and the directions in this book. Be aware that magnetic declination (variance from true north indicated by compass) is significant this far north. Check your map for declination, know how to use a compass, and set yours appropriately.

Many guidebooks provide a laundry list of wildlife generally known to reside in the vicinity. I've tried to be more specific by first naming under the heading "Wildlife sightings" animals that my family, friends, and I saw from each cabin, plus ones sighted *repeatedly* by other cabin visitors. That way, if spotting eagles, porcupines, or bears is your goal, you can find more easily the right cabin to visit. (No guarantees, of course.) This is followed by a more generic, brief list of other wildlife in the area.

Under the heading "Getting there," I've included basic access information, but for even more information (especially on major trails, like the Resurrection Pass Trail) I recommend you pair this book with a good hiking guidebook (see Appendix 3) as well as topographical maps.

You may notice that the cabin-listings format varies slightly throughout the book. Where two or three similar cabins are clustered within a mile or two of each other, especially when they're located on the same body of water, I've described them as a unit. Where the cabins are part of a trail system, but still far apart and with significant differences between them, I've described them singly.

Just to let you know the diverse options awaiting you, I've provided capsule summaries of an extra 56 cabins and huts that I researched but didn't personally visit, using the best available information from land agencies and interviews with rangers. Consult these listings, but please also contact the appropriate land agencies for more details.

I would have liked to visit every single one of the 105 Southcentral Alaska public cabins and huts, but the cost of transportation in Alaska precluded it. (An air charter to some of the more remote cabins can cost $1,000 or more.) If, however, you and 50,000 friends each buy this book, I promise to return to the trail, with pleasure, and make the second edition of this book even more comprehensive. Do you have any corrections, additions, or comments to make? Or just a good public-cabin story to share? I'd love to hear them. They will be used to improve later editions. Please write to me in care of my publisher.

About The Cabins

Cabin architecture

Public cabins are simple structures that rely on their majestic surroundings to impart ambience. Most Forest Service cabins are either Pan Abode or A-frame cabins. "Pan Abode" describes a specific type of square, fitted logs (think aged Lincoln Logs with a coat of dark brown paint). The A-frame Forest Service cabins are wooden frames clad in wood siding, with lofts. The lofts are reached by ladder and are often the warmest and most pleasant part of the cabins. The Forest Service cabins tend to be older and darker inside, usually with small windows.

Most State Park cabins are also constructed of milled, square, fitted logs — usually light-colored spruce. The cabins at Shuyak Island State Park are cedar. In general, the State Park cabins look less utilitarian than the Forest Service cabins. Windows tend to be bigger, and porches larger. An exception is the cabins at Nancy Lake State Recreation Area, most of which are simple, wooden-frame structures that were purchased from private owners and converted for public use. The National Park Service cabins in Kenai Fjords and at Exit Glacier are also wooden-frame, but they are in great shape, and constructed of unpainted, light-colored wood.

There are a few truly rustic, natural log cabins in Southcentral Alaska — the kind one imagines a homesteader crafting without the help of a kit. McKinley Trail Cabin, near Cordova, is constructed of round logs, chinked with moss. Byers Lake #1 Cabin, in Denali State Park, is an old visitor center with a lovely sod roof that sprouts highbush cranberries in summer. The Upper Russian Lake Cabin, on the Russian Lakes Trail (Kenai Peninsula) is also constructed of dark, round logs; it's old and weathered, but appealing in its authenticity. The James Lake Cabin in

Nancy Lake State Recreation Area is constructed of round, minimally finished logs, as is the new Eagle River Nature Center Cabin.

Cabin rules and etiquette

Cabin-users must have a reservation permit or be liable to imprisonment and fines up to $500. Outfitters and other commercial users, and users less than 18 years old, are not allowed to rent cabins. For all the fee cabins in this book, a rental day begins at noon and ends at noon of the next day. Even in remote locations, don't be surprised if someone shows up suddenly, ready to take up residence at just a few minutes past twelve o'clock. Similarly, if you're squatting in a cabin (an illegal activity,

"Lincoln Logs" with handcrafted chair

as stated above) be aware that you're not home-free if no fellow cabin-users arrive in the afternoon or evening. Contrary to one popular notion, there is no time after which a user's reservation is forfeited. (Weary backpackers may show up after midnight with a permit, and they will ask you to leave.)

In nearly all cases, camping next to a cabin is not allowed. Pets are allowed, as long as they're under control and on a leash. Sled dogs and horses must be tied within 100 feet of a cabin. There are fantastic opportunities for fishing and hunting near many of the cabins. Please contact Alaska Department of Fish and Game (see Appendix 1) for the latest information on licenses and regulations.

Gather only dead-and-down wood. Firewood is often scarce near cabins, so Alaska State Parks and the Forest Service ask you to use wood in stoves, and not in outdoor campfires. Don't use driftwood in wood stoves, because the salt corrodes them and increases fire hazards. When you leave, turn off propane or oil (where applicable), close windows, doors and shutters, and pack out your garbage.

What to expect inside the cabins

The cabins are one-room structures with few added features. No electricity. No plumbing. No running water. No automatic heat or light. No bedding. No mattresses. No window coverings. Except where it is

explicitly stated in cabin descriptions, fire wood and/or stove oil is not included. Occasionally, there are a few odd pots and pans (plus some salt, bug spray, and maybe a paperback novel) left by previous visitors, but generally, kitchen supplies are not part of the package. For a handful of exceptions to all these statements, see individual cabin descriptions.

Floors are usually plywood. Outhouses are near all the cabins. Often, there are picnic tables and fire rings outside. (Although sometimes, the picnic tables disappear into the fire rings.) Few cabins have any kind of locking mechanism, and few need one. If your cabin is in a higher-traffic area, bring your valuables (camera, wallet) with you on forays outside the cabin. In general, security is not a problem.

Water is typically either gathered from a lake or creek less than 500 feet from the cabin, or melted from snow, and then purified by filtering or boiling for five minutes. No matter how remote the cabin, do not drink the water directly, since giardia is common throughout Alaska. If you suspect your water source to be glacial, choose the boiling method, since filters will clog after just a few uses.

All the cabins have wooden bunks. A typical room layout might have bunks for six, meaning two sets of bunk beds that each sleep two on the bottom, and one on top. The upper bunks usually aren't railed, so you'll have to watch young children carefully. Often, bottom bunks double as benches on either side of a table, or as the only casual seating in the room. Official cabin descriptions occasionally stretch the truth. A wooden ledge fronting a window — wide and long enough for a 3-year-old to sleep on, say — is described as a bunk. In the case of A-frames, sloping walls may prevent two adults from sleeping on a full-sized bottom bunk. The featured cabin listings in this guide specify how many people might

Upper Russian Lake Cabin interior

be comfortable in a cabin — not just how many are allowed — for just these reasons. If you're not beanpole-thin, there's always the floor.

Most cabins have wood or oil stoves. As stated above, you must bring your own stove oil in most cases, or bring or gather your own dead-and-down wood (not always plentiful, especially in winter, and not always dry). Cutting live trees or standing dead trees is strictly prohibited. Some cabins, especially those maintained by the Forest Service, have tools for sawing and splitting wood, but because these tools are sometimes missing, you should bring your own small axe, hatchet, or folding saw, or be prepared to be comfortable without heat. Some wood stoves work efficiently, converting a wintry room into a sauna. A few warm the room minimally — and that's in summer. Be prepared with extra clothing and properly rated sleeping bags. In nearly all cases, the stoves are intended for heat, not cooking. Kettles can be set on top of flat-topped stoves (not the round ones), but you must bring a camping stove, just to be safe.

Most cabins have a visitor log, a font of local knowledge that I rush to consult as soon as I've set down my backpack. Sherry Simpson's short essay in this chapter was inspired by the logs at Bureau of Land Management cabins near her hometown of Fairbanks, just north of the area covered by this book. South of Fairbanks, we don't have BLM cabins, but Forest Service, State Park and National Park cabin logs have the same flavor (powdered cheddar, in Sherry's world).

Bad Poetry and Other Cabin Pastimes: Visitor Logs
by Sherry Simpson

This is the time of year when many people head outdoors and kill things to eat. My husband and I go outdoors to eat things that could kill us.

Nothing gives us that special rush of living on the edge like renting a Bureau of Land Management recreational cabin and spending the weekend dining on Pringles™, boxed macaroni and cheese, and reasonable-facsimile-brand ham.

Gastronomic punishment isn't why we like these cabins, of course. We like the eight-mile hike into the fringe of the White Mountains, the view from Lee's Cabin, the solitude. We like the way Bureau of Land Management is spending our tax dollars. But mostly we like reading the cabin logs.

BLM encourages public users to jot down useful information in these journals, such as the number of people in the party, mode of transportation, and trail conditions. Instead they get personal confessions, treatises on the value of wilderness, philosophies of life, pointless arguments, and bad poetry. Anyone who wants to peer into the soul of Alaska should browse through these collections.

The logs represent Alaskans of every flavor and fitness level: skijorers (skiers pulled by dogs) and hikers, snowmachiners and dog mushers, bachelor parties and Boy Scouts. Some people have never been out in the northern semiwilds before, and so they use a lot of exclamation points. Others are cool as can be: "Skied in, took a nap, skied back," wrote one overachiever. Outhouse conditions, aurora sightings, dinner menus: No detail is too minor to describe. What varies is the attitude.

Visitor Log from Bald Lake Cabin

Most people thank BLM — just about the only time the agency gets stroked in these parts. But there's always some background mewling. One person wrote three pages that included an entreaty to BLM to add another window so people could sit at the table and gaze at the view while eating. "How do other folks feel on this issue?" asked this perhaps too-civic-minded woman. The only response: "Rocket Science says: Move the table!"

The civic-minded entry also lectured fellow users on the importance of replacing firewood, not leaving food for voles and so on, each suggestion preceded by the statement, "I would encourage people to...." To which yet another critic scribbled, "You would probably want to change heaven if you got there!"

People not only list the other people in their group, they name their dogs — no matter how many (Canvas, Fish, Pavlov, Betsy, Grubby, Tonsil, Dizzy, etc.). Sometimes they draw a team's configuration in the traces.

There's no sense going out in the woods if you can't pick a fight. Running debates erupt occasionally on the usual topics: "Should snowmachines and ATVs be allowed on the trails?" "Are BLM employees taking advantage of their position to hog the cabin?" People send friendly messages to each other, too, saying "hi" to friends, or trading helpful hints: "Watch out for the lantern." "Someone should take a frying pan to Cache Mountain Cabin." "Whatever you do, don't stoke the stove at night or you'll turn those sleeping in the loft into human jerky."

One guy reports finding a questionable [and potentially critter-attracting] use for the rancid margarine others have complained about: "It's great for oiling the door hinges." Another explains how he fixed up the mongrel deck of cards by drawing in extra hearts and weeding out duplicates. "Hey, look, maintaining a BLM cabin is a tough job!" he writes. "Everybody has to pitch in!"

Anyone who thinks poetry is dead should take a look-see through these cabin logs. Turns out it's only wounded. Several people left long, epic poems on the north, prompting satiric responses with such lines as "Jesus had no pop-tarts handy," and "The moose and caribou, they do extol, the gentle hoofbeats of my soul."

Some folks can't resist unburdening themselves of highly personal details. A long passage written entirely in Korean is punctuated by a single phrase in English: "I love Bruce." Another entry describes a marriage proposal. A woman mentions staying here with a friend and concludes: "Perhaps I'm falling in love."

For melodrama, nothing matches the saga of a married couple and their respective lovers who star in several entries, including this one: "I hiked up here with my new friend Zeke and dog Rosebud. Too bad my husband, Sean, couldn't come along but he wanted to spend time with his lover Darcie. But she doesn't want to spend time with him tonight either. It's about time he found out what it's like to be alone." Another visitor urged: "Please feel free to keep sharing." I'm thinking, well, at least the dog got mentioned.

With all these long, detailed remarks, it comes as a relief to encounter the occasional terse summation: "We were here. Cold, scenic, nice. Have fun."

But when it comes time to leave your own mark on the pages, everyone else's eloquence colors the exercise with the tension of an essay question on a high school exam. What if I don't measure up? What if I'm (horrors) boring?

So I spent a lot of time working on this little poem, which I believe captures the essence of our weekend at Lee's Cabin:

> *We came out here for marital bliss*
> *The details of which you'll have to miss*
> *Although we hoped for champagne and brie,*
> *What we got was macaroni and cheese.*

Sherry Simpson teaches journalism at the University of Alaska Fairbanks and writes a column for "We Alaskans," the Sunday magazine of the *Anchorage Daily News.*

How To Reserve A Cabin

There are 105 public cabins in Southcentral Alaska. All but 17 of them require reservations. Each land agency (U.S. Forest Service, Alaska State Parks, and National Park Service) maintains its own cabin rules and reservation system, and can provide the most up-to-date information on cabin and trail conditions.

The **U.S. Forest Service** maintains 42 cabins in the Chugach National Forest. Eighteen of these are located on the Kenai Peninsula, and overseen by ranger stations in Girdwood and Seward. The remaining 24 cabins are located on Prince William Sound, and overseen by ranger stations in Girdwood and Cordova. Many Forest Service cabins are accessible only by boat or plane. Those found on easy-to-reach fishing lakes and major hiking trails (like the Resurrection Pass Trail) are among the best publicized and most heavily booked of Alaska's public cabins — sometimes for weeks or months in advance.

A new reservation system was instituted in October 1998, and as of this writing, the kinks are still being worked out. Bookings are now accepted through a private, national toll-free reservation system based on the East Coast at (877) 444-6777. The reservation center's hours are 6:00 A.M. to 3:00 P.M. (Alaska time) from Labor Day to March 31, and 4:00 A.M. to 8:00 P.M. (Alaska time) the rest of the year. The center's internet address, which wasn't on-line at the time of the writing but is expected to be running by mid-1999, is http://www.reserveusa.com. Current reservations are made on a first-call, first-served basis up to 180 days in advance. (This may change in the near future, allowing you to rent cabins up to a year or more in advance; stay tuned.) You can check cabin availability and reserve dates over the phone or internet with a credit card. You can also make reservations by mail with a check, but they won't

14

be confirmed until your payment is received.

Fees have also changed. Now, Forest Service cabins cost between $25 and $45 a night, depending on cabin location. The reservation charge (previously, a surcharge) is now included in the nightly rate. Your maximum stay varies from three to seven consecutive days, depending on cabin location and season. Again, some of the "maximum stays" for Forest Service cabins have been changed recently; call the reservation center if you have any questions. Cancellations are accepted by phone, or over the internet if the original reservation was made over the internet. You may receive a full refund up to 14 days prior to your arrival date. Cancellations made within 14 days of your arrival will receive a partial refund. Cancellations and all changes are subject to a $10 service fee. After a reservation is made, the center will mail, fax, or e-mail a confirmation voucher. If there isn't time to receive your voucher before your cabin trip, you will be given a confirmation number that will serve as your permit.

The reservation staff answering the phones in New York (or California, when New York lines are busy) know little or nothing about Alaska. They will read you information about the cabin from a cue card, but if you have any serious questions about trail or cabin conditions, it's best to contact the Forest Service in Anchorage, or the ranger district office closest to the cabin or trail you plan to visit (see Appendix 1).

Alaska State Parks (Department of Natural Resources, Division of Parks and Outdoor Recreation) maintains 33 public cabins in state park and state recreation areas in Southcentral Alaska including: 13 cabins at Nancy Lake State Recreation Area north of Anchorage; one on Eklutna Lake; five near Homer; four near Seward; three near Valdez; two in Denali State Park; four in prime sea-kayaking territory on the coast of Shuyak Island; and one on Afognak Island.

Reservations are accepted and cabin information is provided at the DNR Public Information Center in Anchorage at 3601 C Street, Suite 200, Anchorage (907) 269-8400, or at any Alaska State Parks area office (see Appendix 1). The DNR Center staff is very helpful. They have lots of brochures on hand, and some staff members have first-hand knowledge of the cabins. A computer is available at the center if you want to scan lots of cabins and available dates on your own.

Reservations can be made in person or by mail (call first to check availability and receive instructions) up to 180 days in advance. Pay by cash, check, or money order. No credit cards or phone reservations are accepted. Confirmation is made only after payment is received. The nightly fee ranges from $25 to $50, depending on cabin location. The maximum stay varies from three to seven days per month. Remember to ask for a free parking pass so that you don't have to pay extra at the trailhead.

A cabin credit (minus a $5 reservation fee) is offered if a cancellation is received seven days or more before arrival, or if the cabin cannot be used due to events beyond the renter's control (natural disaster, extreme weather, family emergency, or department fault).

For the latest cabin and trail condition information only, you may also call smaller, state recreation area offices and ranger stations closest to the cabin you'll be renting. To check cabin availability, you can also contact the Alaska State Parks cabin web pages at https://nutmeg.state.ak.us/ixpress/dnr/parks/index.dml, but you can't make a reservation over the internet at this time.

The **National Park Service** maintains four cabins in Southcentral Alaska, all within the Kenai Fjords National Park near Seward. Three remote coastal cabins are available for rent in summer only, at Aialik Bay, Holgate Arm, and North Arm. These are accessible by boat or floatplane only. The park also has one cabin, available in winter only, at Exit Glacier north of Seward.

Reservations are accepted by mail (call first to check cabin availability at (907) 224-3175) or in person at the Kenai Fjords National Park office in downtown Seward, on 4th Avenue. The coastal cabins can be reserved after January 1 for that year's summer season. Reservations for

A Hook Point Cabin "score"

Willow Cabin, the winter-only cabin at Exit Glacier, are taken in late fall, after snowfall accumulates and the road is closed. The nightly fee for all Kenai Fjords cabins is $35, payable by check or money order. The maximum stay varies from three to nine consecutive days, depending on cabin location and popularity. Individuals in the same party are not allowed to make sequential reservations to extend this limit. A cabin credit is offered if cancellation is made 10 days or more before arrival.

The **Eagle River Nature Center** ((907) 694-2108) has one cabin for rent. Reservations may be made for up to a year in advance. Call or visit the center in person to check availability. Payment may be made in person, or by phone, fax, or mail with cash, check, or credit card. The reservation will be held only after full payment is received. After you've paid, you'll receive a permit, lock combination (the number is regularly changed to ensure security), and parking pass. There are no refunds for cancellations.

The **Kodiak and Kenai National Wildlife Refuges**, administered by the U.S. Fish and Wildlife Service, both have cabins available for public use. These are the least publicized of Alaska's public cabins. The Kenai cabins are as close as you'll get to old-fashioned backcountry emergency cabins. They are first-come, first-served. Maximum stay is two weeks (just so that you don't get any fancy ideas about setting up permanent housekeeping). Clean up after your stay, or even leave the cabin a little better than you found it. These cabins receive little or no maintenance.

The Kodiak Refuge cabins are fee cabins, reserved by lottery. Write or call the refuge ((907) 487-2600) for an application. You will be asked to make several choices for cabins and dates. Winning applications are drawn on the first business day of January for the rental months of April, May, and June; on the first business day of April for July, August, and September; on the first business day of July for October, November, and December; and on the first business day of October for January, February, and March. Additional reservation opportunities are available at the wheelchair-accessible cabins, Blue Fox Bay and Uganik Lake, for interested users with documented mobility impairments. Both successful and unsuccessful applicants are notified after the drawing date. A notification of fees due ($20 per night), if any, is sent with the lottery results. You must pay within one month or forfeit your reservation. After the lotteries, all unclaimed dates are open to the public for rent on a first-come, first-served basis (see Appendix 1).

The **Mountaineering Club of Alaska** maintains eight huts in the Talkeetna and Chugach Mountains. Reservations and payment are not required, but potential users are urged strongly to become members in the club (see "About the Mountaineering Club of Alaska Huts," page 100).

Cabin Crapshoot: Your Chances to Score

"Impossible," a friend told me when I said I wanted to write a firsthand guide to public cabins. "Can't be done." No, the hard part wasn't paddling among grizzlies or backpacking steep trails, he said. It was getting cabin reservations in the first place.

Another acquaintance, a kayaker who spends plenty of soggy nights camping in Prince William Sound, said he never bothered to rent cabins — much as he wanted to — because he assumed they weren't available. Ever.

So, I conducted a survey. I waited until a bright, hopeful day in early summer (June 8, 1998 to be exact) and attempted to book every cabin in the system, for every possible date until September 1. The results: spontaneity is not completely dead. By June, weekend pickings may be slim, but there are some wonderful cabins less than 50 percent booked, even in summer. Below you'll find the cabins listed in order of least available to most available. The number that follows each cabin name is the number of dates that were open out of a total possible 85 days between June 8 and August 31.

If you see your dream cabin at the top of the list, you'll know to book extra, extra early next year. (The northwest corner of Prince William Sound, and trailside cabins on the Kenai Peninsula are the most solidly-booked cabin regions, in this survey.) If you're planning a last-minute getaway and looking for a fun place to go — anywhere — skip to the bottom half of the list and find the cabins that other travelers tend to forget. (If you can't make it to Cordova, try Nancy Lake State Recreation Area, north of Anchorage.) And remember: many of the same cabins that top the list in summer are easily available in spring, fall, or winter.

Location abbreviations:

AA—Anchorage area;
AI—Afognak Island;
C—Cordova;
C/PWS—Prince William Sound, gateway Cordova;
DSP—Denali State Park;
KBSP—Kachemak Bay State Park, near Homer;
KP—Kenai Peninsula;
NLSRA—Nancy Lake State Recreation Area;
RB—Resurrection Bay, near Seward;
SI—Shuyak Island State Park;
V/PWS—Prince William Sound, gateway Valdez;
W/PWS—Prince William Sound, gateway Whittier;

Cabin	Number of nights available (out of 85)	See page	Cabin	Number of nights available (out of 85)	See page
Swan Lake (**KP**)	2	127	Upper Russian Lake (**KP**)	2	145
Derby Cove (**RB**)	3	187	Harrison Lagoon (**W/PWS**)	3	243
Paulson Bay (**W/PWS**)	3	237	Barber (**KP**)	4	141
Crescent Lake (**KP**)	4	148	Pigot Bay (**W/PWS**)	6	242
Byers Lake #2 (**DSP**)	6	47	S. Culross Passage (**W/PWS**)	8	245
Trout Lake (**KP**)	8	133	Devil's Pass (**KP**)	10	125
Shrode Lake (**W/PWS**)	10	239	Dale Clemens Memorial (**KP**)	12	159
Lagoon Overlook (**KBSP**)	15	175	Romig (**KP**)	15	131
West Swan Lake (**KP**)	16	135	Crescent Saddle (**KP**)	17	149
Coghill Lake (**W/PWS**)	19	244	Martin Lake (**C**)	19	260

Cabin	Number of nights available (out of 85)	See page	Cabin	Number of nights available (out of 85)	See page
Green Island (**C/PWS**)	20	235	Crow Pass (**AA**)	22	41
Upper Paradise Lake (**KP**)	23	153	Aspen Flats (**KP**)	24	143
Nellie Martin River (**C/PWS**)	24	264	Lagoon East (**KBSP**)	25	177
Spruce Glacier (**RB**)	25	191	Eagle's Nest (**SI**)	27	208
Porcupine Glacier (**RB**)	27	190	Caribou Creek (**KP**)	28	118
Sea Star Cove (**KBSP**)	29	180	McKinley Trail (**C**)	31	251
Shelter Bay (**C/PWS**)	35	262	Byers Lake #1 (**DSP**)	36	46
Resurrection River (**KP**)	36	147	Jack Bay (**V/PWS**)	40	247
Nancy Lake #4 (**NLSRA**)	40	71	Yuditnu Creek (**AA**)	40	50
Lagoon West (**KBSP**)	42	177	Lower Paradise Lake (**KP**)	42	158
McKinley Lake (**C**)	42	254	Bald Lake (**NLSRA**)	43	73
Salmon Cove (**SI**)	45	208	East Creek (**KP**)	48	123
James Lake (**NLSRA**)	49	90	Deer Haven (**SI**)	50	209
Fox Creek (**KP**)	50	121	Double Bay (**C/PWS**)	54	263
Nancy Lake #1 (**NLSRA**)	54	69	Red Shirt Lake #3 (**NLSRA**)	56	81
Hook Point (**C/PWS**)	59	256	Mulcahy View (**SI**)	59	207
Nancy Lake #3 (**NLSRA**)	62	70	Port Chalmers(**C/PWS**)	65	263
Power Creek (**C**)	65	258	Softuk Bar (**C**)	66	261
Red Shirt Lake #4 (**NLSRA**)	68	82	Lynx Lake #1 (**NLSRA**)	70	87
Kittiwake (**V/PWS**)	71	246	Red Shirt Lake #1 (**NLSRA**)	72	79
Nancy Lake #2 (**NLSRA**)	76	70	Pillar Lake (**AI**)	78	210
Log Jam Bay (**C/PWS**)	78	264	Lynx Lake #3 (**NLSRA**)	78	89
McAllister Creek (**V/PWS**)	79	246	Tiedeman Slough (**C/PWS**)	80	259
Beach River (**C/PWS**)	81	267	Lynx Lake #2 (**NLSRA**)	81	88
San Juan Bay (**C/PWS**)	82	266	Red Shirt Lake #2 (**NLSRA**)	83	80

Not applicable, not constructed yet, or data not available on date of survey:
Pete Dahl
China Poot Lake
Eagle River Nature Center
Juneau Lake
Callisto Canyon
Moraine Cabin
Kenai Fjords cabins
Kodiak National Wildlife Refuge cabins
no-reservation cabins (Kenai National Wildlife Refuge and Mountaineering Club of Alaska huts).

Packing, Getting There, and Just Before You Go

What to bring to a cabin

The short answer is: everything you'd bring on a backpacking trip. Plus a little extra.

On backpacking trips, it's safe to assume that you can get back to the trailhead on your own. On remote cabin trips, that isn't always the case. Especially if you're dropped off by air or boat charter, you must be prepared for bad weather that leaves you stranded, awaiting pickup, often with no way of hiking out on your own. Being weathered in for three days is not uncommon. The Forest Service advises bringing extra food to last two to five days. Even if you've hiked to a cabin, bring a few extra days' worth of food and extra dry clothes packed in a waterproof bag, just in case.

Cabins aren't always warm, so bring extra clothes, rain gear and/or winter gear, and sleeping bags rated to fit the season. Many cabins are dark, so bring a lantern or lots of candles. The only time cabins don't seem dark at all is when you're trying to sleep. The summer sun doesn't set until nearly midnight at these latitudes, with a ghostly twilight lingering well into the night. If you can't sleep except in a pitch black room — and especially if you're traveling with children, who have a hard enough time settling into a new place — bring large garbage bags and duct tape to cover the windows.

Nearly all public-use cabins are located on water (ocean, river, or lake). Bring a boat or kayak and fishing gear to increase your enjoyment. Many lakeside Forest Service cabins have rowboats, but life jackets are not provided, so bring your own.

Unless you're dropped off and picked up at a cabin, or traveling to a nearby cabin in an area you know well, consider bringing a tent. For many trips, a tent is essential, especially if you're traveling cabin to cabin, or heading one-way to a cabin on a challenging route. Surprises along the trail or along the coast can delay you significantly; being fully prepared to camp will spare you unnecessary anxiety and discomfort.

Finally, even if you're being transported by boat or bush plane, be careful about what you pack your stuff in. Don't load your food and clothes into suitcases, coolers, or grocery-store bags, thinking you'll be able to dump it direct-

Loading luggage for fly-in

ly into a cabin. Quite frequently, you'll be dropped off on a beach at low tide, or on a trail that's "just a little ways" (a few hundred feet to a half-mile or more) from the cabin. The pilot may toss your bags just above a rapidly rising tide line. The rain may be falling. And you may find yourself hauling and double-hauling through brush or up a steep slope, effectively "backpacking" even if that wasn't your intention.

Equipment Checklist

- ☐ Rental Permit
- ☐ Tent (sometimes optional, depending on nature of trip)
- ☐ Camping Stove
- ☐ Camping Pad
- ☐ Sleeping Bag
- ☐ Flashlight
- ☐ Matches, Candles
- ☐ Map, Compass
- ☐ Cooking and Eating Utensils
- ☐ Collapsible Water Jug or Large, Wide-mouth Water Bottles
- ☐ Water Filter or method for treating water
- ☐ Food (for length of stay, plus about three days)

☐ First Aid Kit
☐ Toilet Paper
☐ Insect Repellent
☐ Warm Clothes for all seasons, even summer, including
   Adequate Waterproof Rain Gear
   Layers of Fleece (or synthetic long underwear and outerwear)
   Hat and Gloves
   Extra Wool or Synthetic Socks
☐ #1 Stove Oil (five gallons will last 48 hours in summer, less in winter)
   or Propane as needed (for cabins with oil or propane stoves)
☐ Folding Saw and/or Small Axe or Hatchet (for cabins with wood
   stoves)

Optional

☐ Tent (sometimes essential, depending on nature of trip)
☐ Lantern
☐ Firestarters (helpful in wet areas)
☐ Starter Supply of Wood (for cabins with wood stoves)
☐ Starter Supply of Fresh Water
☐ Signaling Equipment: Two-way Radio or Flares (that can be used to
   hail nearby boats or planes)
☐ Garbage Bags and Duct Tape (for window coverings, screen repair)
☐ Pillow
☐ Fishing or Hunting Gear (and Licenses)
☐ Waders and/or Rubber Boots (for some fishing areas)
☐ Life Jackets (if you intend to be on the water)
☐ Bug Head Net (rarely used, but an option for buggiest areas in summer)
☐ Emergency Blanket
☐ Bear Bell
☐ Boat or Kayak (preferably folding or inflatable if you're traveling by air)
☐ Small Motor (2 to 7.5 horsepower, if you are visiting a Forest Service
   cabin where a rowboat is provided and you prefer speed to silence)
☐ Games, Journals, Books

In Case of Emergency, Break Bindings

Craig Medred, an outdoors editor at the Anchorage Daily News, *Alaska's largest newspaper, has spent 25 years writing about people who mess up. Wilderness accidents, backcountry incompetence, and plain bad luck are his beats. That gives him plenty to write about in Alaska, where the penalties for any kind of ineptitude run pretty steep. Head out hiking or boating without the right gear here, even on a warm, bright summer day, and you could end up sick, hurt, dead, or at least embarrassed — and in one of Medred's columns.*

So, when I asked Craig to list what he thought were the most important things to bring on a cabin trip, I got a surprise.

"Number one: Matches," he suggested. "And number two: Something to read. Because A, you can start a fire with the pages, and B, you have a tendency to get stuck in these places. Especially if you fly in.

Indoor activity at Mulcahy View Cabin

Especially in Prince William Sound. And the thing about being stuck is that if you're stuck at a cabin, it's probably bad enough outside that you're probably also stuck inside *the cabin. You're going to go nuts unless you have something to read or someone you like to play cards with."*

What about dehydrated food or high-tech backpacking gear?

Nope, Craig said. Matches and a book still come first.

"You can go days without food," he said. "You can boil water. What else do you need?"

In Craig's honor, then, here's my own annotated list of recommended Alaska reading, specially geared to cabin trips.

Where the Sea Breaks its Back by Corey Ford

18th century naturalist Georg Steller was the first European to document the wildlife of Alaska's coast. Ford's 1966 classic captures Steller's enthusiasm for discovery, and tells the gory tale of Vitus Bering's tragic last voyage. Recently reissued as a paperback, this book provides excellent reading for coastal cabins, or anywhere the waves slam and the wind howls.

Seven Words for Wind: Essays and Field Notes from Alaska's Pribilof Islands by Sumner MacLeish

Any sea kayaker or sailor learns to fear (or at least respect) the wind. While you're holed up in a coastal cabin, waiting for the sea to calm, read this account of modern life in the stormy Pribilofs.

Disappearance: A Map: A Meditation on Death and Loss in the High Latitudes by Sheila Nickerson

A state poet laureate and essayist, Nickerson weaves history and memoir in this haunting work of literary nonfiction. Good reading for extended cabin trips in remote locales.

Wilderness: A Journal of Quiet Adventure by **Rockwell Kent**
This less-known book, written by an artist who lived in a cabin on a small island in Resurrection Bay, is the perfect companion for any of the Seward-area coastal cabins.

Going to Extremes by **Joe McGinniss**
The author's winter visit to the Crescent Lake Cabin is only one of many Alaska adventures in this funny, insightful, and poignant classic.

No Room for Bears by **Frank DuFresne**
If you're heading into brown bear territory — most of Southcentral Alaska, but especially the Kodiak archipelago or Montague Island in Prince William Sound — bring this classic, pro-conservation book about the beleaguered species.

To the Top of Denali by **Bill Sherwonit**
Sherwonit shares the history of our continent's highest peak, including the bizarre story of the first climbers who conquered the mountain. Good for cabins near or with a view of Denali (Byers Lake #1 and #2 in Denali State Park; Lynx Lake #1 Cabin in Nancy Lake State Recreation Area).

Any poetry collection by Robert Service
The Yukon bard's classic, sometimes corny poetry is good for cabin read-alouds. Bring it along on bitterly cold winter trips to interior cabins (like Exit Glacier or Nancy Lake State Recreation Area), or for gold-rush-era reading on the Resurrection Pass Trail.

The Last New Land: Stories of Alaska, Past and Present **edited by Wayne Mergler**
Spending a summer cabin-hopping but don't know what book to bring? This 791-page anthology covers Alaska authors from Jack London to Nick Jans. It's too heavy to carry on long hikes, but a good bet for fly-in trips.

What to leave at a cabin

Very little. Obviously, you must remove all your garbage. Maintenance crews can't keep up with the mounds left behind, even the well-intentioned stuff, like extra food and magazines left for the next cabin visitors. Food, in particular, is a problem. A great believer in Alaska lore, I once fretted for the stranger who might appear at a cabin after a storm, hoping to find a box of macaroni and cheese inside. But I fret less now that I've visited cabins in bear country. Yes, the big guys really do break in, especially after they've had a taste of human food. If you want to help the next person, leave no cans, boxes, or freeze-dried food, only a few candles or some split firewood. Also, sweep up before you go.

Transportation

Sometimes the only way you can get to a cabin safely or without spending your entire vacation in transit is to charter a boat or airplane. Charter-boat services tend to be more cost-efficient than air services, depending on where you're traveling and how many people are in your party. To some distant locations, however — like Shuyak Island, the outer Prince William Sound islands, or North Arm in the Kenai Fjords — air charters are an equal or better option.

Charter companies come and go quickly, and fares change every year. Appendix 2 in this guidebook lists only a few companies, because it's best to get updated lists of authorized charters (sometimes, with price sheets) directly from the land agencies renting out cabins. Alaska State Parks and the National Park Service will send lists upon request. The Forest Service doesn't publish lists. To find charters that serve Forest Service cabins, first call the chamber of commerce from the closest gateway town (see Appendix 2). If you still can't find one, call the appropriate district ranger office of the Forest Service and someone will help you.

Boat charters/ water taxis

Most boat charters charge a fixed price to various cabin locations, or about $6 per nautical mile for each dropoff or pickup. (Unlike with air-charter rates, that figure includes the captain's return time.) Most water

Boat drop-off in Prince William Sound

taxis can carry up to six people and kayaks — far more than a Cessna 206 can, enabling you to split the cost more ways. Some charters will help you coordinate your trip with other cabin-users; most will not. In 1998, a one-way dropoff at the cabins in northwest Prince William Sound cost about $180 per boatload for Pigot Bay, $200 for Paulson Bay, and $300 for South Culross Passage or Harrison Lagoon. Double those fares if you'd like a pickup as well.

Once you reach farther into the Sound, charter air fares become more competitive. A boat charter to Green Island will cost you about $1,300 round-trip for up to six people. By air from Seward, the same trip would cost about $1,200 for three or four adults, more for a larger party. If you're traveling with a small group, flying probably will be cheaper as well as faster. With a group of six — and certainly, if you want to see the coast along the way — a boat charter would be the better option.

From Homer and Seward, you can get a lift via water taxi to public cabins in Kachemak and Resurrection bays, respectively, for $35 to $50 round-trip, per person.

Air charters

Some cabins can be reached only by small planes equipped with floats (to land on lakes or the ocean) or balloon tires (to land on beach or gravel airstrips). Chartering a small bush plane is an adventure in itself. It's something that all visitors to Alaska — the "flyingest" state in the union, with more pilots per capita than anywhere else — should do at least once. But charter companies don't necessarily make it easy. Many don't publish price sheets, preferring to quote or negotiate over the phone just prior to your trip. In their defense, charter insurance rates are steep, and a price you were quoted in February (when you're planning your trip and booking your cabin) may have changed after the insurance bill comes due in May, jacking up fares overall.

If you have money to blow, you can fly to just about anywhere from Anchorage, the home of dozens of floatplane operations. But more commonly, you'll try to get as close as possible to your cabin destination by road, and only then hop a flight to keep costs down.

While public land agencies and chambers of commerce will get you started, they won't make recommendations. You should call several air-charter companies to compare prices, but as many pilots will take great pains to remind you, the substantially cheaper fare is not always the best deal. You want to fly with someone who is safe and reliable — a pilot who *won't* necessarily pick you up "on time" if the weather isn't good.

How to find the best charter company? Ask around. That's not easy to do if you live out of state, but other companies helping you plan your vacation (a B&B, kayak rental company, local sporting goods store) may be able to confirm a local charter company's reputation. Failing that, go with experience. A company that has stayed in business for 10 to 15 years in a small town can't be too bad — few passengers would fly with them if they were. Charter companies themselves occasionally point disparaging fingers at each other. But really, most of them are very professional. I have been completely satisfied with every pilot and charter company I've used.

Below you'll find a list of four of the most common bush planes available for charter. Sometimes, a company that owns only larger planes will charge you a smaller plane rate, if you're traveling in a small group or with little gear, just to keep pace with the competition. Companies may charge per person, but usually they charge by the planeload, whether or not you fill it. Some companies have set prices for specific dropoff locations, but usually total flight time determines cost.

Plane	Passengers	Total Weight (people/gear)	Typical Hourly Rate
Cessna 185	2-3	750 pounds	$225-$250
Cessna 206	3-4	900 pounds	$250-$300
Beaver	4-5	1250 pounds	$350-$400
Otter	8-9	2000 pounds	$600

If a cabin is 20 minutes by air from the air charter's base, you pay not for 20 minutes of flight time, but rather 40 minutes for a dropoff (to cover the pilot's trip back to the airport). Or you pay for 80 minutes (to cover both dropoff and pickup, a total of four flights for the pilot). So, at $300 per hour, a typical price for a Cessna 206, the total round-trip charge

Floatplane drop-off at Shuyak Island

for a cabin 20 minutes away from the charter's base should be about $400. The obvious way to save money is to fly as part of a larger party, dividing the cost more ways. Once in a while, a charter plane can coordinate your dropoff with a pickup in the same area, allowing you to split the cost with other cabin-users.

Some planes can carry hardshell kayaks by strapping them onto the exterior of the plane. More commonly, paddlers buy or rent folding kayaks, which can be disassembled to fit easily into two luggage-sized bags.

When flying to some coastal cabins, tides must be considered. Discuss this with your pilot when planning dropoff and pickup times.

Finally, here are a few tips from the pilots themselves: Don't try to sneak more gear than you are allowed. The pilots will eyeball or weigh your stuff, and charge you for extra flight time if they have to split the load over several trips. Don't fly with a pilot who seems eager to take risks. If the weather looks bad, if you can't see the ground from your seat prior to takeoff, if your floatplane's float are dragging in the water, or if your floatplane is so overloaded that it requires more than one attempt to lift off from a lake, speak up and get off. Don't pressure a pilot to fly in poor conditions, either to drop you off or guarantee your timely pickup. The man or woman at the controls knows best, and it's your job to be prepared to wait for hours or days, weather depending.

Llaaculnguluni

Long before there were bush planes, the Alutiiq people of coastal Southcentral Alaska had a word for being weathered in: *Sapurluku*. And another word for having trouble with the weather: *Llaaculnguluni*. So, while you're stuck inside your cabin, having a little trouble, consider the experience a cultural one.

It could be worse. Think of Joe McGinniss, author of a classic book about Alaska, *Going to Extremes*. He visited the Forest Service's Crescent Lake cabin, on the Kenai Peninsula. Intent on roughing it, he went alone. In winter. Without a watch, and without any books. "I wanted three days and three nights of unbroken contact with the environment," he wrote. "Total solitude. No escapes of any kind." That's just what he got, too. After a few days of it, he was ready to be home again. Then, the weather turned. Turns out, a blizzard wasn't the only problem. His pilot had broken some ribs, adding some extra time to the delay. But McGinniss didn't know that. In the meanwhile, he stewed. His Crescent Lake chapter — a graphic reminder to anyone who thinks packing a few days' extra food is unwarranted — is excerpted in this book.

Barber Cabin setting

Crescent Lake

from **Going to Extremes** *by Joe McGinniss*

The pilot had been due back on Wednesday, but Wednesday had been a blizzard day, so I'd cut my firewood and eaten my cheese and wished that the moose would return.

On Thursday it was bright and clear and I woke up filled with joy. I could see across the lake again, could see the tops of the mountains, and the sky. The wind had subsided and all was quiet once more. The first noise I would hear would be the noise of the plane. Then I would see it in the sky. I figured the pilot would be there about noon. Whenever noon was. It did not matter. Having endured four days, including two and a half in a blizzard, I could certainly handle an hour or two in the sun. Knowing that so soon I would be out. Climbing into the plane, putting my sleeping bag and food box and snowshoes and unused Coleman lantern in the back, and then bumping along the lake surface through the snow. Then taking off. And rising above the tops of the mountains that had been looming above me for what had come to seem half my life. I would be heading toward Anchorage. Toward people. Toward life. I didn't think I would be able to explain to anyone exactly how it had felt, being here. I didn't think I'd even want to try. I just wanted to go to a movie, and to a place that served pizza, and I wanted to drink beer and play songs on a jukebox and take a hot shower and make love in the bed in my apartment.

But the pilot didn't come. All day, there was nothing in the sky but the sun. All day, not a sound around the lake. I could tell when it was about midday, and then I watched, disbelieving, as the afternoon shadows slowly started to rise up the sides of the mountains to cover the surface of the lake. I didn't cut wood. I didn't take a walk. I just sat on my fully packed duffel bag, in front of the cabin, and watched the sky.

It got dark. There was no plane. I went to bed, filled with bitterness and rage. In the morning, I said, I would walk out. From the far end of the lake there was supposed to be a trail that led, eventually, to a road at a place called Moose Pass. I would get out that way on my snowshoes, dragging my duffel bag through the snow, carrying the lantern and the ax. And I would find someone, somewhere, maybe in this place called Moose Pass, and I would get myself back to Anchorage. And when I reached Anchorage I would go out to the office of the flying service, and I would start swinging the ax. And I would chop the wings off all their planes. Rotten bastards. Sons of bitches. Suppose I had chopped a toe off cutting firewood? Suppose I'd accidentally sawed through my wrist? I could be lying on the cabin floor bleeding to death and these bastards hadn't even come to pick me up. This was the worst moment I'd had in Alaska, by far. I even began to feel anger toward Tom, for loaning me all this crap that had enabled to come here in the first place, and toward the U.S. Forest Service, for having even built this goddamned cabin, and toward anyone who had ever lived in a cabin, in the winter, in the woods. Eventually, beneath the sheer weight of so much impotent rage, I fell asleep.

Finally, before you go

Before your cabin trip, call the office of the relevant land agency closest to the cabin you're visiting (see each cabin's listing) and ask for an update. Some offices provide good, up-to-date information, especially when rangers or maintenance crews have visited a cabin recently. Others do not. The person in charge of taking reservations won't know as much as a ranger. (For U.S. Forest Service cabins, the reservation center is on the East Coast, and the folks answering the phone won't know Alaska at all. Don't even ask, or you'll get a short speech from a cue card written years ago. Instead, call the relevant ranger station directly.)

Rangers themselves have a lot of territory to cover. Ask specific questions. Especially in early summer, you should call to ask if relevant trails are snow-free or cleared of fallen trees. Be skeptical — often, trails are described in better condition than you will find them. (There's no conspiracy here, except that maintenance crews are typically composed of strapping young men and women who don't notice the thick alder and bumpy terrain as much as the rest of us.) If you're planning to visit a lakeside cabin, ask if the lake has thawed — especially in Prince William Sound, some don't thaw until late June. If you're concerned about bears, ask about any recent bear-human interactions in the area. Also, if you plan to fish or hunt, it is essential that you contact the Alaska Department of Fish and Game directly for the latest regulations.

When a trail is described as "primitive," expect to bushwhack. All day, possibly. When a trail is described by a land agency or other guidebooks as a "good, short family trail," well... contributor Jeff Brune has another way to describe that kind of trail. His tale about tackling Crow Pass is a good caveat for this whole book — and all other books of its kind.

Crow Pass Caveat
by Jeff Brune

It was a coup, a con job I played on my family. After living in Alaska for six years, I had finally managed to cajole three generations of the Brunes up to the Crow Pass Cabin for an overnight backpacking trip. Well, not quite yet. We were still in the parking lot. But even getting there took a lot of work — packing, convincing, packing, reassuring — so I was feeling a sense of victory, even at the trailhead.

You have to understand. My family, whom I love dearly, is from Nebraska. About all we do for vacation is go fishing, usually for panfish in the Lower 48 and always with a beer in the hand. This time I wanted to expand their horizons, try something different. Climb a mountain and stay in an alpine cabin. You know, have a life-changing experience or something.

"Why are we doing this?" my nephew Josh grumbled, typical of a high school graduate. "To look for wildflowers or something?" He was clearly craving some salmon-casting action on the Russian River and threatening the group

Top of Crow Pass outhouse

Jeff Brune

dynamics required for a successful journey. I would have to load him down considerably with gear, I thought secretly, before the mutiny spreads. By the time I stuffed his pack and mine, there was little left for my wife, two very young daughters, my 60-something parents, and my older brother.

I chose the Crow Pass Cabin because getting there seemed the easiest — and safest — of the available options. The trail was only 3 miles long and included a 2,080-foot climb, whatever that meant.

A Forest Service flyer described access to the cabin as a "good, short, family trail." Another source, a local guide book, called it "a pleasant day trip into a beautiful mountain wilderness." So, I felt I did my homework and concluded it would be little effort with lots of reward.

Moments from the parking lot, we were slogging our tonnage upward, ever upward, on endless switchbacks, back and forth, through a tunnel of thick alders. Hearts pounded. Bear bells rang. No one spoke. What had I gotten my family into? This sucked.

The alders finally gave way to truly gorgeous mountain views, but the trail led to snow. Thick, mushy, wet snow. It was the middle of summer, for God's sake. June 24 to be exact. Why wasn't this stuff melted by now? Well, the diligent, upward trudging continued, more silence broken by sucking sounds with each heavy step. After two hours of this slurp-hiking, I was beginning to have a mental image of that Forest Service worker who wrote the flyer: An iron-athlete with thighs as thick as sequoias. This evil grin.

Next, the "good" trail (or what we thought was the trail) led us along the edge of the Crow Creek canyon with cascades crashing to rocks far below. By that time, snow gave way to rocky scree and misty, slippery rain, a lovely complement to the precipice below. This is where my poor wife, Christine, was struck by heart palpitations — a somewhat debilitating, but not life-threatening condition she's had since childhood. It's usually prompted by stress, this time by the strain of carrying our hefty toddler in her backpack. So, there she was, lying on the ground and coughing, her usual solution, and trying to get her heart to cooperate.

Everyone was worried: for Christine, for each other, for themselves, all of us strung out along the trail, teetering precariously on the edge. I would call this the low point of the family adventure.

Once past the jaws of death, we took a break and bonded in a big way. Not gushing emotion, but quiet and profound appreciation for each other. It was a timeless moment of warm familial love cradled by a cold, unforgiving mountain landscape. This moment was a true victory, for me and my family. We had succeeded, even before reaching the top.

A full five hours after we left the parking lot, I was the first to see it. The A-frame cabin. "Thar she blows!" I yelled. We were all absolutely giddy.

We hurry to the cabin, drop off our stuff, and run free. Free of heavy packs. Free of worries, except for the trail going down. But that's for tomorrow, *we tell ourselves. Now we're here to enjoy the spectacular mountain scenery. The glacier views. Yes, the wildflowers. Best of all, each other, now that we're alive and well and safe.*

"Safe?" we think. How can this be? We're in an unheated cabin, 3,000 feet straight up in the sky, surrounded by bears and snow. Even the damn out-house is covered to the roof in snow. My poor mother has waited five hours to use the facilities, but we're too tired to shovel. It's the open tundra or nothing.

What is happening to our standards? Who knows? Now it's time to boil some water, eat freeze-dried spaghetti, tell fishing stories, and hunker down on a stiff board for a good night's sleep. Ah, wilderness creature comforts.

In that moment, we actually thought things couldn't be better.

Jeff Brune is an environmental educator at the Campbell Creek Science Center. Formerly, he was a reporter for *Discover* magazine and associate editor for *Scholastic Science World*. He lives with his family in Anchorage.

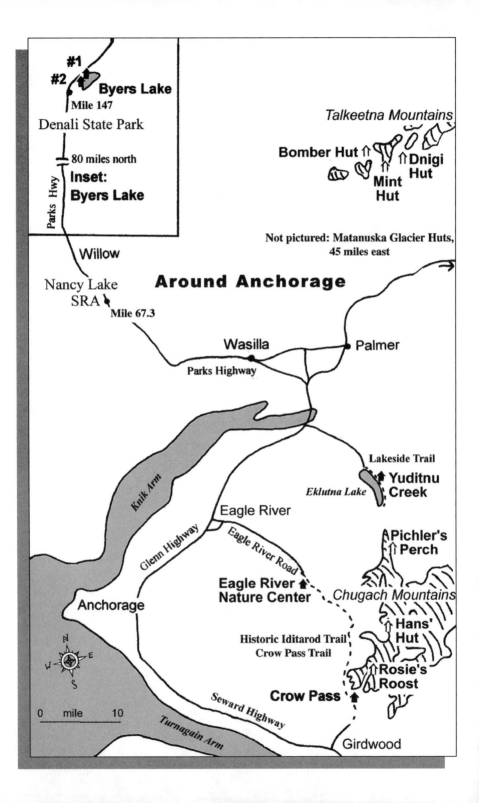

BACKYARD RETREATS FROM THE MATANUSKA-SUSITNA VALLEY TO GIRDWOOD

Our Waldens

"This morning we saw three sheep up the mountain directly behind us. ... The sound of rushing water mixed with the hoot of an owl filled our ears. And woodpeckers. The view of the lake is gorgeous and I wish I could live here. I have been to Walden Pond and as far as I am concerned Henry David Thoreau missed out greatly."

Yuditnu Creek Cabin visitor's log

Crow Pass Cabin. July. We're waiting for a friend to drop by for Saturday morning coffee. Nothing strange in that — except that we are waiting at 3,500 feet, above treeline, in an unheated A-frame cabin perched on the edge of a tundra bowl. Streams of cold fog — the breath of nearby glaciers — sweep past the Crow Pass Cabin's front stoop, obscuring the trail and the knife-edged peaks surrounding us.

"Do you see the runners yet?" I ask Brian, reluctant to sacrifice the warmth of my sleeping bag to fire up the camping stove.

My husband glances at his alarm clock. "7:20. We've got a little while."

"7:20 already?" I say, sitting up abruptly and squinting out the window. "Get dressed! Boil the water!"

35

The night before, it had taken us over two hours to hike three steep miles from the trailhead near Girdwood. Finally, we'd spotted the fuzzy outline of the weathered public cabin. Dwarfed by a ring of craggy peaks, it looked like an ancient cairn. We felt like rare visitors — seemingly the first and only humans to walk this way in years. Until the next morning, that is. That's when the runners appear, dashing out of the fog and passing just feet away from our cabin's front door. Suddenly, the narrow trail that threads through this lonely valley is busier than a downtown sidewalk at noon. Marmots run for cover.

The fastest of over 100 annual Crow Pass Crossing marathoners sprint from the trailhead to the cabin and over the pass in just 27 minutes. When we spot Stewart, the kettle is still cold. He waves and jogs toward us. "You made it," I say, amazed to see a familiar face in such unfamiliar surroundings. We talk for a few minutes as several other runners lope past, disappearing over a small crest. The water still isn't boiling.

"So," Stewart finally asks, "Where's my coffee?"

Brian and I exchange sheepish glances.

"I don't suppose you can wait a little longer..."

"That's OK," our friend says cheerfully, jogging away to catch up with the other runners. "You owe me one."

"We'll get it right next year!" we call after him. I fumble to snap a photo of his retreating back, but it's too late — his red shirt has faded into a wall of grey mist.

"Now what?" asks Brian after a few peaceful minutes, rubbing sleep from his eyes. All the runners are gone. The marmots reappear, chirping and darting over the rocks.

Alaska-style coffee klatch over, we have no other plans. While our friend races the clock, Brian and I put ours away. Now we have only this quiet cabin, the sweep of foggy tendrils through Crow Pass to shape the day's rhythms, and the rest of a mild summer Saturday to explore the wilderness beyond.

〰〰〰

There are 105 public cabins in Southcentral Alaska, many of them remote. Merely getting to them can be an epic quest. But sometimes, what we need most isn't high adventure, just simple retreat.

Walden was just outside Boston — not far from the big city, but far enough to free Thoreau's mind from "worldly engagements," and wild enough to allow him his four-hour saunters through the woods. Only a select handful of public cabins are as quickly, easily, and cheaply reached from Anchorage but they are favorites, especially when we long to escape to the edge of wilderness with visiting family or friends. The Nancy Lakes cabins. Crow Pass Cabin, near Girdwood. The Yuditnu Creek Cabin on Eklutna Lake. The Byers Lake cabins in Denali State Park. All of them are within "Friday night striking distance" of Anchorage, as a friend of mine calls it, and which I define arbitrarily as a maximum three or four hours of combined driving and hiking, biking, or skiing time.

These simple shelters extend our notion of home. We return to them again and again through the seasons, making them our own, celebrating holidays and anniversaries, reunited friendship or rekindled love, or simply celebrating silence. These aren't necessarily the cabin trips that challenge or change us. (Although they certainly can be, since even the most accessible "weekend wilderness" in Alaska can dish up life-threatening surprises.) Most often, they're simply the trips that sustain us. You leave work, pick up friends or family, drive an hour or two, hike or bike or ski an hour or so more — just enough to raise an appetite and calm your nerves — and you're there: away from the glow of city lights, off the grid. And that's what a good weekend cabin — or "Walden" cabin — is all about.

Taking measure of the Crow Pass Cabin

~~~

Byers Lake Cabin #1. September. "You think there are bears here?" my mother-in-law asks for the third time.

She's visiting from Toronto. Her idea of a vacation is a trip to the city: China town, museums, shopping. I've never seen her wear pants before, but she has a pair on today, plus flat-heeled shoes she bought just for this trip. We brought her here to see Denali, the continent's highest peak. She says she's more interested in spending time with her 3-year-old grandson. Preferably inside.

"The bears won't bother us," I say. "Just clap your hands on the way to the outhouse."

"Or," I add, seeing her already tentative smile droop, "Maybe someone could go with you."

There is a long pause as we all fumble in the cabin's deepening darkness, unrolling sleeping bags, searching for candles. Then my visiting brother-in-law speaks up.

"What do you think about moving the car?"

Byers Lake Cabin #1, in Denali State Park, is the only drive-up public cabin in Southcentral Alaska. A paved parking lot ends just a few yards from the handcrafted, sod-roofed log cabin. On this early September evening, our station wagon is the only vehicle in the parking lot, the only manmade object obscuring an otherwise fine view of birch trees flecked with autumn's first yellow leaves.

"You're right," I say. "Maybe I could move it to the other end of the parking lot, out of sight."

"No," my brother-in-law says. "I meant move it closer."

Stuart is worrying about car thieves. Evelyn is worrying about man-eating grizzlies. I'm trying to stifle any wisecracks that might jeopardize family relations.

We spend a night at cabin #1 and then walk the half-mile trail to cabin #2, which sits on the bluff overlooking Byers Lake. Its large picture window provides a fantastic view of Denali — when Denali is visible, that is, which is only one summer day in three.

Many visitors record their disappointments in the cabin's log. "Hoping to get a view of `the great one' from this beautiful cabin window, we anxiously awaited the clouds to clear, to no avail," one person writes in May. And another guest, in August: "Denali flirted with us all weekend, finally revealing a glimpse of her top through the mist on our last evening here."

We're luckier. The mountain stays out for our entire visit. Three full days of clear blue sky, and the blindingly bright outline of snowcovered Denali towering above Byers Lake and a front range of chocolate-brown peaks. My brother-in-law doesn't mention car thieves again. My mother-in-law does mention bears again, but with curiosity instead of panic.

We cook dinner on the porch. Evelyn sits at the picnic table in front of the cabin, staring at Denali. We rest inside the cabin with our 3-year-old son. She stays out on the bluff in front of the cabin, staring at Denali. My mother-in-law enjoys herself — or we think she does. We don't see all that much of her. Mostly, we see her back.

"You want to come read your grandson a book?" we call to her as she stands outside the cabin, her eyes following the imagined routes of distant climbers struggling to make the summit during this amazing spell of clear weather.

"Soon," she says cheerfully. "Soon."

But she doesn't — not right away, anyhow. Denali has cast its spell over her. For a few days, this simple cabin with its views and its silence has pulled her, and us, away from all worries, into a time and space between worlds.

〰〰〰

"Fifty dollars for this?" I once read in a Halibut Cove Cabin visitor log, evidently written by a man who felt he'd been overcharged for a night's stay in a state-owned structure without lights, plumbing, and cable television. But what you're paying for in a public cabin isn't modern amenities. If anything, you're

paying to escape from them.

We may not be able to find five uninterrupted minutes in our electrically wired, multi-level, two-bathroom houses, but in these one-room cabins, the hours unwind as naturally and gently as clouds sailing over mountain tops. Somehow, where there are no "conveniences," there is suddenly far more time: to talk, play cards, read poetry by candlelight. Or simply to enjoy the view.

When you visit a public cabin, you leave behind some of the comforts of home, but there's ample compensation. No one cares if you get sticky with marshmallows. Everyone helps chop the wood. A toddler finds new toys: sticks and pebbles and a pint-sized ash shovel. In summer, it's hard to enforce a bedtime when the midnight sun filters in through the

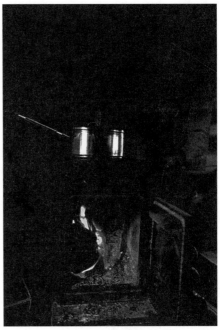

Cabin stove in winter

uncovered windows. In winter, you lay awake listening to the pops and hisses of the black, widebellied woodstove, and take turns climbing down from upper bunks to feed the fire with a fresh birch log.

You hear the sounds your friends' kids make in their sleep, and see what your friends look like in the morning before their first coffee, without mascara or a fresh shave. You tell your big brother — the one who teased you all those years — that he doesn't need to be afraid of the night noises: yipping coyotes, laughing loons. You tell your visiting mother that you're glad she came, and you show her this: Your Walden. And better: Your Alaska.

Not an overpriced lodge, but a cabin: log or wooden-frame walls, the sound of rain and wind, the smell of forest, views of ancient ice or a pristine stream, the taste of wild berries or just-caught fish. Nothing much. Just all the things that money can't buy, and all the reasons many of us in this northernmost state couldn't live anywhere else.

Nancy Lake Cabin #1. January. Seven degrees below zero. After a day of skiing on the frozen lake and an evening of reading Robert Service's "The Cremation of Sam McGee," one person bundles up in his coat, opens the door, and disappears into the darkness, leaving an icy cloud hanging in the doorway. He said he was going to use the outhouse, but he doesn't return. After a while,

someone else pulls on a jacket and heads outside. He doesn't come back either. A third person follows. This is starting to sound like a ghost story, you think; why can't these cabins have indoor toilets, and what are they doing out there in this cheek-burning, molar-piercing cold?

Until finally, everyone is outside the cabin except you, and you finally go out and look up, and there they are: the stars, like you've never seen them. Can't see the Milky Way on your way to the bathroom at home. Can't see the northern lights.

〰〰〰

Yuditnu Creek Cabin. Late April. It's spring, but Eklutna Lake doesn't know it yet. The glacier-fed lake, which will glow turquoise in the summer, is hidden under a milk-colored crust of ice. Even so, we sunbathe on the lake's steep, sloping shore with our friends, their 1-year-old daughter, and our young son as if it's already summer.

On the bicycle ride to the cabin — a satisfyingly bumpy three miles on an old dirt road — butterflies scattered in vertical plumes, just feet in front of our wheels. In the evening we build a fire outside. The adults drink white wine out of tin camping cups and talk about work. Too much work. The toddlers gather twigs to feed the fire. We all listen for owls and wolves; other cabin-users have heard them here, the visitor's log says. We go for a walk the next morning, and smell the rich, damp mustiness of last year's autumn leaves and the perfume of this year's new green shoots — the forest coming alive after a long winter.

"I think I need to quit my job," our friend announces back at the cabin, as we're sweeping it out, preparing to leave. "I need more time," she says.

"For what?" I ask.

"For this."

Snowcapped peak behind Yuditnu Creek Cabin

CROW PASS CABIN

Chugach National Forest (U.S. Forest Service)

"This evening I ran all over various hills, trying to chase the clouds that were rolling in from the valley. Finally, I caught up. I was in the clouds. Just me and the clouds. All I could see was my feet and a small space surrounding them if I looked down, and grey surrounding me. It was like an angel's breath."

Laura, age 13, from Crow Pass Cabin log.

Snapshot: An A-frame cabin, with loft, in the clouds. Alpine base camp for Anchorage hikers; a moderately challenging destination for families.

Location: 3 miles along the Crow Pass Trail, in the Chugach Mountains, near Girdwood.

Elevation: 3,400 feet.

Map: USGS Anchorage A6.

Access: Hiking only.

Available: June 1 through September 30, due to avalanche hazard rest of year.

Best: Path to outhouse is usually shoveled by mid-June. Trail is usually snow-free mid-July through August.

Capacity: Sleeps six on bunks and more, comfortably, in loft. Maximum capacity is eight.

Maximum stay: Three consecutive days.

Cost: $35.

Reservations: Forest Service toll-free reservation center (877) 444-6777, or via Internet at http://www.reserveusa.com. For info on trail and cabin specifics, call the Glacier Ranger District Office, Girdwood, (907) 783-3242.

Caution: Winter avalanche zone. Snow, fog, and cold possible anytime. Trail can be difficult. No stove for heat or cooking in cabin.

Facilities: The 16x16-foot, A-frame cabin has dark brown wood-paneled walls and a green metal roof. Inside you'll find six bunks plus extra space for sleeping bags in the loft, a table, two benches, and shelves. Six-foot-high plexiglass windows, scratched as they are, still let in lots of light. The loft also has good windows and views. There is no stove and the cabin is chilly at night even in summer. Please do not attempt to gather wood or build fires outside the cabin. Any fire rings left by previous guests are illegal (the only wood available above the tundra line is from plundered mining ruins). A narrow front porch and the cabin's outhouse are just feet away from a heavily used hiking trail. Water is available in nearby glacial streams and should be treated before use.

Condition: Poor, with some graffiti. The cabin and outhouse tend to be messier than most because of the number of passersby.

View and surroundings: The weathered, triangle-shaped structure sits above timberline, like an ancient cairn or glacial remnant perched atop a scoured landscape, surrounded by stunning alpine scenery. Steep, snowy slopes (even in summer), waterfalls, and Crystal Lake are visible from the front windows. Waterfalls are audible from a small front porch. Low shrubs and tiny tundra wildflowers fight their way up through steep scree behind the cabin. The climate is cool and wet, and mist often slinks toward the pass, obscuring jagged peaks that rise to over 5,000 feet. A popular, historic trail passes 10 feet in front of the cabin's porch.

Recreation: No fishing. Hunting is limited and tightly restricted by permit. Fireweed, columbine, and other wildflowers brighten the trail and surround Crystal Lake in July and August. Also in August, berries may be ripe for picking en route to the cabin. From the cabin, hiking opportunities abound. Crow Pass and views of Raven Glacier are 0.5 mile past the cabin along the Crow Pass Trail, which continues all the way to Eagle River (28 miles total). The treeless terrain near the cabin makes wandering and wildlife-viewing easy. Mountaineers use this cabin as the first (and most easily reached) of four shelters on the challenging Eklutna Traverse (see page 101 for the others).

Wildlife sightings: Marmots scurry along the trail and burrow under the cabin. Dall sheep, mountain goats, and brown bears sometimes can be spotted on surrounding peaks and slopes. Also in area: black bears, ground squirrels, ptarmigan, and porcupines.

History: The Crow Pass Trail was part of the historic Iditarod Trail connecting Seward, on the coast, with the goldfields of the Interior. Nearly a century ago, trappers, gold miners, and mail-carrying sled-dog drivers braved the steep route, which was improved after gold was discovered in the rocky hillsides of the pass itself. Ruins of the Monarch Mine, a hard-rock ore-extracting operation that closed in 1948, are still visible at mile 2.5 from the Crow Creek trailhead. En route to the cabin, look for the scant remains of a mill and a miner's bunkhouse on the slopes of Jewel and Barnes mountains to the east, and the odd piece of historical machinery just west of the trail, within thundering earshot of the Crow Creek cascades. The public cabin was built in 1969. The avalanche-prone trail, which had fallen into disuse, was reopened for hiking by a Girl Scout trail crew.

For the last 15 years, the Crow Pass Trail has been stampeded by athletes instead of prospectors. Each July, about 100 nimble-footed runners compete in the Crow Pass Crossing, a 28-mile race from the Girdwood end of the trail to Eagle River. The fastest runners pass directly in front of the public-use cabin's porch — a good place to watch the race, if you're so inclined and happen to be spending the night — in under 30 minutes. Those still stumbling past the cabin after the first hour are disqualified from the race.

Getting there: At Mile 90, Seward Highway (35 miles south of Anchorage) turn north onto Alyeska Highway, the road leading into Girdwood and Mt. Alyeska Resort. Drive 2 miles. Turn left onto Crow Creek Road and proceed for 5 more miles. Just after a bridge, the road forks; stay to the right. The trailhead is at the end of the road.

The 3-mile hike to the cabin is rated moderate to difficult, with some rocky and slippery sections. It begins as a steep climb along a well-defined gravel trail through brushy terrain that breaks out onto tundra and scree half-way to the cabin. Near mile 2, the trail divides. Follow either route. The main trail forks to the right and switchbacks up to follow the curve of the slopes and pass within sight of the Monarch Mine ruins. The left fork skirts the powerful Crow Creek cascades before also switchbacking up to the main trail. After hopping across a wide, shallow stream and rounding a bend in the trail, you'll spot the cabin and Crystal Lake.

BYERS LAKE CABINS #1 AND #2

Denali State Park (Alaska State Parks)

Snapshot: Weekend wilderness in high style. Two easy-to-reach cabins — including a traditional, sod-roofed Alaska-style bush cabin — in the shadow of "The High One."

Location: On the shore of Byers Lake in Denali State Park, just off mile 147 of the Parks Highway, 2.5 hours north of Anchorage.

Elevation: 800 feet.

Map: USGS Talkeetna C1 (trail and cabins not shown).

Access: In summer, by car to Byers Lake Cabin #1. On foot, by canoe or kayak, a 0.5 mile trip to Byers Lake Cabin #2. In winter, by ski or snow-machine, add 0.5 mile for both cabins since access road is unplowed.

Available: Year-round.

Best: July and August for berries and bear-sightings; early September for fall foliage; October through March for snow, peace, and quiet.

Sleeps: Five on bunks (a bit of a squeeze) in Byers Lake Cabin #1; Six, comfortably, in Byers Lake Cabin #2. (Six is the maximum capacity for both cabins.)

Maximum stay: Five nights per month.

Cost: $35.

Reservations: DNR Public Information Center (907) 269-8400, or any Alaska State Parks office. For local information on cabin and trails, call the Mat-Su Office (907) 745-3975. Info and cabin availability only via Internet at https://nutmeg.state.ak.us/ixpress/dnr/parks/index.dml

For both Byers Lake cabins

Recreation: Fish Byers Lake for rainbow trout, grayling, Dolly Varden, lake trout, burbot, and whitefish. (It's closed to salmon fishing.) As a state park brochure says, "Byers Lake is a pleasant place to fish — but not a particularly good place to *catch* fish."

There's a rowboat/kayak/rental operation (motorized boats aren't permitted in Byers Lake) at the end of the parking lot, or you can bring your own canoe or kayak. When the skies are clear, there's no better view of Denali (Mt. McKinley) to the west than from the middle of the lake. Berry pickers will find blueberries and cranberries by the gallons in late July and August.

Hiking opportunities, from easy woodland walks to backcountry tundra treks, abound. The cabin makes a great base camp for exploring. The Byers Lake Loop Trail is a 4.8-mile footpath circling the lake and crossing a suspension bridge — a good place to watch salmon in late summer. A moderately difficult 15.2-mile hike (one way) leads south from the Byers Lake campground (0.25 mile from cabin #1) along the Troublesome Creek Trail. A difficult 27.4-mile hike (one way) leads north from the Byers Lake campground along the Kesugi Ridge Trail.

Wildlife sightings: Black bears, trumpeter swans, loons, mergansers, beaver, salmon. Also in the area: arctic terns, brown bear, moose.

History: Once a visitor center, the cabin was made available to the public for rental starting in 1994. Cabin #2 was built in 1994.

Getting there: Drive to mile 147 of the Parks Highway, about 2.5 hours north of Anchorage. **In summer,** to drive to cabin #1, turn east along the road to the Byers Lake campground and park, about 0.5 mile later, in front of the cabin. To hike to cabin #2, park in the picnic area (mile 0.3 of the campground road). The wide trail starts just past a barrier and leads 0.5 mile south along the west shore of Byers Lake to cabin #2. Alternately, if you want to reach cabin #2 by kayak or canoe, park at the boat launch (mile 0.6 of the campground road) and paddle south. The cabin is visible along the lakeshore.

In winter, the campground road isn't plowed, adding about 0.5 mile to cabin access. Park at the Veterans Memorial (just past the summer campground road) and follow the winter trail (signed) about 0.5 mile to cabin #1, or about 1 mile around the west shore of the lake to cabin #2.

BYERS LAKE CABIN #1

Facilities: This is your chance to stay in a traditional Alaska-style log cabin, one of only two public cabins in Southcentral Alaska accessible by road. Once a visitor center, this handcrafted, sod-roofed log cabin was built of large, scribed logs. The cabin's door is massive, with an interesting handle and closing mechanism. If you'd like to bring a padlock with you, the door can be secured while you're out exploring the park (a precaution most cabin-users don't bother with in less-visited areas).

Inside the cabin, you'll find five bunks, a flat-topped wood stove with a clear glass front, and a counter (there's no room for a dining table). Over thirty wooden pegs, charitably installed by a winter visitor with extra time on his hands, give you plenty of places to hang your gear. Unlike most public cabins, this one has blinds on the windows, an effort by Park staff to shield cabin-users from frequent passersby. This cabin is located directly adjacent to a large parking lot and near interpretive signs, after all. Rustic ambience aside, you're not guaranteed seclusion. An outhouse is across the parking lot in front of the cabin. In summer, high bush cranberries sprout from the cabin's roof, forming a lush vegetative toupee.

Gather dead-and-down firewood only. Or you can buy a bundle of wood from the boat concession at the south end of the parking lot, near cabin #1. Pump water from the nearby campground in summer, or purify water from the lake. Bring water or purify melted snow or ice in winter.

Condition: Excellent.

View and surroundings: The cabin is built on a slope, so that the back porch overlooks an amphitheater-like campfire circle, log benches, and a picnic table from second-story height. Sitting on one of two polished burl seats built into the cabin's porch, you can look out beyond the tops of spruce trees to the stars (they shine brightly here) or to the edge of deep-blue Byers Lake. Birch trees, spruce trees with burls (natural knot formations), and berry bushes surround the cabin. The cabin has windows facing all four directions — including north towards the parking lot, just 20 feet away.

BYERS LAKE CABIN #2

Facilities: This light-colored, milled-log cabin has a high ceiling, large windows facing all four directions, green trim, and a wide, covered front porch. A ladder leads to a small, dark half-loft. The cabin has six bunks, shelves, a round wood stove, and lots of floor space. Outside there is a picnic table, fire ring, and clean, well-constructed outhouse.

Gather dead-and-down firewood only. Or you can buy a bundle of wood from the boat concession at the south end of the parking lot near cabin #1. Purify water from the lake in summer. Bring water or purify melted snow or ice in winter.

Condition: Excellent.

View and surroundings: When the mountain is out — about one day in three during the summer — the only view that matters is the one to the northwest. Cabin #2's front windows and porch directly face Denali (Mt. McKinley) and surrounding peaks, about 35 miles away. You can imagine dozens of climbers struggling up the 20,320-foot snowcovered peak, and watch as the massive mountain's summit seems to snag any cloud drifting by. (Really, the mountain creates weather systems of its own, and the perennial scarves of clouds its wears most days are nothing compared to the 150-mile windstorms it occasionally produces.) On a 60-degree morning at Byers Lake, it's amazing to think that not-so-distant climbers are thawing themselves out after a night on the mountain, where summer overnight temperatures can plunge to forty below zero.

The cabin itself sits on a bluff jutting out from the western side of the lake. In late summer, wildflowers surround the cabin. In early September, yellow birch and dark green spruce cast reflections in the calm lake. On misty fall mornings, trumpeter swans glide along the surface of a mirror-smooth lake.

Mom Sherwonit's Byers Lake Bear-Lover's Blueberry Pie

Blueberries on the bush

Ingredients: 3 cups fresh and wild blueberries
¾ cup sugar
⅔ cup water
2-½ tablespoons corn starch
2 tablespoons margarine
1-½ tablespoons lemon juice
½ pint whipping cream
pre-baked pie shell

Mom Sherwonit's directions: Mix 1 cup blueberries with corn starch, sugar and water. Bring to a boil, stirring constantly, adding margarine and lemon juice. Boil until thick. Cool. Fold in 2 more cups of fresh blueberries and chill one hour. Spread whip cream along bottom of cooked pie shell. Pour in berry filling. Cover with remaining whipped cream. When done, share with your friends and family but keep away from bears, which can develop an unhealthy sweet tooth for human foods.

I've always known that Bill Sherwonit must love bears. A geologist in a former life, and presently a nature writer, he has hiked among, photographed, and written about bears extensively, logging many hours among the giants of Alaska. He's been charged once, and come face-to-face with bruins several more times in non-threatening circumstances. It says more about the tolerance of Alaska's bears for humans that he's never been injured by one, given the time he has spent in their company. As a young field geologist, he once had nightmares about bears, but those visions seem to have faded in direct relation to the amount of time he has spent among them. Talking now about the grizzlies of Denali or the coastal browns of Kodiak, he radiates serene calm. He does not carry a gun. As he has written, "My choice is a symbolic gesture of respect to the animal and its world; I'm only a visitor passing through and intending no harm." Compared to him, I am a raving paranoid, and he will probably interpret many of the bear tales and warnings in this book as overly skittish hyperbole.

In any case, Bill was staying at the Byers Lake Cabin with some other writerly folks, wandering the late summer woods and 4.5-mile lakeside trail in search of literary inspiration. I can't vouch for the inspiration, but I know he and his friends found blueberries in abundance. Where there are so many berries, of course, there also are bound to be bears. And in fact, while heading back to the cabin a little too swiftly and soundlessly, Bill ran into one: a startled male, gorging himself in preparation for winter. There was a pause, and then the black bear stepped into the grass and alder, yielding the trail.

Bill survived yet another exciting encounter without a scratch. And the Byers Lake writers brought back enough blueberries for Bill to whip up a delicious blueberry pie, using a recipe he borrowed from his mom, Torie. I missed the cabin trip, but seeing the pie, I was transported back to Denali State Park. The color of the berry filling reminded me of clear, deep blue Byers Lake, with the icy behemoth of Denali (Mt. McKinley) towering in the distance, as glossy white as the pie's whipped cream topping. After eating a delicious wedge, I had to wonder: does Bill really love the bears, or — given that they often appear in tandem — does he simply love the berries?

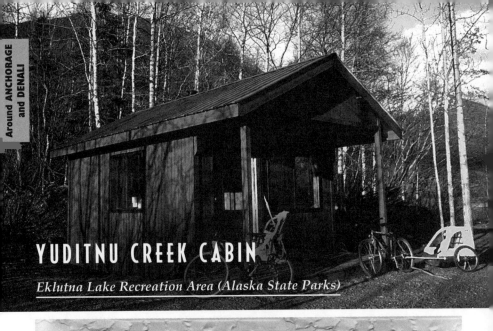

YUDITNU CREEK CABIN

Eklutna Lake Recreation Area (Alaska State Parks)

> *"If two people are to get along without radios, watchmans or any other 'necessary' items we humans seem to need, they must be able to find contentment and happiness in each other. ... P.S. Pete wanted to bring the watchman, but I nixed the idea"*
>
> Yuditnu Creek Cabin log.

Snapshot: Mountain Biking 101 or family base camp. A simple but well-maintained cabin in spectacular surroundings, on the shore of glacial Eklutna Lake.

Location: Next to a wide, sloping rocky beach at the mouth of Yuditnu Creek on the northern shore of Eklutna Lake.

Elevation: 900 feet.

Map: USGS Anchorage B6.

Access: In summer an easy 3-mile trip by foot, mountain bike, horseback, canoe, or motor boat; or by all-terrain vehicle (ATV) Sunday through Wednesday only. Floatplanes are allowed on Eklutna Lake. In winter, a 3-mile trip by cross-country ski or snowmachine.

Available: Year-round.

Best: Late April (or when trail is clear) to September for mountain biking and views of the lake; September for fall foliage; winter for skiing and the silence of a secluded, snowbound valley.

Sleeps: Five, comfortably, on bunks (the maximum is eight). Additionally, a single tent may be erected on the adjacent beach, as long as no more than eight people are in the cabin at any one time.

Maximum stay: 3 nights or one weekend per month.

Cost: $40.

Reservations: DNR Public Information Center (907) 269-8400, or any State Parks office. Info and cabin availability only via Internet at https://nutmeg.state.ak.us/ixpress/dnr/parks/index.dml. For the latest on local trail conditions, there is a ranger station at Eklutna Lake campground (907) 688-0908.

Facilities: The 12x16-foot, minimally furnished cabin has five bunks, a wood stove, a counter (no room for a table), and a small covered porch. Outside are a picnic table, a fire ring with grill, and an outhouse. Only dead-and-down firewood can be gathered; you may want to bring a supply, especially in winter. Purify water from the creek next to the cabin.

Condition: Good.

View and surroundings: Eklutna Lake is the largest body of water in Chugach State Park, a shimmering pool at the bottom of a glacier-carved valley framed by steep mountain walls. From the cabin, you face south across the lake, with a spectacular skyline of peaks to your left. In late spring and early summer, when the lake is still mostly frozen, Yuditnu Creek enters the lake to your right, a warmer plume opening leads in the ice that attract ducks and other waterfowl. The beach itself is wide and sloping, covered with sculpted driftwood and rocks of every size, providing a great playground for children. Thin stands of mostly birch trees, with some spruce, surround the cabin. Access trails linking the cabin to the main Lakeside Trail are fringed with berry bushes. The location of the cabin, off the main trail, provides some seclusion, although hikers, bikers, and tent-campers occasionally do wander the beach.

Recreation: There's lots to do here, with easy access thanks to the gently graded Eklutna Lakeside Trail — an abandoned gravel road now shared by ATVs (Sunday through Wednesday) and non-motorized users. To avoid ATV traffic, visit on Thursday through Saturday, or travel on narrower trails that hug the lake.

The 13-mile Lakeside Trail follows the shore of the lake and beyond, to views of Eklutna Glacier. The trail is good for hiking and even better for mountain biking — it's snow-free in late spring, when other area trails are too muddy, and it's wide enough for bikes towing kid trailers. (You do have to park your bike and continue on foot for the final steep mile of the trail to reach the glacier-viewing area.)

More challenging hikes fan out from the Lakeside Trail. The 2.5-mile Twin Peaks Trail begins near the main trailhead/ parking lot and climbs 1,800 feet into the tundra, with less well-maintained routes continuing even farther into alpine wilderness. From mile 5 of the Lakeside Trail, the 3.5-mile Bold Ridge Trail climbs 3,600 feet to a lookout point. Consult hiking guides (see Appendix 3) for more backcountry treks in this area.

Other activities include: fishing for trout and Dolly Varden at the mouth of Yuditnu Creek; berry-picking, mushroom hunting, and bird-watching along the Lakeside Trail; and canoeing, kayaking, or power-boating on Eklutna Lake (use caution, since the glacial water is cold and winds arise quickly). In winter, snowmachiners and cross-country skiers use the Lakeside Trail and hardpacked routes over the lake ice. Ice climbers can find difficult ice at the end of the Lakeside Trail.

Wildlife sightings: Dall sheep and mountain goats on slopes behind

Eklutna Lake from Yuditnu Creek Cabin

cabin, woodpeckers, owls, eagles, hawks, moose, wolves (often heard, especially in winter), and waterfowl on lake. Also in the area: black bears, brown bears, and lynx.

History: The cabin was built in 1995 by the Anchorage Rotary Club and the Anchorage Snowmobile Club, with help from Alaska State Parks.

Getting there: Take the Eklutna exit at mile 26 of the Glenn Highway, north of Anchorage. Exit east and turn immediately right onto a frontage road, which continues for 0.4 mile to the left turnoff to Eklutna Lake Road. Follow it east as it winds and climbs for 10 miles to the Eklutna Lake Recreation Area. The trailhead is on the northeast side of the parking lot. A boat launch is at the head of the lake for canoeists, kayakers, and powerboaters.

On foot, bike, ski, ATV, or snowmachine, follow the Lakeside Trail (an abandoned gravel road) east. Past the mile 2 post (just before a gravel pit) turn right along a narrower trail, signed PUBLIC USE CABIN #1. As the trail winds toward the lake, it will fork two more times. Turn right both times (signs at each junction will point the way toward the cabin). In winter, snowmachiners and skiers can travel with caution over the lake ice.

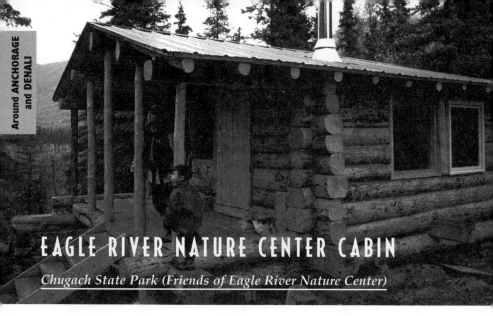

EAGLE RIVER NATURE CENTER CABIN

Chugach State Park (Friends of Eagle River Nature Center)

Snapshot: Year-round naturalist's retreat on Eagle River, or winter base camp for novice cross-country skiers and snowshoers. A new and attractive, easy-access log cabin for wildlife-watchers and families.

Location: About 1.25 miles north of the Eagle River Nature Center, just off the historic Iditarod Trail, next to a small pond and boulder field.

Elevation: 500 feet.

Map: USGS Anchorage A6 and A7.

Access: On foot or ski only along a nearly level trail.

Available: Year-round.

Best: Mid-May to mid-October on foot. December (or when several feet of snow have accumulated to cover the boulder-strewn trail) to March or later on skis. (Winter access without skis is also possible, with minimal postholing, since the trail is usually well-stomped.)

Sleeps: Eight on bunks, the maximum number allowed. (Four or five would be more comfortable.)

Maximum stay: Seven consecutive nights.

Cost: $45.

Reservations: Eagle River Nature Center, located at the trailhead (907) 694-2108.

Facilities: This cozy, rustic 15x16-foot cabin was constructed of beetle-killed spruce, fashioned into natural round logs. Less utilitarian and more lovingly crafted than many public cabins, this volunteer-built structure has a wood floor, exposed rafters, fireplace-style wood stove with a flat top, eight bunks, a small kitchen table, benches, and a covered porch. Windows (with screens and window shades, another handy feature that

Around ANCHORAGE and DENALI

may not hold up to heavy cabin use) face southwest, northwest and southeast. Firewood is provided and stored in an adjacent wood shed. A three-candle lantern is also provided, but you'll have to bring your own candles or purchase them at the Nature Center. The outhouse is a distant 500 feet from the cabin, near the turnoff to the Iditarod Trail. This is one of the only cabins with a door lock. You'll be given a combination code with your permit.

Condition: Excellent.

View and surroundings: The wonderfully secluded cabin faces southwest to the steep, opposite side of the glacier-carved Eagle River Valley with mountains rising to over 5,000 feet both north and south. Next to the cabin is a pond — the home of beavers, a favorite refueling point for ducks and moose, and, unfortunately, a good hang-out for bugs. (Visit in late fall or winter to avoid the latter.) En route to and around the cabin, among stands of spruce and birch, is a beautiful but potentially ankle-wrenching field of lichen-covered boulders. They were deposited here thousands of years ago by a massive rock slide. High bush cranberries and wild roses also grow profusely in the area.

Looking beyond the cabin porch

Recreation: Dramatic scenery, opportunities for wildlife-watching and easy hiking make this a great place to discover nature or introduce friends and family to wild Alaska. The nature center at the trailhead features displays, educational programs, and spotting scopes on a back deck where you can hang out and watch birds visiting feeders. The 0.6-mile Rodak Nature Trail begins at the nature center and features interpretive signs about glaciers, ecology, and the salmon life cycle, plus a viewing deck over a stream where salmon, birds, and occasionally bears can be spotted in summer. The Albert Loop Trail coincides with the Iditarod Trail for its first mile. It starts at the center, passes within 0.25 mile of the cabin, and makes a broad, 3.2-mile loop around the bottom of the valley, through beaver habitat (often flooded, check at the center first), and mixed spruce/birch/cottonwood forest.

From the cabin, you can continue hiking south on the Iditarod Trail all day. The trail, which parallels the glacial, rushing river, is less maintained the farther you go. Good turnaround points are Echo Bend (about 2 miles south of the cabin), The Perch (a rock outcropping about 3 miles from the cabin), or Heritage Falls (about 4 miles from the cabin) — all spots with good views of the valley, river, and 7,000-foot-plus peaks. Twelve miles up the valley — farther than a typical dayhiker using the cabin would manage — you'll reach a ford site across the wide, frigid river that requires caution. From here the trail continues for another 10 steep, rough miles to Crow Pass, site of a Forest Service cabin, and on to the end of the trail, near Girdwood.

This cabin is also one of Alaska's best for beginning skiers and snowshoers. Use it as a base camp for excursions on well-established trails without any fear of snowmachine traffic. The valley is picture-perfect after a fresh snowfall. An added bonus in winter: no bear interactions, fewer bugs, and fewer humans, as well.

Wildlife sightings: Beaver, moose, salmon, river otters, and ducks. Brown bears have been spotted near the cabin and have followed and/or charged people near the nature center in late summer, when the salmon are running. Use caution. Also in the area: wolves, weasels, martens, lynx, and porcupines.

History: The historic Iditarod Trail, a small section of which lies between the nature center and the cabin (and continues on to Crow Pass, near Girdwood) was the famous gold-rush era sled route connecting Seward and Nome. (The modern Iditarod Trail Sled Dog Race bypasses this part of the trail, so you won't see many huskies in this part — only lots of hikers.) Quite a bit more recently, the cabin was built in 1998 by the private, non-profit Friends of Eagle River Nature Center, which took over operation of the original visitor center in 1996 after budget-strapped State Parks staff fingered it for closure.

Getting there: From Anchorage, drive north on the Glenn Highway 10 miles, to the Hiland Road Exit. Bear right and go 2.5 miles to the lighted intersection with Eagle River Road. Turn right and drive 10.6 miles to the end of Eagle River Road, where the Eagle River Nature Center is located. Park at the center (your cabin permit includes the price of parking for up to four cars). Follow the historic Iditarod Trail, which begins behind the nature center, 1 mile to Four Corners (the intersection of Albert Loop and Iditarod trails). The signed right turnoff to the cabin is just beyond this point. Follow the winding, flagged trail over a wooded boulder field until you arrive at the cabin.

Nature-study class in session

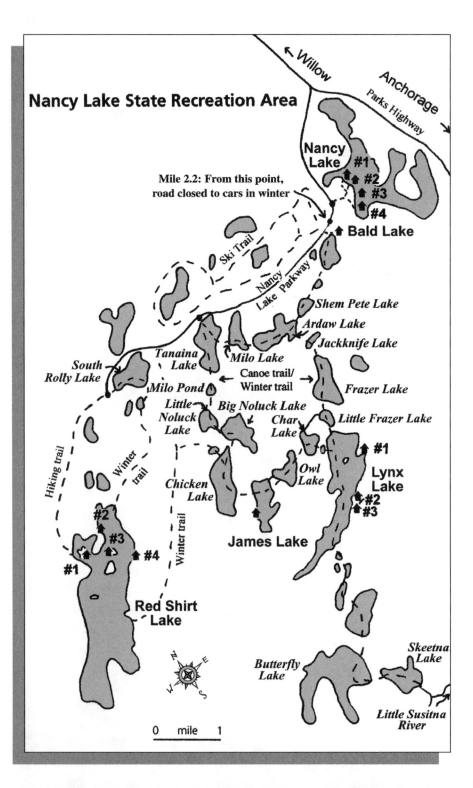

Nancy Lake State Recreation Area

Mile 2.2: From this point, road closed to cars in winter

Loon Country
(Or, a little bitta Minnesota)

"It looks right," I said to Brian as we dipped our paddles into the clear water of Red Shirt Lake, *my excitement mounting with every stroke. A screen of peeling, white-barked trees bordered the opposite shore. A fat loon called once and dove, reappearing a minute later behind us.*

"It smells right," I said, *inhaling the warm, mulchy smell of overripe berries and yellowing birch leaves.*

I held one arm over the gunwales and dipped a cautious finger, then disbelievingly extended my hand in the water up to my wrist. Warm. *And watched froggy-green lily pads slide under our canoe, resurfacing as we passed.* No glaciers. No icebergs.

"This could be Wisconsin," I said to my husband, my giddy voice rising to a shriek. *"This could be Minnesota!"*

Faint praise, you might think. People travel from halfway around the globe to get away from such staid places and come instead to the Alaska of their dreams, a land of superlatives, where the mountains are taller, the vistas grander, the wildlife wilder. Also: the open ocean rougher. And the lakes — especially the glacial lakes — much, much colder.

During summer, when outdoor activity peaks, local newspaper headlines first tittilate, later discourage, and finally exhaust those of us who live here. Hunter missing. Search continues for weekend boaters. Climber found dead. *By July, you don't want to read any more.* White-out. Human error. Wandered for days. Cold shock. Lost. *On summer's hottest day:* Hypothermia blamed. *By August, you're thinking about visiting friends and family somewhere more temperate and less thrilling. Somewhere safe. Maybe Iowa.*

Most Alaska residents were born somewhere else. I grew up in Illinois, and collected mosquito bites every year at Wisconsin summer camps. Visited Grandma at her lakeside cabin in the Ozarks. Eased into adolescence the same summer I canoed the Boundary Waters. I didn't think I'd miss lazy summer days in the flatlands, lakes as small as puddles, muddy portages marked so well that

*the littlest Girl Scout could find her way. I didn't think the sound of a loon
tremoloing at dusk to its mate would bring me close to tears.*

*After moving to Alaska, I mastered the long-voweled lexicon of arctic
lands.* Crevasse. Krummholtz. *After learning those romantic foreign words,
after familiarity bred contempt, an old Midwestern term suddenly began to seem
more exotic.* Skinny-dipping.

*But skinny-dipping here was out of the question, I thought. For a short
while after I moved north, I believed one couldn't swim in an Alaskan lake at all.
Period. The day I first dipped my toes into Kenai Lake, one of our blue-green
glacial beauties, I considered leaving the state. The veins on the top of my feet
throbbed and turned purple, I couldn't feel my toes at all, and I thought:* That's
it. I can't raise a family here. Children deserve to swim with the sun on
their backs, even if it does mean dealing with leeches.

*Turns out that I was completely wrong about the swimming. There are
glacial lakes, like the Kenai, milky and luminescent. And there are lakes that look
fresh but still bear traces of glacial flour and an alpine chill that will induce a
temporary state of amnesia after the briefest dunk.*

*But there are also the shallow, relatively warm lakes of Southcentral's
flatter terrain, including the loon-country lakes of Nancy Lake State Recreation
Area, in the Matanuska-Susitna Valley north of Anchorage. It's where canoeists
of all kinds — serious ones, as well as folks with young kids and uncalloused fingers — can enjoy recreational boating without fear of rapids or icy-cold, sudden-
death water. It's where all of us go to get a little bitta Minnesota.*

*The Nancy Lake State Recreation Area is an approximately 36-square
mile parkland that is both tame and wild. Tame because portage trails are
superbly well-marked and planked, and the area's 13 public cabins, located on a
chain of lovely lakes, take some of the wet and cold out of multi-day paddling (or,
in winter, cross-country skiing). Wild because all but three of the area's three
dozen or so small lakes are closed to motorized boats and floatplanes, and you can
canoe on a sunny autumn weekend, when foliage color is peaking and the nights
are crisp and clear, and still pass only a handful of canoes, or sometimes none at
all. Compared to private lakes in the same region, which are increasingly hemmed
in by private docks and overwhelmed by traffic and noise, the Nancy Lake area is
an oasis of serenity.*

*The loons call — and call they do, every night, from every lake — and
their haunting vibratos seem to carry across thousands of miles, across tens of
years, to the lands of their loon cousins in flatter, gentler country.*

*Red Shirt Lake was our first canoeing destination in the state recreation
area. The 3-mile hike to the lake, where our rented canoe awaited us, was hilly
and hot. (Hot by Southcentral Alaska standards anyway — about 75 degrees.)
The July heat, like the temperate lakewater I would soon discover, surprised me.*

Only two hours north of Anchorage, the Nancy Lake area straddles another climatic zone, influenced by the more extreme (warmer and drier in summer, colder in winter) interior Alaska climate. T-shirt weather felt good, even with clouds of mosquitoes biting.

Tossing our backpacks into our canoe, we paddled an easy half-mile to cabin #3, on its own tiny island in the middle of the lake. At the spacious cabin, which boasts a fantastic wall of picture windows facing the water, Brian broke out his fishing tackle. Within minutes my son was doing something he'd never done in Alaska: standing knee-deep and comfortable in the water, pants rolled up, hands grasping for the turquoise-striped dragonflies crackling like cellophane through the reeds.

Approaching Red Shirt Lake's Cabin #3

With the sun setting, painting the lake pink and orange, Brian cast a few more times and reeled in a northern pike. We stared disbelievingly at the skinny, thrashing fish. I thought we should kill the little invader, but Brian was entranced by its sleek lines and fighting spirit. He let it go.

Pike were introduced in the Mat-Su Valley by well-intentioned anglers who didn't realize that the monsters would take over quickly, gobbling up young salmon, trout, and even waterfowl. State biologists are trying to control the pike problem, which has spread to nearly 100 area lakes. But in the meanwhile, they're a fun fish to have around. They eat voraciously, they fight briefly but valiantly, and they offer yet another reminder of faraway places. Pull a wriggling, needle-toothed 20- or 30- pound pike out of the water — or better yet, in winter, out of a hole in the ice — and you're back in the lands of beer and bratwurst, college football and Garrison Keillor, U.P. and ya-hey.

One pike successfully caught, I begged Brian to set down his rod and hold our baby daughter so I could roll up my own pantlegs and wade before dusk enveloped us completely. He cooperated, but it wasn't enough. Midwestern swimming memories — flashbacks to camps where I'd graduated long ago from pollywog to minnow to shark — were flooding over me. I wished we'd brought bathing suits, but who could have guessed we'd need them?

Never mind, *I thought, and whipped off my shirt and pants. My young son looked on, gleefully incredulous. Then my head was under the dark water and I was home.*

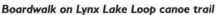

The Red Shirt Lake trip was so satisfying that we immediately planned a more challenging canoe trip for late August: an 8-mile circular route along the Lynx Lake Loop. The 14-lake loop requires 12 portages. (A narrow canoe trail through a reedy channel eliminates the 13th.) Luckily, the portages are mostly level and fairly short — less than 0.25 mile long.

Common loons, as well as one pacific loon and several red-necked grebes, cruised the calm waters alongside us. In three paddling days, we saw only two other canoes, always too far away to hear the paddlers' voices. The portages blistered our fingers and deadened the muscles in our arms, but at the end of every haul we were rewarded with another view, more loons, and another small lake to ourselves.

The names on the map lured us onward, curious to see the next body of water: Owl Lake, Big and Little Noluck lakes, Milo Pond. And on one of the hardest portages, when my triceps threatened to seize up, vast patches of blue-

Boardwalk on Lynx Lake Loop canoe trail

berries, crowberries, and cranberries gave me a face-saving excuse to set the canoe down. We filled a water bottle with four cups of berries so that we'd still be tasting the fruits of loon country when we got back to Anchorage.

At the end of each night's paddle, we built a fire and watched the sun set again from a different cabin. Lynx Lake #2 the first night; James Lake Cabin the second. One guidebook author recommends paddling the Lynx Lake Loop counterclockwise, to put the route's slightly longer portages first. Never mind about the portages, I say. It's your nightly accommodations that should be considered. I recommend the clockwise loop, to put the cabins in order of attractiveness. All three Lynx Lake cabins are charming cottages — tiny, simply built, with pleasant views. But the James Lake Cabin is one of the state park system's finest. Hit it last, or you'll be too spoiled to enjoy any of the others.

James Lake Cabin sits just back from a high hill overlooking a wide sweep of the lake, and fronted by tall grass and a fireweed meadow sprawling down the hill. It's a true log cabin, constructed of honey-colored round logs, with high rafters, and large picture windows facing all four directions. The lake itself is blissfully silent and undeveloped: no jet skis, no floatplanes, no private cabins along the shore.

The James Lake Cabin was built in 1988 by an Operation Raleigh crew of international volunteers, dispatched

James Lake Cabin with rainbow

by Prince Charles to commemorate Sir Walter Raleigh's circumnavigation of the globe. (Other crews participated on projects in remote areas of Chile, Afghanistan, Kenya, and the Arctic.) Young men and women from the United Kingdom, the United States, Canada, Singapore, Australia, and New Zealand formed a canoe flotilla, transporting wood planks to cover the muddy portages en route to James Lake. The U.S. Army dropped off logs for the cabin's construction.

Ten years later, in 1998, one of the volunteers from Singapore returned to James Lake and wrote nostalgically in the cabin's log, "We were pretty young then — 18 to 22 years old — and the beauty of this place enchanted us. It's very reassuring to see this park unspoilt still, and the water still drinkable.... Reading the past few entries, and people's rave reviews of the cabin, I do feel happy and proud to have been responsible for the building of this shelter."

On our way to the James Lake Cabin, dark clouds gathered and stalled just to the south of us. Thunder boomed across the lake. We dug our paddles into the water, anxious to beat the storm. But we were also excited. Thunder is rare in Anchorage. The summery rumbles and a brief burst of hail that followed, sending a nearby pair of rednecked grebes paddle-kicking in zigzag confusion, offered yet another reminder of the Midwest.

By the time we hung our wet clothes in the cabin and stoked a blazing fire, the sky had cleared. A huge double rainbow appeared, arcing east to south. The charged air shimmered. Lily pads on the lake far below gleamed an even brighter green. For many minutes after the storm, silence blanketed the lake. Then a gentle breeze stirred, and the loons began to call again, ushering in dusk.

〰〰

"I love this," I told Brian the next morning, our third and final paddling day, as the morning sun baked the cabin's front porch. He regarded me suspiciously. Perhaps I'd mentioned "Boundary Waters" a few too many times. Or maybe the previous night's tuneless renditions of old Camp Jorn songs had made him wary.

"No, I don't want to move back to the Midwest," I assured him, although he hadn't said a word. "I'm just glad I know where to find a little taste of it."

The sky was cloudless: perfect for canoeing. But also perfect for not canoeing. We sat on the porch, sipping from a final cup of coffee that had turned cold long ago. We lingered until noon, packed up slowly, and then headed north. More tiny lakes. More leg-stretching portages. Mating dragonflies circled our canoe, startling us with their rattling wings. Berry patches offered more face-saving breaks.

On Tanaina Lake, the final lake of the 14-lake loop, a cold northern wind blew in. Just as the gusts hit us, we glimpsed a pink, pyramid-shaped mountain rising, alone, above the horizon.

"Denali," I said, pointing to the ethereal peak, visible over 80 miles away.

Minnesota, Illinois, Wisconsin, and the ghosts of all flat, comforting places were behind us now. Alaska was ahead. We paddled, hunched into the wind, bridging distance and memory.

About Nancy Lake State Recreation Area

There are 13 public-use cabins in the Nancy Lake State Recreation Area, all open year-round and accessible via lake and overland trails from 0.2 to 13 miles long. The area, a 1.5-hour drive north from Anchorage, is popular, family-friendly, and shared by many user groups, from "silent sport" aficionados (hikers, canoeists, and cross-country skiers) to power-boaters and snowmachiners. In one corner of the flat, lake-dotted recreation area, you might spend the evening listening to the whine of jet skis and the bang of distant fireworks. In another corner, only the call of loons will serenade you to sleep.

SUSITNA VALLEY

The cabins themselves vary from simple, dark brown, somewhat weathered structures (on Nancy Lake) to bright, natural-log cabins with porches and extra features (on James and Bald lakes). Each Nancy Lake S.R.A. public cabin has a triangular marker on the shoreline and a sign on the cabin itself. Take care not to trespass on private property. Access, ambience, and cabin styles vary greatly, so plan your cabin getaway carefully. Below you'll find descriptions of all the cabins, divided by location Nancy Lake, Bald Lake, Lynx Lake, James Lake, and Red Shirt Lake.

Nancy Lake S.R.A. has an interesting history. Park facilities were planned in 1968, making this recreation area the oldest state park unit in Alaska. Forward-thinking planners expected the state capital to move from Juneau to nearby Willow, and prepared for the impending population boom by buying up private land, including nearly all the renovated cabins still standing today. (Some of the crudest structures had been hastily erected by land owners "proving up" on free, 5-acre recreational sites purchased earlier from the Bureau of Land Management.) On paper at least, the plans for the recreation area were ambitious: hundreds of campsites, horse corrals, even golf courses. After the capital-move plan died, the state recreation area remained, all the more valuable in its less developed state. Since 1988, the number of cabins available to the public has jumped from five to 13. Only two of them, James Lake and Bald Lake cabins, were built from scratch.

Please note that all the cabins are located in areas where firewood is not abundant. Bring your own (a good idea in winter) or be prepared to scrounge for a while. Gather dead-and-down wood only. Treat lake water in summer. Bring your own supply or purify melted snow or ice in winter.

NANCY LAKE CABINS #1-#4

Nancy Lake State Recreation Area (Alaska State Parks)

Snapshot: Family-friendly cabins for those who don't mind a little company. Four insulated wooden-frame cabins on popular, accessible Nancy Lake, within a 10- to 20-minute hike, ski, paddle, or snowmachine ride from the trailhead.

Location: On the western shore of Nancy Lake, just off mile 67.3 of the Parks Highway.

Elevation: 200 feet.

Map: Alaska State Park brochures: _Nancy Lake State Recreation Area Public Use Cabins, Summer Guide to Nancy Lake State Recreation Area,_ and _Winter Guide to Nancy Lake State Recreation Area._ USGS Tyonek C1 (doesn't show cabins or trails).

Access: In summer, by foot, boat, or canoe. In winter, by ski, dogsled, or snowmachine on hardpacked trails. Airplanes are allowed to land on Nancy Lake (contact Alaska State Parks to check ice thickness in winter).

Available: Year-round.

Best: Late May (after lake thaw) to early September (peak foliage time) for hikers and canoeists. Late November (or when 18 inches of snow has accumulated) to mid-April (lake ice and trail conditions permitting) for snowmachiners, skiers, and mushers.

Capacity: Varies by cabin.

Maximum stay: Five nights per month.

Cost: $35.

Reservations: DNR Public Information Center (907) 269-8400, or Mat-Su Area State Parks Office, (907) 745-3975. Info only, Nancy Lake State Recreation Area Ranger Office, (907) 495-6273.

Misc.: Canoe rentals and paddling information available from Tippecanoe in Willow (907) 495-6688.

About Nancy Lake

Nancy Lake is the most road-accessible of all the state recreation area's lakes, which also makes it the most busy and noisy. Floatplanes and motor boats are allowed here: a campground and boat launch occupy the lake's northern side, and some private houses dot the shore. Still, the public cabins on Nancy Lake's grassy western shore offer an introduction to the northern woods for those who don't want to hike, portage, or paddle far. For a quieter cabin experience, try the new Bald Lake Cabin, which rivals Nancy Lake for easy access. Or visit in winter, when the Nancy Lake cabins provide a good base for exploring cross-country ski trails north of the Nancy Lake Parkway.

For all Nancy Lake cabins

Recreation: Fishing (best just after lake thaw and just prior to freezeup) for rainbow trout, lake trout, whitefish, and Dolly Varden. Blueberries, crowberries, and cranberries, as well as some currants and raspberries ripen from late July through August. Canoeists and boaters valuing easy access over solitude can play along the convoluted, "W"-shaped shoreline of Nancy Lake. Swimming is also popular. Hiking in the area is mostly limited to the cabin-access trails due to muskeg and thick brush. Cross-country skiers can explore 10 miles of cross-country ski trails (off limits to snowmachines) north of the Nancy Lake Parkway. Snowmachiners use the Nancy Lake cabins as a base for zipping all over the rest of the recreation area.

Wildlife sightings: Common loons, red-necked grebes, black bears, and moose. Also in the area: arctic terns, mergansers, eagles, Pacific loons, beaver, brown bears.

History: In 1917, the Alaska Railroad opened access to the lower Susitna Valley. Sparks from passing trains occasionally ignited wildfires that burned in this area. Most of the trees in this young forest (predominantly paper birch, mixed with white spruce) are less than 100 years old. More recently, the invasion of spruce bark beetles is changing the forest again. You may notice pinholes — evidence of the bark-gnawing beetle — in dead or dying, rust-colored spruce trees.

Getting there: There are two access points for Nancy Lake. On the lake's north side, at mile 66.5 on the Parks Highway, there is a campground and boat launch, mostly used by powerboaters. From here, the cabins are 1 to

1.5 miles south. Paddlers may use the boat launch, but most opt for the more convenient canoe-only launch described below.

All other users proceed along the Parks Highway to mile 67.3. Turn left on the unpaved Nancy Lake Parkway. The canoe launch and parking area is at mile 1.6 on the parkway. From here, the cabins are a 0.25- to 0.75-mile paddle southeast.

The main trailhead and parking area for hikers, skiers, and snow-machiners is at mile 1.8 on the Nancy Lake Parkway. The trails to the cabins are easy to walk or ski, but poorly signed at this writing. Many first-time visitors end up backtracking. Watch for new signs and minor trail changes in 1999. A 0.5-mile, wide, gently rolling main trail leads to cabins #2 and #4, with a left turnoff (should be signed) to cabin #1. There is also an unsigned primitive trail to #1 (the old route). The shore between the cabins is thick with devil's club, so resist the urge to take shortcuts if you make a wrong turn. Cabin #3 is surrounded by private land and in summer it can be reached over water only.

Snowmachiners follow the main, packed trail to cabin #4 and then travel over the ice, following the lakeshore left to reach cabins #3, #2, and #1, for a total distance of 0.75 to 1 mile. Skiers may also prefer this route, since the main trail is the most firmly packed.

NANCY LAKE CABIN #1

Capacity: Sleeps six, the maximum allowed (four would be more comfortable).

Facilities: The dark brown, wooden-frame cabin measures 16x16 feet. It has six bunks, table, chairs, counter, round wood stove, outhouse, and deck-sized porch with a rustic log bench. There is an additional picnic table and fire ring with grill outside. This cabin is most frequently rented by canoeists, since it is closest to the carry-in canoe launch at mile 1.6 off the Nancy Lake Parkway.

Condition: Fair.

View and surroundings: The cabin sits about 30 feet back from Nancy Lake on level terrain, connected to the lake by narrow boardwalks. Thick stands of birch and a few spruce trees surround the cabin. To the east are open views of the lake, the opposite, wooded lakeshore, and the distant Talkeetna Mountains. A dozen private cabins and houses are visible across the water. Boat and snowmachine traffic can be heavy. A no-wake zone (not always heeded) and a nesting bird site is just to the north of cabin #1.

NANCY LAKE CABIN #2

Capacity: Sleeps six, the maximum allowed (four would be more comfortable).

Facilities: The dark brown, flat-roofed, wooden-frame cabin measures 12x24 feet. This is the simplest and most weathered of the Nancy Lake structures, but the cabin's wider layout (cabin #1 is 16x16 feet) and slightly larger size overall may help if you're renting with young children and concerned about close proximity to a hot wood stove. The cabin has white interior walls, six bunks, table, chairs, counters, and round wood stove. Outside you'll find a new outhouse, picnic table, and fire ring with grill (no porch).

Condition: Fair.

View and surroundings: The cabin sits about 30 feet back from the water on level terrain, connected to the lake by a narrow boardwalk. Thick stands of birch and a few spruce trees surround the cabin. To the east are open views of the lake, the opposite, wooded lakeshore, and the distant Talkeetna Mountains. A dozen private cabins and houses are visible across the water. Boat and snowmachine traffic can be heavy.

NANCY LAKE CABIN #3

Capacity: Sleeps six, the maximum allowed (four would be more comfortable).

Facilities: The dark brown, frame-construction cabin measures 20x20 feet. A peaked roof, more floor space, and larger, well-positioned windows make this cabin lighter and roomier than cabins #1 and #2. Also, this cabin has a low wall dividing the cooking area from the sleeping area. The cabin has six bunks, counters, table, chairs, and round wood stove. Outside you'll find an additional picnic table and a fire ring with grill (no porch). Cabin #3 is surrounded by private land and must be reached over water only.

Condition: Good.

View and surroundings: The cabin sits about 30 feet back from the water on level terrain connected to the lake by a narrow boardwalk. Thick stands of birch and a few spruce trees surround the cabin. To the east are open views of the lake, the opposite, wooded lakeshore, and the distant Talkeetna Mountains. A dozen private cabins and houses are visible across the water. Boat and snowmachine traffic can be heavy.

SUSITNA
VALLEY

NANCY LAKE CABIN #4

Capacity: Sleeps eight comfortably, the maximum allowed.

Facilities: The 24x24-foot cabin is Nancy Lake's most deluxe, with a covered, extra-large porch, a wall of multi-paned windows with green trim, and a high ceiling with exposed rafters. The roof's wide overhang makes it fairly dark inside, however. While it's still a single-room structure, low wall partitions separate areas within the cabin. The outhouse at #4 is newer and cleaner, too. Don't splurge on all the space if your party is small, however, since this cabin is the hardest to heat of the four. The cabin has 11 bunks (a row of them in front of the east-facing windows double as a window seat), table, counter, round wood stove, benches, and chairs. Outside you'll find an additional picnic table and fire ring with grill. In winter, count on burning three bundles or more of firewood in this roomy cabin.

SUSITNA VALLEY

Condition: Good.

View and surroundings: The cabin sits about 40 feet back from the water on level terrain. Thick stands of birch and a few spruce trees surround the cabin. To the east are open views of the lake, the opposite, wooded lakeshore, and the distant Talkeetna Mountains. Private cabins and houses are visible across the water, and to either side of the public cabin. Boat and snowmachine traffic can be heavy.

BALD LAKE CABIN

Nancy Lake State Recreation Area (Alaska State Parks)

Snapshot: Accessible solitude. The newest cabin in the recreation area, unique for its combination of easy access and quieter surroundings.

Location: On the north shore of Bald Lake, southwest of Nancy Lake and just a few minutes' walk south of mile 2.5 of the Nancy Lake Parkway along a wide, well-maintained trail (signed).

Elevation: 200 feet.

Map: Alaska State Park brochures: *Nancy Lake State Recreation Area Public Use Cabins, Summer Guide to Nancy Lake State Recreation Area,* and *Winter Guide to Nancy Lake State Recreation Area.* USGS Tyonek C1 (doesn't show cabins or trails).

Access: In summer, by foot along an easy 0.2-mile trail. In winter, by ski, snowmachine, or dog sled. No airplanes are allowed on Bald Lake.

Available: Year-round.

Best: Late May (after lake thaw) to early September (peak foliage time) for hikers and canoeists. Late November (or when 18 inches of snow has accumulated) to mid-April (lake ice and trail conditions permitting) for snowmachiners, skiers, and mushers.

Sleeps: Six comfortably, the maximum allowed.

Maximum stay: Five nights per month.

Cost: $35.

Reservations: DNR Public Information Center (907) 269-8400, or Mat-Su Area State Parks Office, (907) 745-3975. Info only, Nancy Lake State Recreation Area Ranger Office, (907) 495-6273.

Facilities: This bright, attractive 16x24-foot cabin is constructed of light-colored, milled logs, with a green metal roof and green window trim.

Compared to other cramped, less-furnished public cabins in the Nancy Lake State Recreation Area, this one has a wealth of sitting, eating, and gear-storing areas. The cabin has seven bunks (two double as a convenient L-shaped bench around the table), large square dining table, counter, shelves, extra bench, plastic chairs, and flat-topped wood stove. Outside are an outhouse, picnic table, and fire ring with grill. A half-loft provides extra room for gear only (no sleeping allowed); and with the dozens of natural wood pegs inside, there's no shortage of places to hang your hat. A covered porch is supported by burl-knotted posts. Extra features include a rustic log bench, a rough-hewn birch chair, and even a boot brush bolted to the porch.

Condition: Excellent.

View and surroundings: The secluded, south-facing cabin perches slightly above and 100 feet back from Bald Lake, with tranquil hilltop views of the water to the east and south. Birch and spruce forest surround the cabin. A wide, gently sloping trail runs downhill to the grassy lakeshore. There are no other developments and little or no activity on Bald Lake.

Wildlife sightings: Loons, black bear, moose, beaver, wolverines, and porcupines (including one that likes to wake cabin-users with an early-morning gnawing routine). Also in the area: mergansers, red-necked grebes, arctic terns, and brown bears.

Recreation: An abandoned one-mile wetlands/ birch forest nature trail heads south from the Bald Lake trailhead at mile 2.2 of the parkway (hike straight ahead from the parking lot, instead of turning left on the wider trail toward the cabin). Some boardwalk planks are rotten or missing on the overgrown trail, but it's still possible to hike with waterproof boots, with good chances of spotting waterfowl along the way.

To paddle Bald Lake, canoeists can portage from the trailhead to a small beach downhill of the cabin, or to a lake access trail just before the cabin, to the right. Either way, the portage is about 0.2 mile (the trail to the cabin is wide and root-free, but hilly). Swimming is also popular. You can fish for salmon and rainbow trout in the lake.

Skiers and snowmachiners can explore over 13 miles of shared trails by crossing the western shore of Bald Lake and following the trail southwest to Shem Pete Lake, then joining up with the Lynx Lake Loop canoe trail system. North of the Nancy Lake Parkway are 10 miles of skiing-only trails, beginning practically across the road from the Bald Lake trailhead, at mile 2.2 of the parkway.

SUSITNA VALLEY

History: The Bald Lake Cabin was built in 1996 and has become the most popular cabin in the recreation area.

Getting there: Drive to mile 67.3 of the Parks Highway. Turn left on the unpaved Nancy Lake Parkway.

    In summer, drive to mile 2.5. The Bald Lake trailhead and summer parking lot (signed) will be on your left. From here, a trail heads to the left and downhill, 0.2 mile, to the cabin. **In winter,** drive to mile 2.2 and park at the winter trailhead. From here, proceed 0.3 mile on skis, snowmachine, or dog sled along the unplowed section of the Nancy Lake Parkway to the Bald Lake trailhead (signed) on your left. See summer directions above.

SUSITNA VALLEY

RED SHIRT LAKE CABINS #1-#4

Nancy Lake State Recreation Area (Alaska State Parks)

Snapshot: Weekend favorites for canoeists who also like to hike. Attractive, insulated wooden-frame cabins of varying designs, all with great views of a less-visited lake.

Location: On Red Shirt Lake, in the southwest corner of Nancy Lake State Recreation Area. Two of the cabins are located on the lakeshore; two cabins are located on their own tiny islands.

Elevation: 100 feet.

Map: Alaska State Park brochures: *Nancy Lake State Recreation Area Public Use Cabins, Summer Guide to Nancy Lake State Recreation Area,* and *Winter Guide to Nancy Lake State Recreation Area.* USGS Tyonek C1 (doesn't show cabins or trails).

Access: In summer, by a combination of a 3-mile hike and a short (1 mile or less) canoe trip. Bushwhacking to cabin #2 is possible, though not recommended. In winter, a moderately challenging 7.5- to 8-mile cross-country ski or snowmachine trip over a closed road and shared winter access trail.

Available: Year-round.

Best: Late May (after lake thaw) to early September (peak foliage time) for hikers and canoeists. Late November (or when 18 inches of snow has accumulated) to mid-April (lake ice and trail conditions permitting) for snowmachiners, skiers, and mushers.

Capacity: Varies by cabin.

Maximum stay: Five nights per month.

Cost: $35.

Reservations: DNR Public Information Center (907) 269-8400, or Mat-Su Area State Parks Office, (907) 745-3975. Info only, Nancy Lake State

Recreation Area Ranger Office, (907) 495-6273.

Misc.: Canoe rentals and paddling information available from Tippe-canoe in Willow, (907) 495-6688. Tippecanoe keeps canoes at the head of the lake, so hikers who have reserved a canoe ahead of time need carry only paddles and life jackets along the 3-mile access trail to the lake.

About Red Shirt Lake

There are many private land parcels on the lake, belonging to a "who's who" of notable Anchorage families. Some use this area as a weekend or holiday retreat. Others commute to the city in summer by floatplane. Motor boats are allowed, but since there's no public boat launch, you may not see a single one. In general, expect some July and August weekends to have a congenially busy, northwoods summer-camp feel. On week-days during the off-season, on the other hand, it is possible to have the entire lake to yourself.

For all Red Shirt Lake cabins

Recreation: Fishing (best just after lake thaw and just prior to freezeup) for rainbow trout, lake trout, Dolly Varden, and whitefish. Northern pike are less picky. Pike up to 30 pounds have been caught in Red Shirt Lake, where the non-native species was first spotted in 1980. Ice fishermen occasionally try their luck here. Blueberries, crowberries, and cranberries, as well as some currants and raspberries ripen from late July through August.

Canoeists can explore the 3-mile long lake (although some islands and shoreside parcels are private, so watch where you pull ashore). Swimming is also popular. Hiking — except for the 3-mile sum-mer access route to the lake — is limited. Hardpacked snowmachine-and-skiing routes criss-cross the lake in winter.

Wildlife sightings: Common and Pacific loons, red-necked grebes, mer-gansers, eagles, black bears, and moose. Also in the area: arctic terns and brown bears.

Getting there: Drive to mile 67.3 of the Parks Highway. Turn left on the unpaved Nancy Lake Parkway. **In summer**, drive 6.5 miles to the the parkway's end, at the Red Shirt Lake trailhead and parking area, across from the South Rolly Lake campground. To hike to the lake, head past the gate opposite the campground and up the closed road. Immediately uphill of the gate, you'll reach a bulletin board directing you left, onto the summer access trail.

The well-marked Red Shirt Lake Trail traverses a scenic, forested ridge west of Arc, Twin Shirt, and Red Shirt lakes. Along the rolling 3-

SUSITNA VALLEY

mile trail — the highest in the recreation area — you'll gain 500 feet of elevation each way, with occasional glimpses of the distant Chugach Mountains. The trail ends at a small hike-in camping area and canoe launch, with chained rental canoes visible along the shore. From the launch, you'll paddle 0.25 to 1 mile, depending on the cabin rented.

In winter, the Nancy Lake Parkway ends at mile 2.2. The remainder of the Parkway becomes an unplowed, multi-use winter trail. To reach Red Shirt Lake, you'll need to continue on skis, sled, or snowmachine for 4.3 miles to the South Rolly Campground. At the campground's boat launch, travel over the lake, following the right shoreline to the creek flowing from South Rolly to Red Shirt Lake. Do not travel on the creek ice itself. The winter trail to Red Shirt Lake, marked with small orange rectangles, parallels the creek for 2.5 miles to the north end of Red Shirt Lake. From there, travel over the ice to your cabin. Total one-way distance from the winter trailhead is 7.5 to 8 miles. Be prepared for varying trail conditions and temperatures that can plunge to 40 degrees below zero.

Cabin view of Red Shirt Lake

RED SHIRT LAKE CABIN #1

Capacity: Sleeps eight comfortably, the maximum number allowed.

Facilities: Red Shirt #1 is a 20x24-foot wooden-frame cabin with a dark brown exterior, light interior walls, and a high ceiling. With its odd assortment of plastic-and-steel chairs and its cracked linoleum floor, it looks more like a small dormitory than a rustic cabin. The dining table inside is extra long, and outside there is a fire ring with grill, and two picnic tables (including one on the large, covered porch). The cabin's twenty windows are its best feature. One wide panel of picture windows faces open water to the east. Another cluster of panes in the cabin's southwest corner offers glimpses of water lapping up against the tiny island's western shore. The cabin also has ten bunks, wood stove, and counter. You can approach the cabin from the small landing areas on the island's east or west sides, although the east side is easier.

Condition: Fair.

View and surroundings: Red Shirt Cabin #1 offers an easy-to-reach, child-friendly, island retreat for canoeing, watching sunrises, and picking berries. The cabin faces south from its own jigsaw-shaped island, tucked behind a screen of birch and spruce trees, less than 50 feet from the water both to the east and west. Twenty windows of varying sizes provide good lake views through the trees in a 180-degree arc. (You can watch the morning sun glimmering on the water without getting out of your bunk, thanks to a row of picture windows in the cabin's east wall.) Less than a quarter-mile from a campground on Red Shirt Lake's northwest shore, the cabin is within earshot of weekend campers, but not easily visible. Mats of fireweed, and cranberry, crowberry, and blueberry bushes surround the cabin, outhouse, and a cleared picnic area just beyond the cabin's front porch.

RED SHIRT LAKE CABIN #2

SUSITNA
VALLEY

Capacity: Sleeps four, the maximum allowed (two would be more comfortable).

Facilities: Red Shirt #2 is a cute little cabin, officially registered as 16x12 feet, but it feels even smaller. It's light and airy inside, though, with windows on three sides. The cabin has four bunks, wood stove, and counter. Outside are an outhouse, picnic table, and fire ring with grill. (No dining table inside and no porch.)

The cabin, tucked behind a miniature meadow of grass and fireweed, is not as clearly visible from the lake as the other Red Shirt cabins, but will come into view as you paddle close to the shore. While the cabin is most commonly (and most sensibly) used by canoeists, this is the only cabin that one *may* reach on foot. Be warned, though, it's not recommended and it's tough going, especially when midsummer vegetation obscures the unmaintained trail. Some late-arriving and unprepared hikers have trouble finding it. If you're determined, it's a 0.75-mile bushwhack around the head of the lake, starting near the camping/canoe-launch area.

Condition: Good.

View and surroundings: Red Shirt Cabin #2 is good for couples or any-one who values privacy over space. The petite structure faces east from the boggy northern shore of the lake, about 40 feet from the water. The cabin is hidden from most boat and floatplane traffic, hemmed in by tall grass, a few skinny spruce trees, and vast patches of fireweed. Just north of the cabin is a beaver lodge.

RED SHIRT LAKE CABIN #3

Capacity: Sleeps six comfortably, the maximum allowed.

Facilities: This is the most deluxe of the four Red Shirt cabins, with lots of eating, sitting, and general hanging-out room. The 24x16-foot cabin's high, sloping ceiling frames a wide wall of picture windows overlooking the water. The dark brown, wooden-frame cabin has six bunks (eight, if you count the double-long, skinny bunk that doubles as a window seat), an indoor picnic table as well as a long counter that serves as a dining table. Outside you'll find an outhouse, picnic table, fire ring with grill, and wide, covered porch with a polished log bench.

Condition: Excellent.

View and surroundings: Red Shirt Cabin #3 faces west from its own tiny, wooded island in the middle of the lake. Perched on a small rise 75 feet back from the water, with a 5x11-foot panel of five picture windows, the cabin offers the best hilltop sunset views to be enjoyed anywhere in Nancy Lake State Recreation Area. It also has the nicest covered porch, supported by skinny unpeeled log posts. A small stony beach, hemmed in by reeds, offers a picturesque spot for pike-fishing. (If you don't have any luck, paddle toward the large, private island just to the south and cast from your canoe.)

RED SHIRT CABIN #4

Capacity: Sleeps six, the maximum allowed (four would be more comfortable).

Facilities: Red Shirt #4 is a dark brown, 12x28-foot wooden-frame cabin with seven bunks, wood stove, and small dining table (no porch).

Condition: Good.

View and surroundings: Red Shirt Cabin #4 is located on the eastern shore of the lake, 30 feet back from the water. The cabin's front steps face north, into the woods. Its west-facing windows provide good, open views of the lake. A modest pocket of sandy beach (think northern Wisconsin, not Hawaii) tucked behind reeds make this cabin a favorite for dedicated dippers. This cabin is second only to #2 for privacy. Canoeists pass by frequently (skinny-dippers beware), but usually at a distance.

LYNX LAKE CABINS #1-#3 AND JAMES LAKE CABIN

Nancy Lake State Recreation Area (Alaska State Parks)

Snapshot: Three tiny cottage-like cabins and one spacious rustic log cabin on the Lynx Lake Loop, a popular and challenging 8- to 10.5-mile canoe trail (or in winter, 13.5-mile multi-use trail) that links 14 tranquil, forest-rimmed lakes in the heart of loon country.

Location: On the eastern shore of Lynx Lake and the western shore of James Lake, respectively, in the middle of the Nancy Lake State Recreation Area.

Elevation: 150 feet.

Map: Alaska State Park brochures: *Nancy Lake State Recreation Area Public Use Cabins, Summer Guide to Nancy Lake State Recreation Area,* and *Winter Guide to Nancy Lake State Recreation Area.* USGS Tyonek C1 (doesn't show cabins or trails).

Access: In summer by canoe with multiple portages along the Lynx Lake Loop canoe system. It is also possible to enter the canoe system and reach the cabins via the Little Susitna River, an all-day trip that requires more canoeing experience. Airplanes are allowed on Lynx Lake; *not allowed* on James Lake. In winter by ski, dog sled, or snowmachine along the Lynx Lake Loop system.

Available: Year-round.

Best: Late May (after lake thaw) to early September (peak foliage time) for hikers and canoeists. Late November (or when 18 inches of snow has accumulated) to March or later (lake ice and trail conditions permitting) for snowmachiners, skiers, and mushers.

Capacity: Four or six, depending on cabin.

Maximum stay: Five nights per month.

Cost: $35.

Reservations: DNR Public Information Center (907) 269-8400, or Mat-Su Area State Parks Office, (907) 745-3975. Info only, Nancy Lake State Recreation Area Ranger Office, (907) 495-6273.

Misc: Canoe rentals and paddling information available from Tippecanoe in Willow, (907) 495-6688. Tippecanoe keeps canoes at the head of road-accessible Tanaina Lake, the starting point of the Lynx Lake Loop. The company insists that renters pay a small additional fee for a portage device that consists of rods and a sling, enabling the canoe to be carried like a stretcher by two people. It helps considerably. If you're planning to tackle the loop in your own private canoe (unless you're going solo) consider acquiring a similar device.

About Lynx and James lakes

Lynx and James lakes are two of the 14 lakes on the Lynx Lake Loop (sometimes also referred to as the Tanaina Lake Loop), an 8- to 10.5-mile canoe route that connects a chain of quiet, wooded lakes via 13 short portages. Most of the portages are 0.25 mile or shorter and are well marked with orange P signs, easily spotted along the shore. A few portages are hilly. Planks cover most of the muddier sections. Lynx Lake, like Nancy and Red Shirt lakes, has many private parcels, allows planes and motor boats, and can be busy on summer weekends. James Lake is undeveloped except for the single, public log cabin on its western shore and is accessible in summer by canoe only. The rest of the lakes on the loop are completely undeveloped and uncrowded, thanks to the challenge of the numerous portages.

For canoeists wanting to combine a cabin trip with camping, there are designated campsites with outhouses on the east and west shores of Ardaw Lake, on the northwest corner of Lynx Lake, and on the portage trail between Little Noluck and Big Noluck lakes, as well as on Skeetna Lake, outside of the Lynx Lake Loop.

For all Lynx Lake and James Lake cabins

Recreation: For the most part, getting there by canoe or cross-country ski is the recreation. Fishing (best just after lake thaw and just prior to freeze-up) for northern pike, rainbow trout, lake trout, whitefish, and Dolly Varden in Lynx Lake. Big and Little Noluck lakes are stocked with rainbow trout. There are some pike and trout in other small lakes. Blueberries, crowberries, and cranberries, as well as some raspberries and currants, ripen from July through August. Swimming in the lakes is also popular. Winter cabin-users who haul along sleds can have a ball on the hair-raising James Lake cabin hill.

Wildlife sightings: All the lakes in the loop, from the 2-mile long Lynx Lake to small Jackknife Lake and even tiny Milo Pond are home to water-fowl, including Common and Pacific loons, ducks, mergansers, and grebes. Also sighted: black bears, brown bears, beaver, moose, eagles, arc-tic terns, swans, and porcupines (especially one dedicated log-gnawer under the James Lake Cabin).

Getting there: Drive to mile 67.3 of the Parks Highway. Turn left on the unpaved Nancy Lake Parkway. **In summer,** continue 4.8 miles to the canoe trailhead (signed TANAINA LAKE LOOP). Downhill from the parking lot you'll find the canoe launch and chained, Tippecanoe rental canoes on the shore of Tanaina Lake. You can paddle the loop clockwise (to reach the Lynx Lake cabins first) or counterclockwise (to reach the James Lake Cabin first and to put the slightly longer portages behind you at the beginning of the trip). The trip can be done in two days, but is best done in three days, allowing you to stay overnight at both Lynx and James lakes.

Mileages vary slightly according to direction paddled and cabin rented, but to give you an idea, a three-day clockwise trip might go as fol-lows. (Note that the 8-mile loop, as described in State Park brochures, is really up to 10.5 miles long if you veer off the most direct route in order to stay at the public cabins.)

Day one: paddling Tanaina, Milo, Ardaw, Jackknife, Frazer, and Little Frazer lakes and finally half-way down along the eastern shore of Lynx Lake to cabin #2, a distance of 4 miles with five portages. (There's no portage between Jackknife and Frazer lakes because a grassy channel connects them.) Day two: paddling back north to the portage connecting Lynx Lake to Char Lake, and onward to Owl Lake and then to the cabin halfway down the western shore of James Lake, a distance of 3 miles with three portages. Day three: paddling back north to the portage connecting James Lake with Little Chicken Lake, then onward to Big Noluck Luck, Little Noluck Lake, Milo Pond, and finally Tanaina Lake, a distance of 3.5 miles with five portages.

Yes, you'll spend as much time out of your canoe as inside it, but in my experience that makes for a rewarding trip, especially for families (and especially if you pack light, so that you never need to double-haul your gear). Young children who can't sit long in a canoe rarely have to wait for more than 10 minutes before they get to stretch their legs on a portage. The same kids who can't hike very far get to rest in the canoe another 10 minutes later, at the next lake. (And along the way, from July through August, there are berries, dragonflies, and the occasional frog hopping across the portage trail to lure them onward.)

In winter, drive to the winter trailhead at mile 2.2 of the Nancy

Lake Parkway. From there, continue on skis, dog sled, or snowmachine for 0.3 mile along the unplowed section of the parkway to the Bald Lake parking lot. A sign indicates the winter route to Lynx Lake. Follow the trail as it heads south, follows the western shore of Bald Lake, heads southwest to Shem Pete Lake, and finally joins the summer-canoe-trail system at the east end of Ardaw Lake. From Ardaw Lake, follow the marked canoe portages and frozen lakes south to Lynx Lake and/or James Lake, depending on the cabin rented. Total distance from the winter trailhead to: Lynx Lake Cabin #1 — 4.0 miles; Lynx Lake cabins #2 and #3 — 4.5 miles; James Lake Cabin — 5.5 miles.

Return the way you came. Or, to continue the loop, follow the summer-canoe-trail system to the trailhead at Tanaina Lake. Then follow the unplowed Nancy Lake Parkway 2.6 miles east to the winter trailhead. The total distance from Lynx Lake Cabin #1 back to the winter trailhead, following the clockwise loop is 7.5 miles; from Lynx Lake #2 and #3 — 8 miles; from James Lake Cabin — 6 miles. The maximum total winter trip distance, if you stay overnight at both Lynx Lake and James Lake cabins, is 13.5 miles for the entire loop. Be prepared for varying trail conditions and temperatures that can plunge to 40 degrees below zero.

LYNX LAKE CABIN #1

Capacity: Sleeps four, the maximum allowed (two or three would be comfortable).

Facilities: This insulated, wooden-frame cabin measures 12x12 feet. It has four bunks, counter, wood stove, outhouse, outdoor picnic table, and fire ring with grill. (No dining table.) Antlers hang lopsidedly over the door, adding a rustic decorative touch.

Condition: Good.

View and surroundings: The cabin perches on the slightly elevated, north side of a small peninsula, on the eastern shore of Lynx Lake, over-looking the water. Windows cleverly clustered in the cabin's northeast corner offer a glimpse of Denali (Mt. McKinley) and Mt. Foraker across the lake — only on a perfectly cloudless day, but worth the gamble. Note that the small island west of the peninsula is private property.

LYNX LAKE CABIN #2

Capacity: Sleeps four, the maximum allowed (two or three would be more comfortable).

Facilities: Painted trim and multi-paned windows make this clean, 12x12-foot cabin look more like a tiny cottage. It has four bunks (including one under a pretty multi-paned window that doubles as a nice west-facing window seat), counter, wood stove, outdoor picnic table, and fire ring with grill. (No dining table inside.) A shared, two-hole outhouse is on a wide trail halfway between cabin #2 and cabin #3. (The two cabins are about 250 feet apart and would be perfect for renting in tandem with another couple or small family.) The cabin isn't visible from the lake; look for a small white triangle marked C on the shore and a canoe landing and a small trail, which leads 100 feet back to the cabin.

Condition: Good.

View and surroundings: The west-facing cabin is back from the water, surrounded by birch and spruce trees and hidden behind a narrow corridor of tall grass. In summer, the vegetation cuts off most lake views, but it also provides a nice buffer to potential noise and traffic, since private parcels and cabins flank the Lynx Lake cabins.

From the cabin's well-lighted interior

LYNX LAKE CABIN #3

Capacity: Sleeps four, the maximum allowed (two or three would be more comfortable).

Facilities: Like Lynx Lake Cabin #2, this 12x12-foot cabin has the quaint features of a tiny cottage, with white interior walls and the additional charm of a small, sheltered porch. The cabin has four bunks (including one that doubles as a window seat), wood stove, counter, outdoor picnic table, and fire ring with grill. (No dining table.) A shared, two-hole outhouse is on a wide trail halfway between cabin #2 and cabin #3. (The two cabins are about 250 feet apart and would be perfect for renting in tandem with another couple or small family.) The cabin isn't visible from Lynx Lake; look for a small white triangle marked C on the shore and a canoe landing and a small trail, which leads 100 feet back to the cabin.

Condition: Good.

View and surroundings: This cabin turns its back on Lynx Lake and instead faces east, overlooking tiny Bains Pond. A cluster of windows on the cabin's southeast corner provide tranquil views of the pond and surrounding birch/spruce forest. Downhill and to the east, a primitive road runs between cabin #3 and the pond.

JAMES LAKE CABIN

SUSITNA VALLEY

Capacity: Sleeps six comfortably, but allows a maximum of seven.

Facilities: This 16x24-foot rustic cabin, constructed of honey-colored round logs, is one of only two log cabins — and the most secluded structure of any kind — in the Nancy Lake State Recreation Area. The well-insulated cabin has six bunks, including two that serve as a convenient L-shaped bench next to a square dining table. It also has a counter, wood stove, outhouse, and outside picnic table with fire ring. For a decade, James Lake Cabin visitor logs included reports of a sauna in the vicinity. Occasionally, cabin-users even erect signs. Alas, the James Lake "sauna" is the Loch Ness monster of Nancy Lake S.R.A. Of course, if you are a devoted non-skeptic, head north of the outhouse, through the devil's club, and take a left at the old birch tree....

Condition: Excellent.

View and surroundings: The cabin is reached by a short, steep trail that cuts though a meadow of neck-high fireweed as it climbs about 50 feet above the lake. Perched on the top of a grassy hill, fringed by birch and spruce trees, the cabin overlooks the water to the south and east, with views across the lake to the distant Chugach and Talkeetna mountain ranges. From the picnic table and fire ring, next to a massive birch tree, you overlook the lake, too. From this fine vantage point, visitors have reported watching beaver — and once, a bear — swimming in the lake below. Large windows on all sides, including two triangular-shaped windows near the rafters, bring light inside the high-ceilinged cabin and offer great views as well.

SUSITNA
VALLEY

Beyond The Backyard: The Eklutna Traverse

by Peter Porco

At the edge of Whiteout Glacier, below the waiting comfort of a small A-frame cabin, we skied along the spine of an immense snowdrift. It was perhaps a quarter-mile long, created by winds that rushed all winter around a corner of the mountain and carved a deep trench in the snow between the glacier and the mountainside.

The drift was a bizarre-looking formation, resembling a gigantic serpent. But it was only one more weird feature in an entire landscape of strange beauty. The peaceful basin of the glacier spread like a huge white sea for miles around. Mountains and ridges rose beyond it like giant ships.

We had been traveling through this wilderness for three days now. But until I stood on the back of the serpent, I hardly saw any of it. My mind had other things to think about: the open blisters on my heels, the 60 pounds of gear on my back, the ego-wounding pace set by the two men I followed, often from far behind. But now came relief from all of that. The third long day of arduous April skiing was over. We were home for the night. The aluminum-sided, A-frame Whiteout Glacier Hut (a.k.a. Hans' Hut) was our shining city on a hill.

From all appearances, we might have been standing anywhere in the remote reaches of Alaska. The view from the glacier was hardly recognizable. Which was the strangest sensation of all. For we were standing just then in the heart of Chugach State Park barely 30 miles from the Hotel Captain Cook, halfway along the easily accessible "Eklutna Traverse."

Easily reachable, maybe, but not easy. The Eklutna Traverse crosses four glaciers on its rugged 40-mile course from Girdwood to Eklutna. Travelers climb 5,000 feet into the mountains no matter which end they start from. During the trek, they descend and reclimb another 2,000 feet.

Easing the journey are a public cabin and three mountain huts situated along the way. But visitors to the shelters are few, park officials say. Only about 75 people a year visit the Rosie's Roost or Whiteout Glacier huts. For good reason perhaps. Much of the year including nearly all of winter the Eklutna Traverse is a dangerous journey, susceptible to avalanches in several sections.

About 30 years ago, two people died in an avalanche while climbing down from one of the Eklutna huts in a snowstorm.

Spring and summer are the safest times to travel. But the Eklutna Traverse can be dangerous then, as well. Just two weeks before our own trip, an Anchorage climber, Randy Howell, broke through the snow on the Whiteout Glacier and fell nearly 50 feet into a narrow crevasse. Howell escaped unhurt, thanks to having been roped to another skier. But he lost his pack, laden with about $2,000 worth of climbing and camera equipment, in the fall. Fierce winds prevented the group from retrieving the pack. Then an avalanche nearly caught a member of the party on their trip back to town.

Now Howell, a 32-year-old offshore drilling inspector for the federal government, was back on the Eklutna Traverse with hopes of retrieving his pack. And I was along for the ride. We were joined there by retired civil engineer Dick Griffith, a 63-year-old legend in Anchorage climbing circles, famed for his long, solo treks across the Arctic, his wilderness savvy, his penchant for leaving men half his age behind on the trail.

Which was exactly what Griffith began to do as soon as we began our journey in the late sun of a recent Sunday evening. We had barely parked our car in Girdwood at the snowy terminus of Crow Creek Road before Griffith shouldered his pack, latched his skis, and vanished down the trail. There's nothing elaborate about Griffith's crosscountry skiing style. It's fairly straightforward. He doesn't skate-ski in the modern style, but prefers a tried-and-true diagonal stride, with a little double-poling thrown in on occasion. He wears single-leather ski boots that he says are good to 40 or 50 below zero.

Leaving Whiteout Glacier Hut

Wayne Todd

"You just gotta keep moving," Griffith says. And that's what he does. Howell and I brought up the rear.

Our plan was to ski that night to Crow Pass Cabin, an elevation gain of about 2,000 feet, taking advantage of the cool evening temperatures that stabilize the snow and reduce avalanche hazards. The next day we planned to ski on to Rosie's Roost. There we expected to be joined by six other skiers who would begin the morning after we did — among them, Griffith's son, Barney, and four women.

The trek up to the Crow Pass Cabin is far from easy. By the time we entered the ravine, it was nearly dark. From there we embarked on a nerve-rattling climb on skis along the short, steep sides of the gully. Griffith took us straight up the creek bed, rather than on the normal foot trail that crosses wide, steep slopes loaded with snow.

Minutes after starting, my weight on the snow caused an area as wide as a house to suddenly settle with a loud "whomp!" A drop like that is often followed by a slide. But there was some brush anchoring the snow and I was safe. We continued on, my slow pace holding the others in check. The moon was full. It shone high on the slopes above us while we skied in the semi-darkness of the ravine. We could see, but we couldn't judge depth or distance.

Eventually we strapped our skis to our packs and in the moonlight climbed a long, steep slope that put us less than half a mile from the Crow Pass Cabin. By the time I stumbled into the shelter, it was nearly 2 A.M. We'd been traveling for eight hours. Two other people were there, surprised anyone would be showing up at the hour we did. They didn't plan to tackle the traverse; they had simply been skiing in the nearby hills.

Dick, Randy, and I quickly got down to the business of melting snow for hot drinks. Then we spread out our bags on the hut's wooden floor. I quickly fell asleep. The next morning was stunning clear skies and a strong sun. But having arrived late, we slept in for most of it. We didn't return to the trail until the early afternoon.

Before starting out, we had wondered about the conditions on the Raven Headwall — a fairly steep, 500-foot slope at the head of the Raven Glacier that we had to climb to reach the Eagle Glacier. Griffith had wanted us to be at the headwall early in the day, before the sun began softening the snow too much. But that was no longer possible. We were left hoping the slope would be reasonably stable.

The four-mile trip to the headwall carried us deeper into the Chugach Mountains. Just beyond Crow Pass we got our first glimpse of the "7,000-footers": Mount Yukla, Mount Kiliak, Korohusk, and Old Soggy rising above Eagle River. The Raven Glacier itself is a surprise — a long, white-and-blue tongue shooting suddenly out a small valley on the right. To get on it, we had to traverse broad, steep slopes that gave me pause. Alone and trailing, I stayed in Griffith's tracks, following the master more or less blindly. I just hoped he was right.

Chances were good that he was. This was Griffith's 12th journey over the Eklutna Traverse, which might stand as a record of some sort. Usually the trip requires four to seven days to complete. Incredibly, Griffith finished his very first traverse, in 1978, in a single day. "But I was younger then," he says now.

Once on the glacier, we roped up — a far more complicated process than simply tying in to a rope. Glacier travelers wear "ascenders" — devices that help them climb out of a crevasse if they fall in. Other attachments — cords, slings, carabiners — hang off the ski traveler like baubles off a gypsy.

The exertion of climbing the 2,000 feet to the headwall was aggravated by the broiling sun. A relentless sun may be loved in Anchorage, but it's enough to hide from when magnified by the blinding snow of a glacier.

We reached the base of the headwall at 4:30, just in time to see our trailing party two miles down the glacier. They were only a few hours behind. The headwall itself appeared safe, despite having received half a day of direct sunlight. There was no sloughing of snow we could see. Even the bergschrund — a large crevasse between the glacier and the mountainside — was fully covered by the apparently stable snow.

The headwall was about as safe as he'd ever seen it, Griffith said. Still, we climbed it carefully, skis lashed to our packs. We stayed close to the rocks for protection. Once over the top, we stood on the southwest fork of the Eagle Glacier. Rosie's Roost Hut awaited 2,000 vertical feet down-slope, about two miles to the north.

Griffith and Howell started off unroped. I followed them. A mediocre skier at best, I kept my climbing skins on to slow me down. I stuck to Griffith's tracks. Even so, traveling over the unknown snowbridges of a glacier is far more risky for a skier who falls as I did on several occasions than it is for the skier who doesn't fall.

A few hours later, however, I reached the hut. Pains, shivers, and fatigue ebbed away as I drank as much hot soup as there was time to boil.

The Eklutna hut system (excluding the Crow Pass Cabin, managed by the U.S. Forest Service) may not compare with the great lodges of Switzerland's Haute Route, but they're still a welcome sight. Built in the 1960s by the Mountaineering Club of Alaska, the huts provide a bare floor and a sleeping loft where visitors can roll out their bags, protected from the wind and snow. Theoretically, the huts allow a skier to travel the Eklutna Traverse without a tent or backpacking stove. But leaving such items behind entails risk. The huts can be hard to find in a storm, as some of the log entries in the Whiteout Glacier Hut bear witness.

But on a clear day, the huts command dramatic vistas. From Rosie's Roost we scanned the Eagle Glacier in three directions, including the far end of the valley where the glacier spread out like a primordial ice sheet. That Monday night, however, we didn't concern ourselves with the landscape. We were too preoccupied with thoughts about why the other six members of our party had failed to arrive. *Griffith thought they were only three hours behind us, judging from the last time we saw them. But they never showed up that night.*

"They're gonna hear from me about this," Griffith joked. "I guess it was my fault. I told them they could make it in one day."

Some members of their group were probably too tired to climb the headwall, we decided. They probably bivouacked on the glacier digging a hole for shelter. Or perhaps they returned to the Crow Pass Cabin.

By morning there was still no sign of them. But Griffith was confident that his son, Barney, probably the strongest member in their party, was in control of the situation. He scribbled a note to him on a piece of paper and left it on the table. Then we departed.

Looking to the left after crossing the main branch of the Eagle Glacier, we could see all the way down the Eagle River Valley to Knik Arm — the first real sign of how close we were to Anchorage. The Eagle River is also an "escape" route for those who need to leave the area quickly, when bad weather socks in. The only problem comes in knowing how to negotiate the messy, crevasse-scored lobe of the lower Eagle Glacier. Of course, Griffith knows. He's done it.

From there we began the 2,000-foot climb to the Whiteout Glacier, following a northeastern fork of the Eagle Glacier. Halfway up is a level area. It was there that Howell had fallen into the crevasse and lost his pack. We roped up again. The glacier appeared badly broken with crevasses. By early afternoon, we reached the spot where he'd fallen, which Howell had taken care to mark with climbing wands — slender stakes made visible with surveyor's tape. Amazingly, the wands were still standing despite two weeks of wind, snow, and sunshine.

But finding the pack, Howell knew, would require different tricks and different luck. Howell's tumble may have been one of the more spectacular crevasse falls anyone has taken and lived to tell the tale. It illustrates some of the very real dangers of the Eklutna Traverse.

At the time of the fall, Howell was roped to another skier. They were traveling in a party of seven, proceeding in the opposite direction than we were. He had just carved a left turn, Howell says, when the snow gave way over a crevasse. He dropped 10 feet down, where he found himself hanging by his rope.

His rope partner had reacted well, throwing himself to the ground in an effort to arrest Howell's fall. Howell's skis had landed on the backside of a small snow mound inside the crevasse. He held a nub of ice on the wall of the crevasse with his left hand. It was all that kept him from falling backward and deeper into the crevasse. If he could pull himself more fully onto the mound, Howell reasoned, he'd be stable and only a few feet below the surface.

But as his partner began cinching the rope between them, Howell was pulled backward and off balance. Standing on the snow mound was no longer possible. Shouting messages to another party member who'd anchored himself at the lip of the hole, Howell let the others know he was about to deliberately fall back deeper into the slot. They needed to belay him. Howell only expected to drop another 10 or 15 feet, since he was held by a taut rope. But when he let go of the nub and fell backward, the rope sliced into the snowbridge and Howell watched the narrow walls of the crevasse shoot past him on both sides.

He fell nearly four stories.

"Luckily, I had my pack on," he says now. "It took all the abuse."

When he finally stopped, his body was wedged between the walls of ice. His arms were crossed in front of him. He was able to move them only upward. He could not undo the straps of his pack nor work anything else except his rope and harness connections directly in front of him. Meanwhile, his rope partner had been jerked toward the edge of the crevasse and probably would have plummeted in had another skier not jumped on top of him.

Eventually, Howell was thrown another rope. The others anchored themselves and both ropes into the surface snow, then tried to pull Howell free, using carabiners and other gear to devise a pulley system. But every time they'd heave away, the snow anchors would pull loose. The combination of Howell and his pack was too much weight for the loose snow at the surface.

Finally, he was able to hoist himself a few feet on one of the ropes, shed his pack, and switch his weight to the new rope believing all along that his backpack was still tied into the first rope. But in the confusion of lines and carabiners, it wasn't properly fastened. Howell was lifted to the lip, pulling out still more anchors as he frantically clawed his way through an overhanging snow bulge to reach the surface. When his companions pulled on the other rope, it came up empty.

Howell was cold. He'd been down in the slot for 45 minutes. One of his companions was even colder. The weather was turning bad. After a roped descent into the crevasse by one of the others proved futile, the group proceeded to Rosie's Roost Hut to wait for clear weather and to resume the search. But winds that roared up to 50 mph kept them pinned down for several days. Finally, they gave up on the pack. Using a compass in a whiteout, they navigated their way to Goat Ridge. From there, they descended to Girdwood, kicking off an avalanche along the way.

Before returning to the crevasse, Howell had given himself a one-in-five chance of finding his pack. Now he discovered the crevasse had filled with snow. The odds for finding his $2,000 pack dropped sharply. Digging down through the spot over where he assumed it to be, Howell opened the snowbridge, then rappelled down inside, with Griffith belaying him from above by a second rope.

But he didn't get far. The rappel rope stopped 25 feet down blocked by ice and snow. Howell climbed out. He moved 10 feet down the length of the crevasse and dug again. Entering the crevasse once more, he was stopped once again. In the two weeks since his fall, the high winds had crammed the crevasse with snow.

Finally, we gave it up.

Resting on the glacier after the effort, we spotted a member of our miss-

ing party skiing down the other fork of the glacier, toward the Whiteout Glacier Hut. The others were finally drawing near. We started up again ourselves, but soon stopped to see what progress the others were making.

One of them, Barney Griffith, was coming quickly across the Eagle Glacier toward us. He caught us a little later. Some members in their party had bad feet and some were just slow, he said. They'd all slept in a trench beneath the headwall the previous evening. A little farther up the glacier, Barney and his father dropped their packs, then skied down to the others to carry the packs for some of them.

Howell and I headed up to the Whiteout Glacier Hut.

That was the only night the nine of us stayed in the same shelter. Griffith planned for the three of us to be back in Anchorage the next evening. The other six wanted to ease off his pace and stay at Pichler's Perch, the A-frame overlooking lower Eklutna Glacier.

I, too, wanted to ease off. Of the traverse's 40 miles, we still had 23 to go. I dreaded the next day, especially since the last 13 miles promised to be a forced march across the basically flat terrain around Eklutna Lake. My heels had open blisters by now. How would they take kicking and gliding for 13 miles? So I considered throwing in with the other six and coming out a day later. On waking the next morning, however, I heard a different song. Refreshed and feeling stronger, I decided I wanted to be home that night. I'd go the full 23.

As usual, Griffith and Howell charged ahead, leaving me behind to ski those huge glacial basins alone. The terrain between the two huts is mostly benign. The eight miles to Pichler's Perch, where they waited for me, are all a gradual downhill romp beneath great roaring mountains. I went at my own pace

Pichler's Perch

Wayne Todd

and had the most relaxed time of the trip.

The Eklutna River Valley, among the best-known ski tours in the entire mountain wilderness east of Anchorage, has a long history of use by Natives, the Army, and recreationists. Pichler's Perch is the most-visited of the three glacier huts. But even at that, its logbook only showed about 15 parties a year. Many of them climb the 3,000 feet to the hut, stay a night or two, then return to their cars at the north end of the lake. Among them, a logbook entry by a party led by Griffith: "July 5, 1986 The First American Direct Baby Assault on the hut. Mary Stonebreaker, age 10 weeks youngest baby ever in the hut (we think)."

Soon after I reached the hut for a lunch break, Griffith bolted down the glacier. Howell and I roped up for the next part of our journey — the crevasse-raked snout of Eklutna Glacier that tumbles dramatically for thousands of feet down a narrow canyon.

The bliss of a morning dawdle on the glacier became then an afternoon of trying to stay on my feet skiing under a heavy pack. Besides keeping my balance, I also had to avoid getting tangled in the 75 feet of rope separating Howell, an avid downhill skier, and myself. But Howell was patient. We soon reached the braided bars of the river.

Until then I vaguely remembered Griffith saying something earlier about "double-poling," but it had no physical reality for me. I knew we'd probably be skiing seven miles across the still-frozen lake, but I saw myself in a kick-and-glide slog. But when we hit the gravel bars — still largely covered by ice-encrusted snow — you could say a bright light exploded in the dim caverns of my mind. For six miles along the river and seven on the lake, Howell and I double-poled it bending from the waist in rhythmic motions. I felt like someone working the levers of a railroad handcar.

We cruised. Starting at 6 P.M., Howell reached the end of the lake by 9. I made it by 9:15. We had covered the last 13 miles at a rate of about 3.5 miles an hour. Roughly equal to an easy nonstop lope.

Griffith, who'd gotten there two hours earlier, came out to meet me a mile from the end and graciously offered to help with my pack. I let him have it. What the heck, I thought. It's over. What did I have to prove?

Five years ago, I traveled the Eklutna Traverse in the opposite direction with a party that took a week to do it. This time, we finished it in three days.

Peter Porco is an *Anchorage Daily News* reporter. This story originally ran in a 1990 issue of "We Alaskans," the newspaper's Sunday magazine. Since then, not much has changed on the Eklutna Traverse, which remains one of Southcentral Alaska's little-known wonders. And by the way, adventurer Dick Griffith is still double-poling along, as adventurous at 72 as he was at 63.

About the Mountaineering Club of Alaska Huts

The Mountaineering Club of Alaska (MCA) maintains eight, primitive mountaineering huts on public lands in the Chugach (location of the "Eklutna Traverse") and Talkeetna mountains. The huts, which are more basic than the public cabins described in this guide, are available for use as needed through membership with the club. If other travelers arrive, you will be expected to share space. No reservations or payment are required. However, the MCA asks that hut-users purchase a very reasonable, annual club membership for $10 (family membership, $15). That's less than half the cost of a single night's permit for a State Park or Forest Service cabin. The MCA, which relies on volunteers to maintain the shelters and operates on a shoe-string budget, needs future hut-users' support. In exchange for membership, the MCA sends its members "Scree," a newsletter, which contains — among other things — trip reports and access notes of critical interest to prospective hut-users. The newsletter will also keep you up to date on future hut/cabin developments. For example, the club has discussed building a more deluxe, "European-style hut" on Eklutna Lake, near some excellent ice-climbing areas.

In general, existing huts are small, unheated, unfurnished, single-room shelters located in glacial alpine areas. Some of the older huts, built in the 1960s and 70s, are weathered, but volunteers repair them as needed. All of the huts are constructed of metallic siding and roofing over a wood floor. Unlike most public cabins, the huts have stoves and lanterns, but bring your own fuel. Leave no food, since bears may visit all the hut areas.

Access to most of these structures — unlike the others in this guide — requires mountaineering experience, equipment, and avalanche-safety training. The capsule listings that follow don't include access information, which is detailed (especially when there are multiple routes) and changing (glacial retreat has affected the Eklutna Traverse route, where three of the huts are located). Note that Crow Pass Cabin, sometimes mentioned in conjunction with the huts because it is also used by mountaineers on the Eklutna Traverse, is a Forest Service cabin (see page 41).

For more information, regularly updated hut-fact sheets ($0.25 each) can be purchased at Alaska Mountaineering and Hiking, an Anchorage store that serves as the Mountaineering Club of Alaska's informal headquarters.

EKLUTNA/MATANUSKA /TALKEETNA HUTS

In Brief:
Eklutna Traverse Huts, South to North, in the Chugach Mountains

ROSIE'S ROOST

Chugach State Park (Mountaineering Club of Alaska)

Kirk Towner

Location: Eagle Glacier, about 3.5 miles from the toe of the glacier (5.5 miles northeast of Crow Pass Cabin, 5 miles north of Goat Mountain, 18 miles southeast of Eagle River Visitor Center).

Elevation: 3,900 feet.

Map: USGS Anchorage A6.

Access: With mountaineering experience, via at least five possible routes (Whiteout Glacier, Blackout Pass, Eagle River, Raven Glacier, and Goat Mountain routes). Contact MCA for details.

Available: Year-round, but usually used in summer.

Sleeps: Twelve.

Maximum stay: No limit.

Cost: No fee.

In brief: The uninsulated, unheated A-frame hut, built in 1968, has a two-burner Coleman cookstove, limited cookware, and a lantern (no beds, no radio, no fuel). There is no outhouse. In summer, look below the hut to the north for meltwater.

Reservations: No reservation required. For info, write Mountaineering Club of Alaska at Box 102037, Anchorage, AK 99510. Or visit Alaska Mountaineering and Hiking, an Anchorage outdoor equipment store at 2633 Spenard Rd. (907) 272-1811.

HANS' HUT (A.K.A. WHITEOUT GLACIER HUT)

Chugach State Park (Mountaineering Club of Alaska)

Kirk Towner

Location: Whiteout Glacier, about 3 miles south of Whiteout Pass (5 miles north of Rosie's Roost hut, 8 miles south of Pichler's Perch hut).

Elevation: 6,000 feet.

Map: USGS Anchorage A6.

Access: With mountaineering experience, via Eklutna or Whiteout glaciers. Contact MCA for details.

Available: Year-round, but usually used in summer.

Sleeps: Twelve.

Maximum stay: No limit.

Cost: No fee.

In brief: The unheated, uninsulated A-frame hut, built in 1968, has a two-burner Coleman cookstove, limited cookware, and a lantern (no beds, no radio, no fuel). There is no outhouse. Water is available from a creek 120 feet southeast of the hut in summer.

Reservations: No reservation required. For info, write Mountaineering Club of Alaska at Box 102037, Anchorage, AK 99510. Or visit Alaska Mountaineering and Hiking, an Anchorage outdoor equipment store at 2633 Spenard Rd. (907) 272-1811.

Good advice: "It is common for parties to get stranded at Hans' Hut. Don't try to second-guess the weather and visibility by not taking enough food and fuel, or by heading out into a storm. Relax. Read a book. It always gets better." (Mountaineering Club of Alaska.)

PICHLER'S PERCH

Chugach State Park (Mountaineering Club of Alaska)

Wayne Todd

EKLUTNA/MATANUSKA
/TALKEETNA HUTS

Location: Eklutna Glacier, about 8 miles north of Hans' Hut (16.5 miles south of the Eklutna Lake parking lot).

Elevation: 4,550 feet.

Map: USGS Anchorage B6.

Access: With mountaineering experience, via Eklutna Glacier. Contact MCA for more details.

Available: Year-round, but usually used in summer.

Sleeps: Eight to ten.

Maximum stay: No limit.

Cost: No fee.

In brief: The unheated, uninsulated A-frame hut, built in 1964, has a two-burner cookstove and a lantern (no beds, no radio, no fuel). A trickle of water is about 30 yards southeast of the hut in summer. This is the most weathered of the three Eklutna Traverse huts. The floor could use some repair.

Reservations: No reservation required. For info, write Mountaineering Club of Alaska at Box 102037, Anchorage, AK 99510. Or visit Alaska Mountaineering and Hiking, an Anchorage outdoor equipment store at 2633 Spenard Rd. (907) 272-1811.

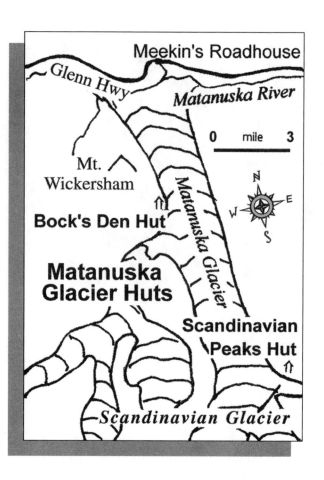

In Brief:
Matanuska Glacier Huts, In The Chugach Mountains

BOCK'S DEN HUT

Chugach Mountains (Mountaineering Club of Alaska)

Location: Matanuska Glacier, just west of the glacier and southeast of Mt. Wickersham, 9.5 miles from the parking lot at the terminus of Matanuska Glacier (8.5 miles from the Scandinavian Peaks Hut).

Elevation: 3,050 feet.

Map: USGS Anchorage C2.

Access: By air, landing on a Super Cub strip about 1.5 miles from the hut. (The strip is bumpy and requires tundra tires, but it is cleared of brush and rocks.) On foot, with mountaineering experience, over the Matanuska Glacier. Contact MCA for details.

Available: Year-round.

Sleeps: Six.

Maximum stay: No limit.

Cost: No fee.

In brief: Built in 1992, the unheated, uninsulated hut has a two-burner Coleman stove and lantern (no beds, no radio, no fuel). An outhouse hasn't been built yet. Keep waste at least 200 feet from the hut area. Follow a game trail south for about 150 feet to find meltwater in the stream.

Reservations: No reservation required. For info, write Mountaineering Club of Alaska at Box 102037, Anchorage, AK 99510. Or visit Alaska Mountaineering and Hiking, an Anchorage outdoor equipment store at 2633 Spenard Rd. (907) 272-1811.

Misc.: For information on charter flights to the hut, contact Meekin's Air Service in Palmer (907) 745-1626.

SCANDINAVIAN PEAKS HUT

Chugach Mountains (Mountaineering Club of Alaska)

Bill Romberg

EKLUTNA/MATANUSKA
/TALKEETNA HUTS

Location: On the Scandinavian Glacier, about 18 miles from the parking lot at the terminus of the Matanuska Glacier.

Elevation: 5,150 feet.

Map: USGS Anchorage C2.

Access: By air, landing on a gravel Super Cub strip about 700 feet from the hut, or on the Matanuska Glacier, south of the hut, in winter. The strip requires tundra tires but is in excellent shape. A small taxi stand for storing gear is next to the strip. By foot with mountaineering experience, a minimum two-day trip (sometimes longer) traveling up the glacier for the entire route. Contact MCA for details.

Available: Year-round.

Sleeps: Twelve.

Maximum stay: No limit.

Cost: No fee.

In brief: The A-frame hut has no heat, but it is insulated. Built in 1990, it has a two-burner Coleman cookstove and lantern (no beds, no radio, no fuel). An outhouse is about 90 feet northwest of the cabin. To find water in summer, look about 120 feet behind the hut for small rivulets draining from the ice; these may be frozen in the morning.

Reservations: No reservation required. For info, write Mountaineering Club of Alaska at Box 102037, Anchorage, AK 99510. Or visit Alaska

Mountaineering and Hiking, an Anchorage outdoor equipment store at 2633 Spenard Rd. (907) 272-1811.

Misc.: For information on charter flights to the hut, contact Meekin's Air Service in Palmer (907) 745-1626.

In Brief:
Talkeetna Mountains Huts, West to East

BOMBER HUT

Talkeetna Mountains (Mountaineering Club of Alaska)

Location: Bartholf Creek Valley, 1.5 miles north of Bomber Glacier (8 miles from the Reed Lakes trailhead).

Elevation: 3,900 feet.

Map: USGS Anchorage D6.

Access: With mountaineering experience, via Reed Lakes Trail and Bomber Glacier, or via Snowbird Glacier. Contact MCA for more details.

Available: Year-round, but usually used in summer, or in early spring for skiing.

Sleeps: Seven to nine.

Maximum stay: No limit.

Cost: No fee.

In brief: The hut has no heat, but it is insulated. Built in 1990, it has a two-burner Coleman cookstove and lantern (no beds, no radio). An outhouse is about 60 feet away. In summer, water is available about 150 feet from the front door among boulders, or from several other creeks nearby.

Reservations: No reservation required. For info, write Mountaineering Club of Alaska at Box 102037, Anchorage, AK 99510. Or visit Alaska Mountaineering and Hiking, an Anchorage outdoor equipment store at 2633 Spenard Rd. (907) 272-1811.

EKLUTNA/MATANUSKA
/TALKEETNA HUTS

MINT HUT

Talkeetna Mountains (Mountaineering Club of Alaska)

Mark Miraglia

Location: Little Susitna River Valley, about 9 miles from the Motherlode Roadhouse (0.5 mile from Mint Glacier).

Elevation: 4,350 feet.

Map: USGS Anchorage D6.

Access: With mountaineering experience, via Reed Lakes Trail and Penny Royal Glacier. Or via Susitna River Valley; mountaineering experience not necessarily required but avalanche-safety knowledge *is* required. Contact MCA for more details.

Available: Year-round, but usually used in summer.

Sleeps: Twelve.

Maximum stay: No limit.

Cost: No fee.

In brief: Built in 1971, this is one of the more attractive MCA huts, with an arctic entryway/enclosed porch. It has a two-burner Coleman cook-stove and two lanterns (no beds, no radio). An outhouse is about 75 feet away. In summer, water is easily found in the creek north of the hut.

Reservations: No reservation required. For info, write Mountaineering Club of Alaska at Box 102037, Anchorage, AK 99510. Or visit Alaska Mountaineering and Hiking, an Anchorage outdoor equipment store at 2633 Spenard Rd. (907) 272-1811.

DNIGI HUT

Talkeetna Mountains (Mountaineering Club of Alaska)

Location: Moose Creek Valley, about 13 miles from the end of Buffalo Mine Road.

Elevation: 4,150 feet.

Map: USGS Anchorage D6.

Access: Via Moose Creek Trail, Eska Creek - Moose Creek benches, or Mint Glacier and Grizzly Pass. No glacier travel or mountaineering experience required (except for Mint Glacier route), but backcountry hiking and orienteering experience are necessary because of the location, distance, and difficulty of creek crossings. This is a two-day trip on foot. Contact MCA for more details. Snowmachiners also use the hut.

Available: Year-round.

Sleeps: Six to eight.

Maximum stay: No limit.

Cost: No fee.

In brief: The hut has no heat, but it is insulated. Built in 1995, it has a two-burner Coleman cookstove and lantern (no beds, no radio). An outhouse is about 60 feet away. In summer, water is easily found in the creek east of the hut.

Reservations: No reservation required. For info, write Mountaineering Club of Alaska at Box 102037, Anchorage, AK 99510. Or visit Alaska Mountaineering and Hiking, an Anchorage outdoor equipment store at 2633 Spenard Rd. (907) 272-1811.

EKLUTNA/MATANUSKA /TALKEETNA HUTS

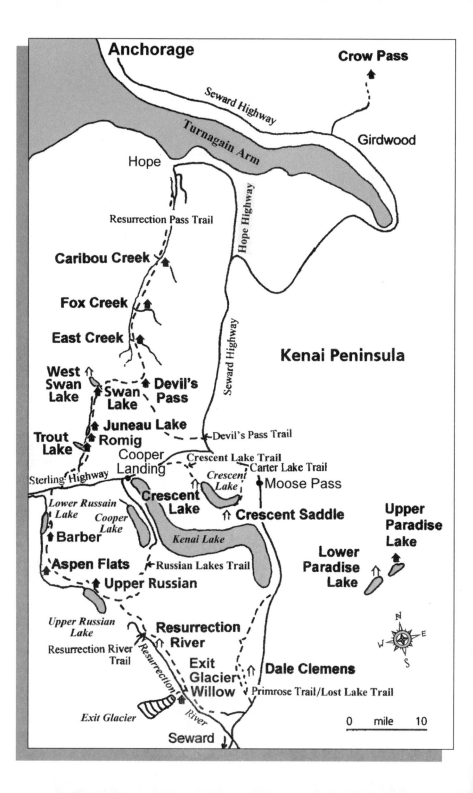

Part II   CABIN-TO-CABIN ON THE KENAI

Popular Peninsula Bays, Lakes, and Trails (Including Seward and Homer)

Any Season, Any Speed: Resurrection Pass Trail

by Brian Lax with Andromeda Romano-Lax

Stewart's mild Scottish brogue was chipper, despite the miserable weather forecast. "Newspaper says it's going to rain all week," he reported as we headed down the Seward Highway to Hope, the starting point for our Resurrection Pass hike. Already, I'd been preoccupied about how I was going to keep up with my friend's fast hiking pace on this popular 39-mile trail, one I'd aspired to tackle for several years. Stewart once summited Mt. McKinley twice, in back-to-back trips. But he is phenomenally modest, rarely even using the word "climb" for his adventures.

Earlier in the year, Stewart had strolled the entire Resurrection Pass Trail in a single day, wearing nothing but shorts, T-shirt, and a small fanny pack. I, conversely, have stretched 3-mile walks into all-day epic adventures — thanks to the toddling pace of my usual companions, my 6-month-old and 4-year-old children. This time, the kids were staying at home. I felt sure I could make it all the way from Hope to Cooper Landing, but I also knew it wouldn't be easy.

Together, Stewart and I represent the gamut of "Rez Pass" hikers, from ultramarathoners and mountain bikers who finish the trail in a single day with energy to spare, to less experienced or child-toting walkers who spend a challenging week conquering the same distance. It says something about the Resurrection Pass Trail's beauty that such a diverse crowd considers it a trail worth attempting. Outsiders, in particular, consider it a perfect introduction to the area, offering a taste of nearly everything Alaskan: spruce/aspen forest, tundra, secluded trout lakes, and bubbling creeks. There's history along the trail, too. The well-trod route was first established by 1890s prospectors traveling from Resurrection Bay to the goldfields near Hope. Recreational gold-panning is still allowed on the northernmost section of the trail.

Stewart and I were approaching the trail from different athletic perspectives, but at least we had something to worry about together: the weather. A tropical storm system off the Pacific coast threatened to batter the Kenai Peninsula with wind and rain. There was no way we were going to postpone our trek, however. Not when I'd booked the trip six months earlier, rising at 4:59 A.M. on a dark March morning to call the East Coast reservation center as soon as it opened. That was the only way we could be sure of getting the particular cabins we wanted for an average eight miles-per-day pace.

Storm systems aside, we were tempting fate by traveling on the cusp of the season. In Alaska, autumn arrives early and can slide into winter in just a few colorful weeks. Five days of rain were likely, but snow was a possibility, too. Stewart could have made a jab about how our slow pace would condemn us to being soaked longer than necessary. Instead, he simply beamed all the way to the trailhead. "I'm excited, actually," he said. "I got to bring along my new umbrella."

My legs ached within hours of our start, but not without reward. The trail follows a rushing creek, often climbing above it. Five miles into our hike, we reached a canyon where we could view the churning water far below, gushing around large boulders. Caribou Creek Cabin, our stop for the first night, sits

Devil's Pass

Stewart Ferguson

opposite the creek from a 3,700-foot slope, burned to increase moose habitat. My back felt sore from shouldering a heavy pack, but less so after I chatted with a passing hunter. He'd shot a moose high up on the slope, and had to pack 100 pounds of meat down the slope and eight miles north, to the trailhead in Hope. And then he had to return, repeating the trip three times in all. My physical efforts seemed minor by comparison.

The next day dawned cool — about 40 degrees, but without the expected torrential rains. Small patches of blue sky sent our spirits soaring. Instead of solid gray gloom, our steady climb from forest to tundra rewarded us with bursts of color. We'd chosen the second week of September for a trip out of necessity. It had been the only time work and family schedules coincided, allowing us enough free time for the hike. In fact, we'd lucked out. Each evening, small clouds of biting flies harassed us, but the mosquitoes had mostly disappeared. The air smelled sweet and musky, saturated with the scent of overripe highbush cranberries and frost-softened rose hips. The aspen trees blazed like torches, their high leafy crowns a brilliant gold. The poplars and birch trees added more bright yellows and light oranges.

Fall colors were at their peak, and yet the countryside was blissfully silent and nearly empty. Designated a National Recreation Trail, and regularly named by various national magazines as a top hiking and biking trail for Alaska visitors, the Resurrection Pass Trail attracts between 8,000 and 10,000 users each year — heavy traffic for these parts. But we passed only two or three people a day: a few more hunters, a few mountain bikers.

At the end of the second day ("always the hardest," Stewart assured me), with my shoulders sore from the rubbing of my pack, and my legs burning, Stewart suggested we drop our packs at the cabin and get a sneak preview of higher terrain.

"Just for a quick run up to the pass," he said brightly. I laughed. Then I realized he was serious. Politeness required that I feign careful consideration. Careful, **brief** consideration.

"How far is it?" I asked.

"Just four miles, round trip. And without our packs!"

I begged off, thankful I had no desire — or energy — to compete.

Stewart simply wasn't accustomed to leisure. Or to solid shelter. He usually camps on ice fields — in wind chills of up to sixty below — where you cook your food as soon as you enter your tent, and then dive into a sleeping bag. Here, too, he intended to maintain his rigorous camping routine each night: heat a cup-of-soup, then prepare a proper dinner, and then sleep. But log walls and a wood stove conspired to change years of conscientious alpine habits. By the second night, Stewart was beginning to relax. There was time to read, time to twiddle around with the fire or wander the nearby woods, time and space to play cards. "It's quite luxurious, really," he remarked. Luckily, Stewart had brought along a hefty political thriller — just the thing to keep him contentedly occupied while I ministered to all my blisters.

There was another reason my friend began to appreciate the cabins. Along the trail, we saw mostly small critters: swans, eagles, ptarmigan, and a porcupine waddling away from us with his quills erect, in prickly indignation. But this narrow trail was really a big-game highway. For what seemed like miles we followed moose tracks along the trail. Then black bear tracks, clearly following the moose tracks. And finally, brown bear tracks — each one as big around as my head — following the moose, the black bear, or both. Stewart stopped waxing quite as poetically about tent life. A roof — and better yet, a firmly closed door — had its place in the woods after all, we agreed.

Every day, the weather got better and better. The hard rains never came. Stewart became even more cheerful, something I had not thought possible, once we got into the 2,600-foot pass. For a mountain climber, higher is always better. But I was happy, too — awed by the scenery spreading in radiant colors all around us. The tundra blazed a half-dozen shades of red. The lichen-covered boulders glowed electric green. If anything, the overcast sky seemed to enhance the brilliant jewel tones under our feet.

We'd lucked into the perfect season. And as mismatched as we were in terms of our hiking abilities, I'd managed to bring the perfect hiking partner. His quick, rolling gait kept me going. I felt like I'd converted him, at least temporarily, to another way of enjoying this trail, at a pace slow enough to pick blueberries and crowberries, take photos, or pocket the occasional interesting rock for my young son waiting at home.

When even Stewart's company couldn't distract me from my cumulative weariness, though, I gained inspiration from the tales of fellow hikers who had conquered this popular trail ahead of us. "Last 11 miles tomorrow for Grandma Kay (age 73) and her five sherpa-daughters," wrote an Anchorage woman in the 1996 Fox Creek Cabin log. "Here's to the rare pleasures only crazy dreams can bring. Fifty years in Alaska and Mom finally hikes Resurrection Pass Trail."

Descending Resurrection Pass, heading back toward the highway and to our families, it began to sprinkle enough for us to finally put on our raingear. It only lasted a half-hour, but that was enough to inspire Stewart to pop out his colorful umbrella. He held it at a jaunty angle, giving its handle an occasional spin. The creek ran behind him, separated into flowing terraces by a series of large beaver dams.

It was worth a little soggy weather for this final parting image: Fred Astaire, suddenly planted on the edge of Alaskan wilderness. I stepped a little more quickly, buoyed by my friend's patient good humor, as he twirled and twirled, inviting the rain to pour.

About the Resurrection Pass Trail

Heading south on this century-old trail, you'll climb from 500 to 2,600 feet, passing no roads or towns along the way. (You will pass plenty of other people, though — this hike is popular, especially in summer.) The grade is mostly gradual, with a few steep switchbacks. In places, the trail is blocked by fallen trees — an added challenge for mountain bikers. Snowmachiners consider the trail narrow in spots, but bikers and hikers should have no problem.

Pace on the trail varies considerably. Some ultramarathoners and mountain bikers tackle the route in one day. On foot, a trip of three to seven days is more typical, with five days (at an eight mile-per-day pace) probably the most common. By mountain bike, the trip can be divided more comfortably over two or three days.

In fall, hunters use the trail and lakes to gain access to game-rich country. In winter, the trail is less busy — the perfect place for an epic cross-country ski or snowmachine trip through deep snow and ever-changing conditions. At higher altitudes, snow lingers well into early summer. The trail is closed to vehicles, including snowmachines, from February 16 through November 30 and to horses (mountain bikers are asked to observe this closure also) from April 1 through June 30, due to mushy, spring trail conditions.

Most of the year, especially from July through October, the cabins are heavily booked. Six of the trail's nine public cabins made the Chugach Forest's top 15 most popular cabins (by number of nights booked) in 1996: Trout Lake, #2; Juneau Lake, #3; Caribou Creek, #5; Romig, #6; Swan Lake, #11; and Devil's Pass, #12. This should alert you to the fact that you'll need to plan ahead, especially if you're renting a chain of cabins. You probably won't stay at every cabin on the trail, but every other cabin may be as wide a stretch you can manage com-

From Devil's Pass Cabin

KENAI–Hope to Cooper Landing

Brian Lax

fortably, especially if traveling with kids.

Another option is to alternate cabin rentals with tent camping. Thirteen designated campsites are located on short spurs off the main route. If you can stay at only one cabin, you might choose Juneau Lake, the newest and brightest log cabin, built in 1998 after the original Juneau Lake Cabin was destroyed by fire. The trail can be hiked in either direction, but if you start from Hope and camp until you reach Juneau Lake, 29.1 miles along the trail (with 9.5 mostly downhill miles left to go), you'll be ready for a luxurious break.

The total length of the Resurrection Pass Trail is 38.6 miles, but if you're a stickler for details, note that each cabin-access trail leading off the main route will add a few tenths of a mile. All the cabins and short access trails (less than 0.1 to 0.5 mile) are well marked and easy to find. Access notes below are described from a southbound orientation. Only the West Swan Lake Cabin lies far off the main trail, at the west end of a lake ringed by thick vegetation. It is best reached by floatplane.

When visiting all cabins, gather dead-and-down wood only. Firewood is not abundant and it may take a while to scrounge enough for a fire. (At the Devil's Lake Cabin, there is no timber and an oil stove is provided, instead.) Lakes or creeks are near all the cabins. Treat all water sources.

To hike the whole trail, you'll need USGS maps B8, C8, and D8; or the Trails Illustrated™ map, *Kenai National Wildlife Refuge/Chugach National Forest*. For a longer trip, continue south on the contiguous Russian Lakes and Resurrection River trails, a 71-mile journey from the trailhead near Hope to Exit Glacier trailhead, near Seward.

History: Gold was discovered in Resurrection Creek in 1888. In the following decade, more than 7,000 prospectors poured into the mining towns of Hope and Sunrise, on the shore of Turnagain Arm. About half of them traveled overland, landing at Seward and stampeding north along the Resurrection Pass Trail. Traffic along the trail slowed when a railroad was constructed between Seward and Girdwood. Nature reclaimed parts of the trail until 1965, when the Forest Service reopened it to the public. Most of the cabins were constructed in the 1960s and early 1970s on preexisting sites of "trespass cabins" built on Forest Service land by trappers and anglers. They're mostly Pan Abode-style cabins (think aged Lincoln logs with a coat of dark brown paint) or wooden A-frames.

Getting there: To hike southbound, start at the Hope trailhead. Drive 71 miles south of Anchorage on the Seward Highway and turn west onto the Hope Highway. Drive 16 miles and turn left (south) at the Forest Service sign onto Palmer Creek Road. The road forks. Take the right fork,

KENAI-Hope to Cooper Landing

Resurrection Creek Road, following Forest Service signs to the trailhead (a total of 4 miles from the highway).

To hike northbound, start at the Sterling Highway trailhead. Drive south of Anchorage to mile 52 of the Sterling Highway, just past the second Kenai River bridge near the small community of Cooper Landing. Alternately, the trailhead for Devil's Pass Trail, which links up to the Resurrection Pass Trail after the Devil's Pass Cabin (heading northbound), is at mile 39 of the Seward Highway.

Cabin Planner/Resurrection Pass Trail Mileage Table

Numbers in parentheses indicate additional mileage of cabin-access trails longer than 0.1 mile. Cabin locations are provided in miles southbound from the Hope trailhead and northbound from the Sterling Highway trailhead.

Cabin/trailhead	Southbound location	Northbound location	Miles to next cabin south	north
Hope trailhead	Mile 0	Mile 38.6	7.1	N.A.
Caribou Creek	Mile 7.1	Mile 31.5	5.6	N.A
Fox Creek	Mile 12.5(+0.2)	Mile 26.1(+0.2)	2.1	5.6
East Creek	Mile 14.4	Mile 24.2	7.0	2.1
Devil's Pass	Mile 21.4	Mile 17.2	4.9	7.0
Swan Lake	Mile 25.8(+0.5)	Mile 12.8(+0.5)	3.8	4.9
West Swan Lake	off trail	off trail	—	—
Juneau Lake	Mile 29.1	Mile 9.5	0.9	3.8
Romig	Mile 30	Mile 8.6	2.3	0.9
Trout Lake	Mile 31.8 (+0.5)	Mile 6.8 (+0.5)	N.A.	2.3
Sterling Hwy trailhead	Mile 38.6	Mile 0	N.A.	7.3

KENAI-Hope to Cooper Landing

Brian Lax

CARIBOU CREEK CABIN

Chugach National Forest (U.S. Forest Service)

KENAI–Hope to Cooper Landing

"A triumphant return after 18 years when I was on a ski trip with my mother-in-law.... Much easier on mountain bikes with Zachary, 15 years old, who wasn't even a gleam in the old man's eye in the winter of 1980."

Caribou Creek Cabin log.

Snapshot: First stop or quick taste of the trail. A simple 12x14-foot log cabin within a day's hike of the Hope trailhead.

Location: Just off mile 7.1, Resurrection Pass Trail, south of Caribou Creek bridge.

Elevation: 1,000 feet.

118

Map: USGS Seward B8 or Trails Illustrated™, *Kenai National Wildlife Refuge/Chugach National Forest.*

Access: By foot or ski; by mountain bike or horse (except April 1 - June 30); or by snowmachine, December 1 through February 15.

Available: Year-round.

Best: June through September for hikers; July through September for mountain bikers; December to February 15 for snowmachiners; and December through March or later (trail conditions permitting) for skiers.

Sleeps: Six on bunks (three or four would be more comfortable).

Maximum stay: Three consecutive nights from May 15 through August 31. Seven consecutive nights the rest of the year.

Cost: $35.

Reservations: Forest Service toll-free reservation center, (877) 444-6777 or via Internet at http://www.reserveusa.com. For info on trail and cabin specifics, call the Seward Ranger District Office, (907) 224-3374.

Facilities: The Pan Abode cabin (a style of log cabin, as described above and in the introduction) has six bunks, with the lower bunks doubling as benches next to a dining table, counter, and a large, flat-topped wood stove. Outside are an outhouse, fire pit, wood shed (not stocked), thermometer, and small front stoop. A whimsical, fragile-looking swing hangs from a birch tree next to the cabin.

Condition: Remodeled in 1991, this cabin and outhouse are in good condition — one rank better than the cabins just to the south. Because this cabin is the closest to the trailhead, litter is sometimes a problem.

View and surroundings: The cabin sits at the edge of a grassy meadow, facing Resurrection Creek 30 feet away, surrounded by spruce forest with open views of steeply rising mountains. Watch for moose on the slope to the west — a controlled burn area, managed as moose habitat. The cabin has larger front and back windows, and smaller windows on each side. It is reached after crossing Caribou Creek, and is located just off the trail (signed) but shielded from most traffic by a screen of trees.

Wildlife sightings: Moose, porcupine, black bears, caribou, and Dall sheep. Also in the area: brown bears, mountain goats, and wolves.

Recreation: Fishing in the area is poor. Berries ripen mid-July through mid-September. This cabin is near a 1.5-mile long recreational gold-panning area, which begins at the Hope trailhead and follows Resurrection Creek. A private claim is just south of the public panning area, so it's

KENAI-Hope to Cooper Landing

essential that you know what you're doing and where you are, unless you want some old-fashioned trouble. Fine gold can be panned from gravels along the creek. Suction dredges (4-inch or smaller) are permitted from May 15 to July 15 with a permit from the Alaska Department of Fish and Game. Obtain the excellent, free "Gold Panning" Forest Service booklet, full of how-to tips, panning locations, history, and even a little Robert Service poetry.

Brian Lax

FOX CREEK CABIN
Chugach National Forest (U.S. Forest Service)

Snapshot: Off the trail. A simple 12x14-foot log cabin in a quiet side-valley.

Location: Off mile 12.5, Resurrection Pass Trail, just north of Fox Creek.

Elevation: 1,500 feet.

Map: USGS Seward C8 or Trails Illustrated™, *Kenai National Wildlife Refuge/Chugach National Forest.*

Access: By foot or ski; by mountain bike or horse (except April 1 - June 30); or by snowmachine, December 1 to February 15.

Available: Year-round.

Best: July through September for hikers and mountain bikers; December to February 15 (for snowmachiners); December through March or later (trail conditions permitting) for skiers.

Sleeps: Six on bunks (three or four would be more comfortable).

Maximum stay: Three consecutive nights from May 15 through August 31. Seven consecutive nights rest of the year.

Cost: $35.

Reservations: Forest Service toll-free reservation center, (877) 444-6777 or via Internet at http://www.reserveusa.com. For info on trail and cabin specifics, call the Seward Ranger District Office, (907) 224-3374.

Facilities: The dark brown, Pan Abode cabin has six bunks, with the lower bunks doubling as benches next to a dining table, counter, and a small, flat-topped wood stove. Outside are an outhouse, fire pit, wood shed (not stocked), thermometer, and small front stoop.

Condition: Fair, with some floor and outhouse damage (possibly from a gnawing porcupine).

View and surroundings: The cabin faces south to a grassy area with low willow bushes and scattered spruce trees. Ridges rise to the south, east and west; a steep, forested slope hems in the cabin from behind. The cabin is not visible from the main trail. To reach it, you'll follow the access trail (signed) off the main trail, north of the Fox Creek bridge crossing, and hike about 0.2 mile. Fox Creek is about 200 feet south and not visible from the cabin itself.

Wildlife sightings: Porcupine, caribou, and black bears. Also in the area: moose, brown bears, Dall Sheep, mountain goat, and wolves.

Recreation: Fishing in the area is poor. Berries ripen mid-July through mid-September.

KENAI–Hope to
Cooper Landing

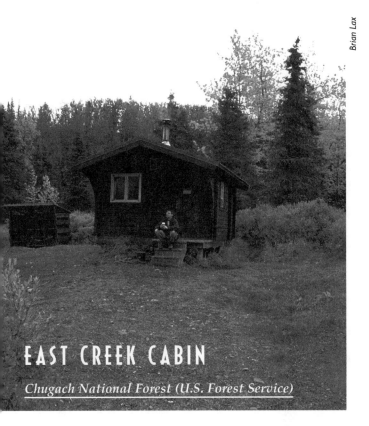

Brian Lax

EAST CREEK CABIN
Chugach National Forest (U.S. Forest Service)

Snapshot: Taste of sourdough. A simple 12x14-foot log cabin with an Alaska-style food cache.

Location: Mile 14.4, Resurrection Pass Trail.

Elevation: 2,200 feet.

Map: USGS Seward C8 or Trails Illustrated™, *Kenai National Wildlife Refuge/Chugach National Forest.*

Access: By foot or ski; by mountain bike or horse (except April 1 - June 30); or by snowmachine, December 1 to February 15. From here south to the pass, the trail can be difficult to follow after a heavy snowfall.

Available: Year-round.

Best: July through September for hikers and mountain bikers, December to February 15 for snowmachiners, December through March or later, trail conditions permitting, for skiers.

Sleeps: Six on bunks (three or four would be more comfortable).

Maximum stay: Three consecutive nights from May 15 through August 31. Seven consecutive nights rest of the year.

Cost: $35.

Reservations: Forest Service toll-free reservation center, (877) 444-6777 or via Internet at http://www.reserveusa.com. For info on trail and cabin specifics, call the Seward Ranger District Office, (907) 224-3374.

Facilities: The dark brown, Pan Abode cabin has six bunks, with the lower bunks doubling as benches next to a dining table, counter, and a small, flat-topped wood stove. Outside are an outhouse, fire pit, wood shed (not stocked), and small front stoop. This cabin's most interesting feature is a small, authentic Alaska-style food cache — basically a miniature cabin on stilts with a removable ladder, allowing you to store your edibles away from marauding beasts.

Condition: Fair, with some graffiti.

View and surroundings: The cabin faces west with good views of mountain slopes to the south and west. Open grassy areas with low willow shrubs and scattered spruce and mixed hardwoods surround the cabin. East Creek is 100 feet away but not visible from the cabin itself. Access is by a sidetrail (signed) about 150 feet off the main trail, just north of East Creek.

Wildlife sightings: Porcupine, caribou, black bears, brown bears, and moose. Also in area: Dall sheep, mountain goats, and wolves.

Recreation: Fishing in this area is poor. Berries ripen mid-July through mid-September.

KENAI-Hope to
Cooper Landing

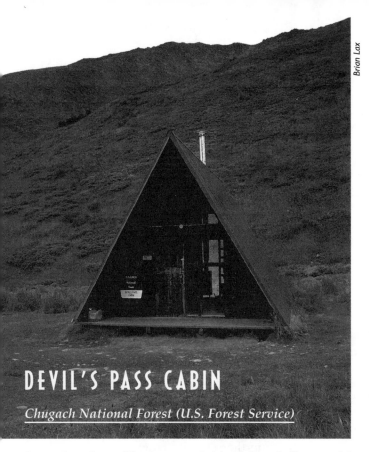

DEVIL'S PASS CABIN

Chugach National Forest (U.S. Forest Service)

Snapshot: Some like it steep. A 16x16-foot A-frame cabin surrounded by tundra and narrow valleys, with multiple access options.

Location: At the intersection of Devil's Pass Trail and mile 21.4 of the Resurrection Pass Trail.

Elevation: 2,400 feet.

Map: USGS Seward C8 (use C7 also if approaching via Devil's Pass Trail) or Trails Illustrated™, *Kenai National Wildlife Refuge/Chugach National Forest.*

Access: By foot or ski along the Resurrection Pass Trail; by mountain bike or horse (except April 1 - June 30); by snowmachine, December 1 through February 15, along the Resurrection Pass Trail; or by foot or mountain bike in summer or fall only along the 10-mile long Devil's Pass Trail (Devil's Pass Trail is not recommended in winter due to avalanche hazards). Resurrection Pass Trail is difficult to follow at this elevation after a heavy snowfall. Whiteouts are frequent above treeline.

Available: Year-round.

Best: July through September for hikers and mountain bikers; December to February 15 for snowmachiners; December through March or later (trail conditions permitting) for skiers on Resurrection Pass Trail. Mid-June through September only for Devil's Pass Trail users.

Sleeps: Six on bunks (comfortably, with plenty of extra room in the loft).

Maximum stay: Three consecutive nights from May 15 through August 31. Seven consecutive nights rest of the year.

Cost: $35.

Reservations: Forest Service toll-free reservation center, (877) 444-6777 or via Internet at http://www.reserveusa.com. For info on trail and cabin specifics, call the Seward Ranger District Office, (907) 224-3374.

Facilities: The dark brown, A-frame cabin has a dutch door, six bunks, loft, table and benches, and an oil stove (#1 stove oil not included). Outside are a narrow front porch and an outhouse.

Condition: Fair.

View and surroundings: The cabin sits above treeline, a spectacular setting in summer, when wildflowers blanket the area, or in early fall, when the tundra glows a half-dozen shades of red. Large windows face open views south and north along Resurrection Pass Trail and east into Devil's Pass valley. Both valleys are narrow with stark ridges rising on either side to 4,000 feet. Juneau Creek is 15 feet from the cabin, visible from the loft.

Wildlife sightings: Dall sheep on surrounding mountainsides, marmots, ptarmigan, bears, caribou, and northern harrier hawks.

Recreation: Fish for Dolly Varden at Devil's Pass Lake, less than 1 mile southeast of the cabin along the Devil's Pass Trail. Berries ripen mid-July through mid-September.The open tundra invites off-trail hiking to several nearby ridges.

KENAI-Hope to Cooper Landing

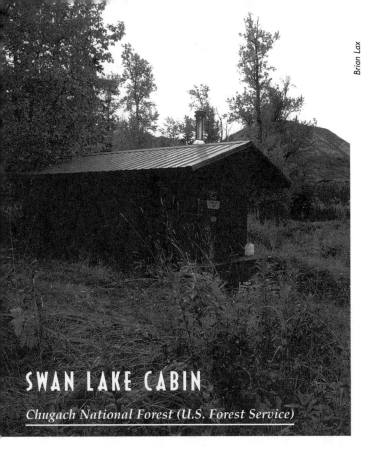

SWAN LAKE CABIN

Chugach National Forest (U.S. Forest Service)

Snapshot: Lakeside retreat for weary travelers. A 12x14-foot log cabin two-thirds of the way (southbound) along the Resurrection Pass Trail.

Location: About 0.5 mile off Mile 25.8, Resurrection Pass Trail; on the southeast corner of Swan Lake.

Elevation: 1,400 feet.

Map: USGS Seward C8 or Trails Illustrated™, *Kenai National Wildlife Refuge/Chugach National Forest.*

Access: By foot or ski; by mountain bike or horse (except April 1 - June 30); by snowmachine, December 1 through February 15. Note that from here north to the pass, the trail can be difficult to follow after a heavy snowfall. By floatplane, 30 minutes from Moose Pass, 15 minutes from Cooper Landing.

Available: Year-round.

Best: July through September for hikers and mountain bikers; December to February 15 for snowmachiners; December through March or later (trail conditions permitting) for skiers; mid-July through August for salmon anglers.

Sleeps: Six on bunks (three or four would be more comfortable).

Maximum stay: Three consecutive nights from May 15 through August 31. Seven consecutive nights the rest of the year.
Cost: $45.
Reservations: Forest Service toll-free reservation center, (877) 444-6777 or via Internet at http://www.reserveusa.com. For info on trail and cabin specifics, call the Seward Ranger District Office, (907) 224-3374.

Facilities: The dark brown, Pan Abode cabin has six bunks, with the lower bunks doubling as benches next to a dining table, extra bench, counter, and a large, flat-topped wood stove. Outside are an outhouse, fire pit, wood shed (not stocked), and porch with bench. A rickety, flat-bottomed rowboat is included (bring your own life jackets).

Condition: Fair to good.

View and surroundings: The cabin sits 75 feet back from Swan Lake, a lake squeezed between two nearly-4,000-foot mountains, facing west. The lakeshore is grassy, with scattered birch, spruce, high bush cranberry and wildflowers in a rolling terrain. A campground is on the north side of the lake. The cabin is reached by a 0.5-mile spur off the summer trail. The winter trail, however, passes within 100 feet of the cabin.

Wildlife sightings: Black bears, moose, beaver, swans, and shorebirds. Also in area: brown bears, caribou, and wolves.

Recreation: Fish Swan Lake for rainbow trout, lake trout, Dolly Varden, and sockeye salmon. Sockeyes spawn in the Swan Lake outlet during mid-July and August. Berries ripen mid-July through mid-September.

KENAI-Hope to
Cooper Landing

Brian Lax

JUNEAU LAKE CABIN

Chugach National Forest (U.S. Forest Service)

Snapshot: Best of the trail. A new, brighter, natural wood log cabin with great lake views.

Location: Mile 29.1, Resurrection Pass Trail; on the eastern shore of Juneau Lake.

Elevation: 1,350 feet.

Map: USGS Seward C8 or Trails Illustrated™, *Kenai National Wildlife Refuge/Chugach National Forest.*

Access: By foot or ski; by mountain bike or horse (except April 1 - June 30); by snowmachine, December 1 through February 15; by floatplane, 20 minutes from Moose Pass, 10 minutes from Cooper Landing.

Available: Year-round.

Best: June through September for hikers; July through September for mountain bikers; December to February 15 for snowmachiners; December through March or later (trail conditions permitting) for skiers.

Sleeps: Six on bunks (three or four would be more comfortable).

Maximum stay: Three consecutive nights from May 15 through August 31. Seven consecutive nights rest of the year.

Cost: $45.

Reservations: Forest Service toll-free reservation center, (877) 444-6777 or via Internet at http://www.reserveusa.com. For info on trail and cabin specifics, call the Seward Ranger District Office, (907) 224-3374.

Facilities: After a series of dark cabins, the blond wood accents and more decorative doors and windows of this log cabin are a treat for the eyes. This cabin was rebuilt by volunteers in 1998 after the original Juneau

Lake Cabin — one of the oldest cabins in Chugach National Forest — was burned down accidentally by young hikers. This new cabin, which could be mistaken for a private home in suburbia, has a different layout than its Pan-Abode predecessor, with six bunks, a fireplace-style wood stove with glass front, counters, and a table with three benches. Although it has some improved features (a ramp and two doors) it isn't officially "to code" for wheelchairs; still, fly-in users with limited mobility will appreciate the changes. Outside are a new outhouse, firepit, and raised porch with bench. A rowboat (in better shape than average) is provided; bring your own life jackets.

Condition: Excellent. Built in 1998.

View and surroundings: The cabin faces west from a rise above Juneau Lake, providing great views across the water. Windows face north, west and south. The cabin is surrounded by shrubs (dwarf birch, willow, and woodland plants), scattered spruce, birch, and aspen trees. The cabin overlooks the trail.

Wildlife sightings: Moose, black and brown bears. Also in area: wolves.

Recreation: Fish Juneau Lake for rainbow trout, whitefish, burbot, and grayling. Berries ripen mid-July through mid-September.

KENAI–Hope to
Cooper Landing

Brian Lax

ROMIG CABIN
Chugach National Forest (U.S. Forest Service)

Snapshot: Tackling the trail, or just fishing. A dark and utilitarian 12x14-foot log cabin within a long day's hike of the Sterling Highway trailhead.

Location: Mile 30, Resurrection Pass Trail; on the southern shore of Juneau Lake.

Elevation: 1,300 feet.

Map: USGS Seward C8 or Trails Illustrated™, *Kenai National Wildlife Refuge/Chugach National Forest.*

Access: By foot or ski; by mountain bike or horse (except April 1 - June 30); by snowmachine, December 1 through February 15; by floatplane, 20 minutes from Moose Pass, 10 minutes from Cooper Landing.

Available: Year-round.

Best: June through September for hikers; July through September for mountain bikers; December to February 15 for snowmachiners; December through March or later (trail conditions permitting) for skiers.

Sleeps: Six on bunks (three or four would be more comfortable).

Maximum stay: Three consecutive nights from May 15 through August

31. Seven consecutive nights rest of the year.

Cost: $45.

Reservations: Forest Service toll-free reservation center, (877) 444-6777 or via Internet at http://www.reserveusa.com. For info on trail and cabin specifics, call the Seward Ranger District Office, (907) 224-3374.

Facilities: The dark brown, Pan Abode cabin has six bunks, with the lower bunks doubling as benches next to a dining table, counter, and a flat-topped wood stove. Outside are an outhouse (across the main trail), fire pit, thermometer, and porch. A rowboat is included (bring your own life jackets).

Condition: Fair.

View and surroundings: This cabin is situated in a soggy, buggy area, and its location directly on the trail may infringe on your privacy. Its access to decent fishing in both Juneau Lake and Juneau Creek and proximity to the south trailhead make it popular nonetheless. The cabin faces north, in a clearing ringed by tall spruce, scattered birch, and willow on rolling terrain. While it sits above the lakeshore, it offers limited views of the water.

Wildlife sightings: Moose, black and brown bears. Also in area: wolves and Dall sheep.

Recreation: Fish Juneau Lake for rainbow trout, lake trout, whitefish, burbot, and grayling. Juneau Creek offers Dolly Varden, rainbow trout, and grayling. Berries ripen mid-July through mid-September.

KENAI-Hope to
Cooper Landing

TROUT LAKE CABIN

Chugach National Forest (U.S. Forest Service)

Snapshot: Taste of the trail, or just fishing. A more secluded, 14x14-foot A-frame cabin within a day's hike of the Sterling Highway trailhead.

Location: About 0.5 mile off mile 31.8, Resurrection Pass Trail; on the northern shore of Trout Lake.

Elevation: 1,200 feet.

Map: USGS Seward C8 or Trails Illustrated™, *Kenai National Wildlife Refuge/Chugach National Forest.*

Access: By foot or ski; by mountain bike or horse (except April 1 - June 30); by snowmachine, December 1 through February 15; by floatplane, 20 minutes from Moose Pass, 10 minutes from Cooper Landing.

Available: Year-round.

Best: June through September for hikers; July through September for mountain bikers; December to February 15 for snowmachiners; December through March or later (trail conditions permitting) for skiers.

Sleeps: Six on bunks (comfortably, with plenty of extra room in the loft).

Maximum stay: Three consecutive nights from May 15 through August 31. Seven consecutive nights rest of the year.

Cost: $45.

Reservations: Forest Service toll-free reservation center, (877) 444-6777 or via Internet at http://www.reserveusa.com. For info on trail and cabin specifics, call the Seward Ranger District Office, (907) 224-3374.

Facilities: The dark brown, A-frame cabin has six bunks, loft, a dutch door, table and four benches, L-shaped cook area, and an extra-large wood stove — lots of it new, thanks to a recent refurbishment. Unlike most A-frames, this one has small, ventilating windows to cool the cabin when the wood stove is working overtime. Outside are an outhouse, narrow porch, and firepit. A flat-bottomed rowboat is included (bring your own life jackets).

Condition: Good. Refurbished and resanded in 1998. Because this cabin is close to a trailhead, litter is sometimes a problem.

View and surroundings: The cabin sits slightly above the lake, facing south, surrounded by rolling hills forested with spruce, birch, and willow. Floor-to-ceiling plexiglass windows face north and south, with views of the lake from the loft. The cabin is 0.5 mile off the main trail (signed), providing some privacy, although anglers also use the cabin-access trail and lakeshore.

Wildlife sightings: The area is used heavily by moose and maintained as prime habitat through controlled burning. (Brian spent a peaceful morning here watching a mama moose and calf browsing down at the lake, their bulbous noses and twitching ears periodically buried in the water.) Also in area: black and brown bears, wolves, and Dall sheep.

Recreation: Fish Trout Lake for lake trout, rainbow trout, and whitefish. Juneau Creek offers Dolly Varden, rainbow trout, and grayling. Berries ripen mid-July through mid-September. Even if you don't hike the rest of the Resurrection Pass Trail, the section northbound to this cabin is worth the effort, especially at mile 4.5 from the Sterling Highway trailhead (2.3 miles south of the cabin), where Juneau Falls plunges from a steep gorge.

KENAI–Hope to
Cooper Landing

In Brief:

WEST SWAN LAKE CABIN

Chugach National Forest (U.S. Forest Service)

Location: Northwest corner of Swan Lake; near (but not connected by trail to) the Resurrection Pass Trail.

Elevation: 1,400 feet.

Map: USGS Seward C8 or Trails Illustrated™, *Kenai National Wildlife Refuge/Chugach National Forest.*

Access: By floatplane, 15 minutes from Cooper Landing or 30 minutes from Moose Pass. This cabin is recommended as a fly-in only. Bushwhacking along the lakeshore is possible but extremely difficult and requires orienteering. Limited winter access by ski or snowmachine (December 1 through February 15) requires crossing a frozen lake; use caution.

Available: Year-round but mostly used in summer and fall.

Sleeps: Four comfortably (maximum is eight).

Maximum stay: Seven consecutive nights.

Cost: $45.

In brief: This 12x14-foot cabin, popular among anglers and hunters, has a wood stove and rowboat (life jackets not included). Wildlife include moose, black and brown bears, caribou, and wolves. Fish Swan Lake for rainbow trout, Dolly Varden, and sockeye salmon. Sockeyes spawn in Swan Lake's outlet during mid-July and August.

Reservations: Forest Service toll-free reservation center, (877) 444-6777 or via Internet at http://www.reserveusa.com. For info on trail and cabin specifics, call the Seward Ranger District Office, 224-3374.

KENAI-Hope to Cooper Landing

Biking With The Beetle: Russian Lakes Trail and Crescent Lake Trail

Singletrack. Single. Track.

I rolled those words around my mouth as I pedaled, wondering why I hadn't taken them seriously until now. My bulging panniers rubbed against boulders and snagged on bushes. The excess gear (a camping pillow, extra water jugs) had to go. My partner's bike trailer — several inches too wide for the trail itself — had to go, too, or it would drag him sideways down the next sloping hill. We left all of it hidden in the brush behind an enormous cottonwood tree, with a note saying we'd return on foot to haul it back out.

I'd never mountain biked before, except on wide, flat, tire-pampering asphalt. Now, nine hours into a bruising ride on the Russian Lakes Trail, sweat and mosquito repellent streamed down one cheek. My forearms ached from hours of bullying my bike along a narrow, alder-choked trail and over at least 30 beetle-killed, wind-toppled trees. Luckily, the summer sun at these northern latitudes hovers just above the horizon until nearly midnight or I would have been toiling in darkness. Even so, the temperature was dropping fast and my legs, wet from fording several icy mountain streams, throbbed with a creeping chill.

At 11:00 P.M., several hours into a fatigued trance, I squinted ahead and spotted it. The Forest Service cabin's roof jutted just above neck-high bushes. Shelter. My knees weakened with gratitude. (Literally. For the umpteenth time, I fell off my bike — this time, into a ditch of spiny devil's club.)

My partner and I entered the dark, empty cabin. There was no lock; no innkeeper or campground host to greet us; no fellow campers to pressure us into idle chatter. We closed the door on clouds of mosquitoes and on our own nervous thoughts, lit a fire and hung our wet socks to dry. The kettle hopped and rattled on the red-hot stove. We breathed in the smell of woodsmoke and the warm, waxy perfume of candleflame. We ate a simple, hot dinner on a wood-plank table. From the shadows of the cabin, we stared out the small window into a small patch of lavender midnight sky that refused to darken completely.

A deep, dreamless sleep beckoned, but this still, contented moment was too precious to lose to slumber. Thoughts of the day's travails dissolved into a foggy, mellow state of satisfaction. Snug in our cabin, we felt safe, warm, and blissfully alone — the only residents of the only manmade structure for dozens of square miles around, in some of the wildest country within an easy half-day's drive of Anchorage, the state's biggest metropolis.

Not bad for about $35 a night, plus a little sweat. Okay, a lot of sweat. But worth it.

I'd misjudged the difficulty of the Kenai's popular mountain-biking trails. I hadn't realized that backcountry bicycling means shoulderwide tunnels through dense alder, and wheel ruts so narrow and deep that less-than-perfect steering sends you popping out of the groove and careening wildly into tree trunks, spiky thickets, and stinky marsh puddles. Sometimes, you can't see the trail at all. During our late May trip, we had to wheel our bikes across a wide patch of soft snow. One sideways slip and we would have tumbled hundreds of feet down an avalanche chute. At summer's lush peak, grassy meadows obscure part of the trail completely.

Of course, if you're a mountain biker, you love challenges: the maze of obstacles, the roots and rocks, the skinny trail. And even we novices get such a thrill from speeding through the woods that the regular dismounts, wobbles and crashes are worth the trouble. But there's another hazard to consider in these parts: beetles. Tiny ones — as small as the lead tip of a pencil. You're probably laughing. You're thinking that your knobby, macho treads could roll over an entire village of small insects without even registering the bumps. And they could, if beetles lived on the ground. Instead, spruce bark beetles burrow under the bark of trees. The trees die, a storm blows, and suddenly, you have not "singletrack," but no track — dead, skinny spruces everywhere, often too high to jump without dismounting and too long to swerve around. "Mountain biking" becomes a euphemism for hiking into the night with an overloaded bicycle perched painfully over one shoulder.

The beetles have been chewing their way across the Kenai Peninsula since the mid-1980s, leaving a trail of dried-out, rust-needled spruces. The infestation

Biking the Russian Lakes Trail

has just about run its course in the north half of the Kenai, but for the next five years, those dead, dry trees will continue to snap and fall — almost always perpendicular to a trail, from the perspective of a cyclist (or cross-country skier, for that matter).

"You get a big wind event out of Cooper Landing, and you have trees crashing down all over the place," says U.S. Forest Service entomologist Ed Holsten, who adds that he's flown over the handlebars of his own bike after meeting up with a horizontal spruce.

The Cooper Landing area is one of the Kenai's windiest corners, thanks to snow-topped mountains and gust-funneling valleys that make the area so scenic and popular for hiking, biking, and cross-country skiing in the first place. As of this writing the effects of the last Noah-sized torrent, in 1996, are still seen on the Russian Lakes and Crescent Lake trails. Forest Service crews try to clear popular trails at least once each month. When they've passed through recently, you may get to enjoy a relatively easy ride. But often the Forest Service is busy with non-beetle-related tasks, like rebuilding bridges and rerouting trails after floods.

None of this should discourage you from biking the 21-mile Russian Lakes Trail (a one-way route starting from Cooper Lake and ending at mile 52.6 of the Sterling Highway). Or the 12.8-mile round-trip Crescent Lake Trail, a smoother, somewhat easier trail. It just means you should take your time, revel in the challenge, and enjoy spending a night or two at the public cabins along the way. Fall is an especially nice time. Summer's jungle-like growth has died back, and spruce needles and yellow leaves blanket the trail, maximizing your chances to pedal instead of push.

Since the distances of both trails are relatively short, some avid mountain bikers zip through in a single day. (The real maniacs finish one trail, and then head down the Sterling Highway a bit farther and bike the 39-mile Resurrection Pass Trail as well.) But they miss half the fun: spending a night in the Forest Service's oldest cabin, a handcrafted log structure on the shore of Upper Russian Lake. Or fishing for rainbow trout on a rushing stream just yards in front of the Aspen Flats Cabin. Or angling for grayling from the Crescent Lake Cabin. Or just resting on a cabin's front porch, grateful legs hanging down over the edge, and watching that midnight sun finally and reluctantly go down.

A night's stay in a cabin along the way not only rests the shoulders and quads, it soothes the ego. Waking at the Upper Russian Lake Cabin to the smell of fresh cottonwood buds in the air, I almost forgot how many times I'd fallen off my bike the day before. I tried not to notice the scratches and yellowing bruises on my legs. I tried not to think about all those tree-gnawing beetles. I got back on that bike again — lifting one tender leg up high to do so— and thought about the next warm, welcoming cabin ahead.

And as I pedaled, chin held high, I practiced my new word, so that I wouldn't forget it: Single. Track. Single. Track. Singletrack.

About the Russian Lakes Trail

The Russian River is world-famous for sportfishing and in summer, during two sockeye salmon runs, its banks are crowded shoulder-to-shoulder and sometimes several rows deep with anglers trying to hook a Russian red. (Some of the anglers only manage to hook one another.) Meanwhile, a few miles up the Russian Lakes Trail, toward Barber Cabin, the action slows. A few more miles on the narrowing trail toward Aspen Flats Cabin, most angling ends, and the trail is quieter still. And beyond that point, somewhere next to a clear, rushing stream folded between canyon walls, you may forget entirely about other humans.

The Russian Lakes Trail is a satisfying 21.5-mile, three-cabin traverse through the forest, best done in two to three and a half days. It's also a nice a trail to tackle piecemeal, however. The more developed, wheelchair-accessible trail to Barber Cabin at Lower Russian Lake (3.3 miles from the Sterling Highway trailhead) is great for families and anglers. The more secluded and rugged trail to Upper Russian Cabin (9.5 miles from the Cooper Lake trailhead) is a wonderful, long day's hike or bike (even if you head back the way you came). Wherever you end up, you'll have water outside your cabin door: large, mountain-rimmed lakes at Barber and Upper Russian cabins, or a sparkling, fast-flowing stream just off the Aspen Flats Cabin's front stoop.

The traverse can be done in either direction. Starting from the Cooper Lake trailhead is much easier, since you're heading downhill most of the way (from 1,300 feet to 350 feet, with some rolling hills in between). Many people go the other way, though, especially when they're connecting this trail with Resurrection Pass Trail to the north and/or Resurrection River Trail to the south (which intersects the Russian Lakes Trail midway between the Upper Russian Lake Cabin and Cooper Lake trailhead).

The trail is closed to vehicles, including snowmachines, from February 16 through November 30 and to horses (mountain bikers are asked to observe this closure also) from April 1 through June 30, due to mushy, spring trail conditions. Winter travel is possible to Upper Russian Lake and Aspen Flats Cabin from the Cooper Lake trailhead. The Forest Service does not recommend travel to Barber Cabin from the Russian River campground because of avalanche hazards along Lower Russian Lake. In early summer (or until the Forest Service has had a chance to remove them) fallen trees are common along the trail. Call the Seward Ranger District for trail-condition updates. In summer, lush cow parsnip and fast-growing alder can obscure parts of the trail, especially in sunny clearings; be ready to do some grassy wading, if not exactly bushwhacking.

When visiting all cabins, gather dead-and-down wood only. It is in fair supply. Treat all water sources.

Getting there

To start at the Sterling Highway trailhead, drive south of Anchorage to mile 52.5 of the Sterling Highway and turn left onto the road to the U.S.F.S. Russian River campground (signed). Drive through the campground (about 1 mile) to the trailhead at the far end. **To start at the Cooper Lake trailhead,** drive south of Anchorage to mile 48 of the Sterling Highway and turn left at Snug Harbor Road, just past the first bridge over the Kenai River. Continue 11 miles up the unpaved Snug Harbor Road. The small parking area and trailhead (signed) is on the left side of the road. Note that in winter, neither the Russian River campground-access road nor the last 2.5 miles of Snug Harbor Road to the Cooper Lake trailhead are plowed.

Cabin Planner / Russian Lakes Trail Mileage Table

Numbers in parentheses indicate additional mileage of cabin-access trails longer than 0.1 mile.

Cabin/trailhead	Eastbound location	Westbound location	Miles to next cabin east	west
Sterling Hwy trailhead	Mile 0	Mile 21.5	3.3	N.A.
Barber	Mile 2.6 (+0.7)	Mile 18.9 (+0.7)	7.3	N.A
Aspen Flats	Mile 9 (+0.2)	Mile 12.5 (+0.2)	3.2	7.3
Upper Russian	Mile 12	Mile 9.5	N.A.	3.2
Cooper Lake trailhead	Mile 21.5	Mile 0	N.A.	9.5

KENAI–Moose Pass to Seward

BARBER CABIN

Chugach National Forest (U.S. Forest Service)

Snapshot: Easy-to-reach lake retreat. A larger, wheelchair-accessible log cabin perfect for families and anglers.

Location: On the eastern shore of mountain-ringed Lower Russian Lake, off a 0.7-mile sidetrail from mile 2.6 of the Russian Lakes Trail.

Elevation: 400 feet.

Map: USGS Seward B8 or Trails Illustrated™, *Kenai National Wildlife Refuge/Chugach National Forest.*

Access: By foot; by wheelchair (see note under facilities) or jog stroller; by mountain bike or horse (except April 1 - June 30). Trail closed to motorized vehicles from May 1 to November 30. By floatplane, 25 minutes from Seward, 20 minutes from Cooper Landing. Winter travel is unsafe between Russian River campground and south end of Lower Russian Lake.

Available: Year-round, though winter travel is not recommended between Russian River campground and south end of Lower Russian Lake.

Best: Late May through September for hikers or bikers.

Sleeps: Five on bunks, comfortably.

Maximum stay: Three consecutive nights from May 15 through August 31. Seven consecutive nights the rest of the year.

Cost: $45.

Reservations: Forest Service toll-free reservation center, (877) 444-6777 or via Internet at http://www.reserveusa.com. For info on trail and cabin specifics, call the Seward Ranger District Office, (907) 224-3374.

Facilities: The spacious, 16x20-foot rustic cabin is constructed of dark, round logs with a brighter, natural-colored wood interior. Inside are five bunks, table, benches, large flat-topped wood stove, lots of wooden pegs for hanging gear, a mirror, and — a rarity in Forest Service cabins — plenty of extra floor space. Outside are a deck-sized porch with rails and bench, extra-wide outhouse connected to the cabin by a boardwalk, and even a birdhouse attached to the cabin's exterior. The large fire ring, surrounded by plank benches, is a great place for toasting s'mores and watching darkness settle over the lake. Ramps circle the building and lead to an accessible boat dock. A rowboat is included (bring your own life jackets). Wheelchair users, please note: the 3.3-mile, gently rolling trail to the cabin gains 50 feet in elevation, has a high crown and deep gravel. While it was fully accessible when first constructed, changes from weather and heavy use may have made it too rugged for some users.

Condition: Excellent.

View and surroundings: The cabin sits in a large grassy clearing, facing Lower Russian Lake, flanked on each side by spruce, birch, and black cottonwood trees. The narrow lake is a deep-blue ribbon wedged between steep, 4,000-plus-foot peaks. From its center (a short, easy row in the Forest Service-provided boat) you can look south to the Skilak Glacier, a glistening branch of the 700-square-mile Harding Icefield farther south. To reach the cabin, you hike an addition 0.7 mile along a wide, gravel sidetrail (signed) off the main Russian Lakes Trail. There's no guarantee of privacy, however, since anglers also use the cabin-access trail and lakeshore.

Wildlife sightings: moose and lots of waterfowl, including loons, ducks, and mergansers. Also in area: black and brown bears, lynx, and wolves.

Recreation: Fish for rainbow trout in Lower Russian Lake, and for sockeye salmon downstream of the Russian River Falls. There is exceptionally scenic hiking or mountain biking uptrail, toward the Aspen Flats Cabin, over 7 miles away. The narrow trail crosses several icy, plunging creeks and winds along the high, tundra-clad edge of a valley scarred by wildfires.

KENAI–Moose Pass to Seward

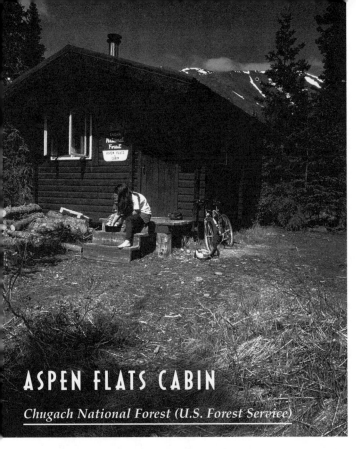

ASPEN FLATS CABIN
Chugach National Forest (U.S. Forest Service)

Snapshot: Views of the rushing Russian, off the main trail. A simple 12x14-foot log cabin on the banks of a famous sockeye salmon river.

Location: Between Lower and Upper Russian Lakes, off mile 9 of the Russian Lakes Trail from the Sterling Highway trailhead.

Elevation: 600 feet.

Map: USGS Seward B8 and Kenai B1; or Trails Illustrated™, *Kenai National Wildlife Refuge/Chugach National Forest.*

Access: By foot; by mountain bike or horse (except April 1 - June 30); by snowmachine or skis from the Cooper Lake trailhead only (may be icy or difficult to follow after heavy snowfall). Winter travel is unsafe between Russian River campground and south end of Lower Russian Lake. Trail is closed to motorized vehicles from May 1 to November 30.

Available: Year-round.

Best: Late May through September for hikers, mid-June through September for mountain bikers.

Sleeps: Five on bunks, comfortably.

Maximum stay: Three consecutive nights from May 15 through August 31. Seven consecutive nights the rest of the year.

Cost: $35.

Reservations: Forest Service toll-free reservation center, (877) 444-6777 or via Internet at http://www.reserveusa.com. For info on trail and cabin specifics, call the Seward Ranger District Office, (907) 224-3374.

Facilities: This dark brown, Pan Abode log cabin has six bunks, two of which double as benches next to a small dining table, a new flat-topped wood stove, shelves, and a counter. Outside are a fire pit, outhouse, and a small front stoop. There is no boat at this location.

Condition: Fair.

View and surroundings: The cabin sits about 0.2 mile off the main trail in flat, boggy terrain, thickly carpeted with blueberry and cranberry bushes. It faces west across the Russian River — straight, deep, and fast-flowing — about 50 feet from the cabin's front stoop. Mountains rise to 5,000 feet behind the cabin.

Wildlife sightings: This is prime habitat for moose and waterfowl, including harlequin ducks and mergansers, which bob in the smooth current of the Russian River. Brown bears are commonly spotted during the river's salmon runs. Use caution along the trail. Also in the area: black bears and wolves.

Recreation: Fish the river for Dolly Varden and rainbow trout. Fishing for sockeye salmon upstream of Russian River Falls is not permitted. Hikers and bikers can explore varying terrain — muskeg, meadows, and high-canopied forest — along the trail, toward either the Upper or Lower Russian lakes cabins. Abundant berries ripen in late July through September.

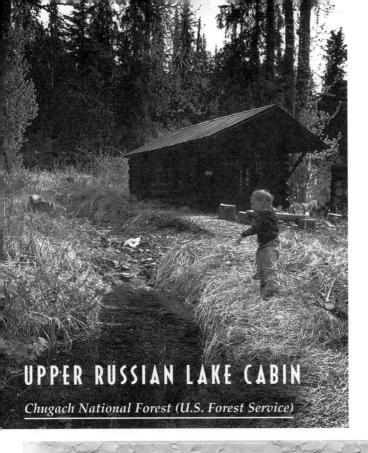

UPPER RUSSIAN LAKE CABIN

Chugach National Forest (U.S. Forest Service)

"Someone previously broke the stove. We fixed it with a beer can. Snowmachined in, listened to owls hoot, and blew up propane tanks with a shotgun. Life is good."

Upper Russian Lake Cabin log.

Snapshot: Rustic seclusion: A century-old traditional log cabin overlooking Upper Russian Lake.

Location: On the northeast shore of Upper Russian Lake, on the Russian Lakes Trail, 9.5 miles from the Cooper Lake trailhead.

Elevation: 700 feet.

Map: USGS Seward B8 or Trails Illustrated™, *Kenai National Wildlife Refuge/Chugach National Forest.*

Access: By foot; by mountain bike or horse (except April 1 - June 30); by ski or snowmachine from the Cooper Lake trailhead only (may be icy or difficult to follow after heavy snowfall). Winter travel is unsafe between Russian River campground and south end of Lower Russian Lake. Trail closed to motorized vehicles from May 1 to November 30.

Available: Year-round.

Best: Late May through September for hikers, mid-June through September for mountain bikers.

Sleeps: Six on bunks (four would be more comfortable).

Maximum stay: Three consecutive nights from May 15 through August 31. Seven consecutive nights the rest of the year.

Cost: $35.

Reservations: Forest Service toll-free reservation center, (877) 444-6777 or via Internet at http://www.reserveusa.com. For info on trail and cabin specifics, call the Seward Ranger District Office, (907) 224-3374.

Facilities: This round-log rustic cabin is dark inside and out, with a cold stone floor (instead of the typical plywood), multi-paned windows, six bunks, small table and benches, flat-topped wood stove, shelves, and a counter. Outside are a wood shed, outhouse, and fire pit with stumps and logs for seating. The rowboat that was destroyed a few years ago has been replaced. (Bring your own life jackets.)

Condition: Fair. (But who's complaining? This cabin has been a haunt for hunters, prospectors, and recluses for decades.)

View and surroundings: The cabin sits back from the lakeshore, surrounded by grass, cow parsnip, and lots of old cottonwood trees, including some standing dead ones. Upper Russian Lake, three miles long and often riffled by winds, shimmers in the distance. A stream runs past the cabin, just five feet off to the side, bubbling over smooth stones. Cooper Mountain, at 5,270 feet, looms over the area to the northeast.

Wildlife sightings: Beaver, eagles, and lots of waterfowl, both on the lake and in the many ponds and creeks on the way to the cabin from the Cooper Lake trailhead. Moose, brown and black bears. Also in area: Dall sheep and wolves.

Recreation: Fishing for salmon is prohibited near the cabin (and anywhere upstream of the Russian River Falls). There is excellent fishing for Dolly Varden and rainbow trout in Upper Russian Lake.

KENAI–Moose Pass to Seward

In Brief:

RESURRECTION RIVER CABIN

Chugach National Forest (U.S. Forest Service)

Location: Off a short cabin access trail along the Resurrection River Trail, 1.5 miles upstream from the Martin Creek bridge (6.5 miles from trailhead on Exit Glacier Road).

Elevation: 500 feet.

Map: USGS Seward A8, B8, or Trails Illustrated™, *Kenai National Wildlife Refuge/Kenai Fjords National Park.*

Access: By foot; by mountain bike or horse (except April 1 through June 30); by snowmachine (Dec. 1 through April 30); or by cross-country ski. The trail is difficult to follow on skis due to steep side hills; follow streambed. Note that winter mileages are about 5 miles longer because Exit Glacier Road is unplowed (see Exit Glacier Cabin listing for parking and access). The trail is wet in summer and poorly maintained as of this writing.

Available: Year-round. Use caution in summer when bears congregate along river.

Sleeps: Four, comfortably (maximum of eight).

Maximum stay: Three consecutive nights May 15 through August 31. Seven consecutive nights the rest of the year.

Cost: $35.

In brief: Since flooding in 1996, the perennially wet Resurrection River Trail has been awaiting long-term repairs. As of this writing, a washed-out bridge and trail markers had not been replaced. Hunters and occasional hikers are still visiting the area and renting the cabin, which overlooks a small pond with views of surrounding mountains. The 12x14-foot cabin has a wood stove. Reputedly, claw marks on the exterior walls are testament to the heavy brown bear population in this area. Especially when salmon are spawning, use extra caution. Due to the condition of the trail, it's not an easy jaunt anytime. Contact the Forest Service for an update. Wildlife include moose, black and brown bears, Dall sheep, wolves, and beavers. The 16-mile trail connects with the Russian Lakes Trail four miles east of the Upper Russian Lake Cabin, which in turn connects with the Resurrection Pass Trail for a 71-mile traverse between Seward and Hope.

Reservations: Forest Service toll-free reservation center, (877) 444-6777 or via Internet at http://www.reserveusa.com. For info on trail and cabin specifics, call the Seward Ranger District Office, (907) 224-3374.

In Brief:

CRESCENT LAKE CABIN

Chugach National Forest (U.S. Forest Service)

Location: On northwest shore of Crescent Lake; 6.5 miles from the trail-head, which starts at the end of Quartz Creek Road, off mile 44 of the Sterling Highway.

Elevation: 1,450 feet.

Map: USGS Seward B7 (edges of C7 and C8 also needed to show all of Crescent Lake Trail); or Trails Illustrated™, *Kenai National Wildlife Refuge/Chugach National Forest.*

Access: On foot; on bike or horse (except April 1 through June 30); by snowmachine (Dec. 1 through April 30) or skis from Carter Lake Trail and over the southern side of frozen Crescent Lake only, due to extreme avalanche danger on the Crescent Creek Trail in winter and early spring; by floatplane, 15 minutes from Moose Pass, 20 minutes from Cooper Landing.

Available: Year-round; use caution in winter due to avalanche hazards.

Sleeps: Four, comfortably (maximum of eight).

Maximum stay: Three consecutive nights from May 15 through August 31. Seven consecutive nights the rest of the year.

Cost: $45.

In brief: This very popular cabin is located on one of the Kenai Peninsula's smoother, more gradually ascending singletrack trails, making it a favorite of mountain bikers and hikers. Fly-in anglers also come to fish the lake and Crescent Creek for trophy-sized grayling (con-tact the Alaska Department of Fish and Game for special regulations). Wildlife include moose, brown and black bears, and Dall sheep. Mining operations may be visible along the trail; respect private property. The 12x14-foot cabin has a wood stove. A rowboat is provided. (Bring your own life jackets.) Bushwhacking between the Crescent Lake Cabin and Crescent Saddle Cabin, farther east, is not recommended. The unmain-tained trail crosses a deep creek and several avalanche chutes, which may be dangerous even in summer.

Reservations: Forest Service toll-free reservation center, (877) 444-6777 or via Internet at http://www.reserveusa.com. For specific info on trail and cabin specifics, call the Seward Ranger District Office, (907) 224-3374.

KENAI-Moose Pass to Seward

In Brief:

CRESCENT SADDLE CABIN

Chugach National Forest (USFS)

Location: South shore of Crescent Lake at the saddle; 7.5 miles from the Carter Lake trailhead, which starts at mile 33 of the Seward Highway.
Elevation: 1,450 feet.
Map: USGS Seward B7 (C7 also required to show Carter Lake Trail); or Trails Illustrated™, *Kenai National Wildlife Refuge/Chugach National Forest.*
Access: By foot; by mountain bike or horse (except April 1 through June 30); by snowmachine (Dec. 1 through April 30) or skis from Carter Lake trailhead only, due to extreme avalanche danger on the Crescent Creek Trail in winter and early spring; by floatplane, 15 minutes from Moose Pass, 20 minutes from Cooper Landing.
Available: Year-round.
Sleeps: Four, comfortably (maximum of eight).
Maximum stay: Three consecutive nights from May 15 through August 31. Seven consecutive nights the rest of the year.
Cost: $45.
In brief: This 12x14-foot cabin, with oil stove and rowboat (#1 stove oil and life jackets not included) is most popular among fly-in anglers. Wildlife include moose, black and brown bears, mountain goats, Dall sheep, and trophy-sized grayling. (Contact Alaska Department of Fish and Game for special regulations). Access on foot is moderately difficult. The old Carter Lake Trail is primitive; expect high grass and brush. Bushwhacking to the Crescent Lake Cabin, farther west, is not recommended.
Reservations: Forest Service toll-free reservation center, (877) 444-6777 or via Internet at http://www.reserveusa.com. For info on trail and cabin specifics, call the Seward Ranger District Office, (907) 224-3374.

KENAI-Moose Pass to Seward

Stewart Ferguson

WILLOW CABIN
PUBLIC USE CABIN

EXIT GLACIER WILLOW CABIN

Kenai Fjords National Park (National Park Service)

Snapshot: Views of Alaska's ancient ice, with all the comforts of home. A modern, fully furnished cabin for winter recreationists at the foot of a glacier.

Location: At the end of Exit Glacier Road, just north of Seward, in the only road-accessible corner of Kenai Fjords National Park.

Elevation: 400 feet.

Map: USGS Seward A7 (doesn't show Exit Glacier Road); or Trails Illustrated™, *Kenai Fjords National Park.*

Access: Cross-country ski, snowshoe, snowmachine, or dog sled on a 7.3-mile section of closed, snowpacked road.

Available: Winter only, after Exit Glacier Road has been closed due to accumulated snow (usually December), until about April. Call the National Park Service at (907) 224-3175 to check the road condition and cabin availability.

Best: December to April.

Sleeps: Eight on bunks, comfortably.

Maximum stay: Three consecutive days.

Cost: $35.

Reservations: Kenai Fjords National Park office in downtown Seward, 1212 Fourth Ave., (907) 224-3175.

Caution: Winter temperatures near the glacier are lower than at Seward. The river valley may be windy and the road icy. Use caution when exploring near Exit Glacier. Stay off the ice; the glacier is active and calves, even in winter. If traveling with dogs, beware of moose, which are prone to stress in winter and have been known to charge and kill unrestrained pets in the area.

Facilities: Willow Cabin is used by National Park staff and volunteers as a summer residence and is rented to the public in winter. Next door are Cottonwood Cabin (not for public rental), the larger Alder Cabin (the residence of a winter caretaker), and a two-hole outhouse. Behind Alder Cabin is an outdoor water pump that freezes each year, usually in January.

From inside, Willow Cabin looks more like a motel room or apartment than a cabin. There are two bedrooms with a full-sized double bunk in each, mattresses, bureaus, and closets. The living area has a sofa. The kitchen area has chairs and a table, a large cooking area, counters, sink (no running water), cooking utensils, pots and pans, dishes and flatware. A propane range with oven, a heater, and wall lamps provide plenty of heat and light, with the neighboring caretaker *typically* on duty, ensuring an adequate supply of propane. A bulletin board provides safety information and clean-up instructions. Even though the cabin looks like a motel room, don't forget to pack out your garbage.

No pets are allowed in the cabin. Dogs must be restrained at all times on leashes less than six feet long. A wide porch with overhang provides some shelter from the elements.

Condition: Excellent.

View and surroundings: Willow Cabin's large front windows and porch directly face Exit Glacier, 0.5 mile away and luminescent even under a layer of snow. All three Park Service cabins sit in the middle of a lightly wooded, glacial-outwash valley, ringed by mountains. There is no direct sun in winter, but moonlight plays against the steep, snowy slopes nearby and sounds reverberate through the valley. Especially in early spring, nearby avalanches and cracking glacier ice occasionally add to the symphony.

Wildlife sightings: Moose, mountain goats, and bald eagles are frequently seen. On several occasions, wolverines — notoriously reclusive animals — have been bold enough to peer in the cabin's windows and nibble on ski poles left outside. Also in area: coyotes, wolves, and (in spring) black bears.

Recreation: In addition to the main road to the cabin, there are side trails for snowmobiling, skiing, snowshoeing, and mushing. From the cabin, a trail (not maintained, but usually hardpacked by snowmobile) leads 0.5 mile to the terminus of the glacier. An unmaintained trail continues along the north side of the glacier, to Harding Ice Field, for more experienced snowshoers and backcountry travelers only. No hunting or fishing.

KENAI–Moose Pass to Seward

Getting there: Turn west onto Exit Glacier Road, 3.7 miles north of Seward (about 3 hours south of Anchorage). Follow the road 1.3 miles to a gate, which marks the end of the maintained part of the road. Park next to the gate. The 7.3-mile section of closed road is usually hardpacked and nearly level, making travel moderately easy, except when a layer of ice coats the road. Expect to ski or snowshoe for 3 to 5 hours, one-way. The road parallels the braided Resurrection River, bordered by thin stands of mixed spruce/hardwood forest. Peaks over 4,000 feet high flank the river valley. Landmarks along the way include: the Chugach National Forest boundary (signed), near mile 2 of the closed section of road; Paradise Creek (where you'll finally spot the sun to the south if traveling midday in winter) at mile 5.3; and the bridge over Exit Creek at mile 5.7. After the bridge, you'll pass a closed campground before coming to a short side-trail (signed PUBLIC USE CABIN) on your left. Follow the trail past Cottonwood Cabin to Willow Cabin. The larger Alder Cabin, home of the winter caretaker, is about 200 feet away.

Exit Glacier view near cabin

Stewart Ferguson

UPPER PARADISE LAKE CABIN

Chugach National Forest (U.S. Forest Service)

> *"The weather's been gracious enough the last couple of days to afford us a peek of Wolverine Glacier, some of Nellie Juan's glaciers and river, this valley, and peaks beyond ... At 4,700 feet, it seems the world's all yours — what a rush!"*
>
> *Upper Paradise Lake Cabin log.*

Snapshot: Paradise for fly-in anglers or anyone wanting to experience alpine wilderness. A simple, secluded log cabin in scenic high country.

Location: On the northwestern shore of Upper Paradise Lake in the Kenai Mountains.

Elevation: 1,340 feet.

Map: USGS Seward B6 or Trails Illustrated™, *Kenai National Wildlife Refuge/Chugach National Forest.*

Access: By floatplane, 15 minutes from Moose Pass or 25 minutes from Seward; by foot, with backcountry hiking and orienteering experience only. The cabin is 10 miles east of the Seward Highway in the Paradise Valley (about a two-hour drive south of Anchorage). There is no maintained trail.

Available: Year-round.

Best: June through August.

Sleeps: Six on bunks (four would be more comfortable).

Maximum stay: Three nights from May 15 through August 31. Seven nights the rest of the year.

Cost: $35.

Reservations: Forest Service toll-free reservation center, (877) 444-6777 or via Internet at http://www.reserveusa.com. For info on trail and cabin specifics, call the Seward Ranger District Office, (907) 224-3374.

Facilities: This 12x14-foot dark brown, Pan Abode cabin has a recently added arctic entryway (sheltered doorway). Inside you'll find six bunks, a table and benches, counter, shelves, and flat-topped wood stove. The outhouse is perched atop a hill behind the cabin. A rowboat is included. (Bring your own life jackets.) Purify water from the lake. Firewood is not abundant at this near-treeline cabin. You'll have to row across the lake and scrounge for dead-and-down wood; it's better to bring all you need.

Condition: Good.

View and surroundings: Snow-covered mountains, glaciers, krummholz (stunted spruce trees) and tundra surround this lakeside cabin, a humble structure dwarfed by the alpine wilderness. The cabin sits on the north shore of a small nub of boggy peninsula, jutting into the middle of Upper Paradise Lake. A 5,083-foot mountain slopes up from the lake's far shore, visible from the cabin's front window. (Jeff, a friend, likened the leaning, snow-streaked mountain to a massive, breaking wave — precisely the way I think of it now.)   To the east and the northwest — directly over the outhouse — rise mountains heavily plastered with glaciers. A waterfall plunges down the steep slope at the head of the lake. Even when the wind isn't blowing, just looking around makes you shiver.

The lakeshore, 40 feet from the cabin, has a pebble beach scattered with countless small pieces of driftwood — used to good effect as natural, gnarled hooks within the cabin. The small peninsula is mostly brushy muskeg. (The boggy patch behind the cabin was nicknamed "Baby Moose Meadow" by one cabin-user.) Song- birds dart around the cabin, over short, dense stands of willow and alder. There are some larger trees on a rise north of the cabin, but most of the surrounding slopes are above treeline.

Wildlife sightings: Eagles (especially at stream outlet), beaver, black bears, and moose. Also in area: brown bears and mountain goats.

Recreation: Fishing for grayling is the number one reason to come here. There are several good fishing holes. Try rowing to the outflow stream on the south side of the small peninsula (toward the western shore of Upper Paradise Lake). In a weekend, some anglers will catch absolutely zip, while others reel in hundreds.

Photographic opportunities are plentiful and wildflowers

abound, especially along the small beach in front of the cabin. A partial tally in July included columbine, lupines, geranium, fireweed, Jacob's ladder, cinquefoil, bottlebrush, daisies, monkshood, and chocolate lilies. Salmonberries ripen in August.

There is no trail hiking, but backcountry enthusiasts who don't mind getting wet and weary have bushwhacked in several directions. Hiking up to the saddle at the northeast head of the lake, you can glimpse Wolverine Glacier and the wild country beyond. The twisting gravel bars of Paradise Valley also invite exploration with map and compass. Backcountry skiing on virgin slopes is also possible.

Getting there: Reachable mainly by chartered floatplane, this can be an expensive trip, but the flight itself is a sightseeing experience worth the price even before you reach the cabin. You'll see twisting glacial rivers, lush valleys, hidden waterfalls plunging from high peaks, and possibly mountain goats perched on nearly vertical slopes.

Upper Paradise Lake Cabin with floatplane

KENAI-Moose Pass to Seward

Grayling al Florencio
(or Kenai Peninsula Mexican Fish Soup)

Ingredients for two adults (double recipe for more):
> one large can tomatoes
> half large onion
> 2 or 3 serrano or jalapeno peppers
> 2 potatoes, sliced thin
> oil for frying
> lime
> a tin of herring or mackerel in Tabasco sauce, discreetly packed
> with luck, some grayling

Directions: Cut potato, onion, and jalapeno in thin slices and fry until soft. Add can of tomatoes and another can of water to make a soup. Now, if you have some grayling, clean it (gutted and head off), cover it with water, and boil it in a deep frypan, just until the flesh is white and falling apart. Peel back the skin and remove chunks of fish to toss into the soup. (If you haven't used too much water, the boiling water will be flavorful, so add that too.) If you don't have grayling, toss in the tinned herring or mackerel. Before serving, squeeze lime on top.

This recipe was taught to me by Florencio, a Copper Canyon Tarahumara Indian with a flair for improvisation. It was his spicier version of "stone soup," which, according to a timeless children's story, is simply a stone boiled in a pot of water. Plus, maybe, a carrot here, or a potato there, or whatever

you happen to have on hand, the sum of which ultimately makes a wonderful con-
coction that is all the better when eaten on a chilly lakeshore or riverbank following any sort of disappointment (the burros running away, or — in this
Alaska version — the lack of fish after a $450 floatplane charter and a long day
of angling). As long as you start with a watered-down can of tomatoes, a little
onion, a tin of fish, and some spice, anything else you add will taste good.

    This recipe answers the question: what do you bring to eat on a cabin
fishing trip? You need to be prepared to eat even if the fish don't bite (macaroni
would be an insult). But if you do catch fish, you also want to use most or all of
your backup ingredients, so that you're not lugging around unnecessary weight.
If you're cooking dinner while the optimistic anglers of your party are still out
in the rowboat, you can have a comforting meal ready for their return without
insulting anyone. If they return with arms full of fish, you can say, "Fantastic!
I've been waiting with the broth to poach it in." If they return empty-handed,
you can say, "No problem. I happened to pack some herring." Just don't let them
know you packed the canned fish, a key ingredient, until this critical moment, or
you may be accused of infecting the party with low expectations and bad luck.

    Grayling is the fish used here, because it is an easy fish to catch in the
lakes where it lives. When it's biting — usually in early and late summer, when
it's not too sluggishly warm outside — even children and inexperienced anglers
manage to land a few with ease. It's a delicate fish (some people liken the flavor
of the flesh to lemon and thyme), with lots of small bones. While it can be fried,
it falls apart, which is why I like putting it into soup.

    If you catch something firmer, larger, and more full-flavored, like a
salmon, skip the soup, wrap the fish in foil, and throw it on a fire.

**Author's son Aryeh with
fresh-caught grayling**

KENAI-Moose Pass to
Seward

In Brief:

LOWER PARADISE LAKE CABIN

Location: On the shore of Lower Paradise Lake, in the Kenai Mountains.
Elevation: 1,200 feet.
Map: USGS Seward B6 or Trails Illustrated™, *Kenai National Wildlife Refuge/Chugach National Forest.*
Access: By floatplane, 15 minutes from Moose Pass or 20 minutes from Seward. There is no trail into Paradise Valley. Access on foot is possible with backcountry bushwhacking and orienteering experience only.
Available: Year-round.
Sleeps: Four, comfortably (maximum of eight).
Maximum stay: Seven consecutive nights.
Cost: $45.
In brief: This 12x14-foot cabin with wood stove is popular for fly-in grayling angling and hunting. With no road or trail access, the cabin offers seclusion and spectacular views of glaciated peaks. Wildlife include moose, black and brown bears, and mountain goats.
Reservations: Forest Service toll-free reservation center, (877) 444-6777 or via Internet at http://www.reserveusa.com. For info on trail and cabin specifics, call the Seward Ranger District Office, (907) 224-3374.

KENAI–Moose Pass to Seward

In Brief:

DALE CLEMENS MEMORIAL CABIN

Location: On the winter route of the Lost Lake/Primrose Trail, 4.5 miles from the Lost Lake trailhead in summer, 2.5 miles in winter. (The trailhead is located in the Lost Lake Subdivision, mile 5 of the Seward Highway.)

Elevation: 1,750 feet.

Map: USGS Seward A7, B7; or Trails Illustrated™, *Kenai Fjords National Park*.

Access: By foot; by mountain bike or horse (except April 1 through June 30); or by snowmachine (Dec. 1 through April 30), skis, or snowshoes. Often trail is not snow-free until mid-June.

Available: Year-round.

Sleeps: Four, comfortably (maximum of eight).

Maximum stay: Three consecutive nights from May 15 through August 31. Seven consecutive nights the rest of the year.

Cost: $45.

In brief: This 14x18-foot cabin is one of the newer and more attractive Forest Service cabins, with lots of windows and views of towering Resurrection and Mount Ascension peaks (4,700 and 5,700 feet, respectively). It has a propane stove, with propane *sometimes* available although rangers won't guarantee it (contact the Seward Ranger District to inquire). If you do bring propane, it must be in a 20-pound cylinder to match the fittings. In winter, the cabin is 2.5 steep miles from the trailhead (in a subdivision 5 miles north of Seward). In summer, the winter route is too boggy, so you must follow the more gradually climbing main trail and then loop back along a 1.5-mile spur, for a total of 4.5 miles from the trailhead. Wildlife include moose, black and brown bears, wolves, mountain goats, and ptarmigan. Abundant salmonberries ripen in summer. Hikers can continue north along the scenic, alpine Primrose Trail (15 miles total) and fish for rainbow trout in Lost Lake.

Reservations: Forest Service toll-free reservation center, (877) 444-6777 or via Internet at http://www.reserveusa.com. For info on trail and cabin specifics, call the Seward Ranger District Office, (907) 224-3374.

KENAI-Moose Pass to Seward

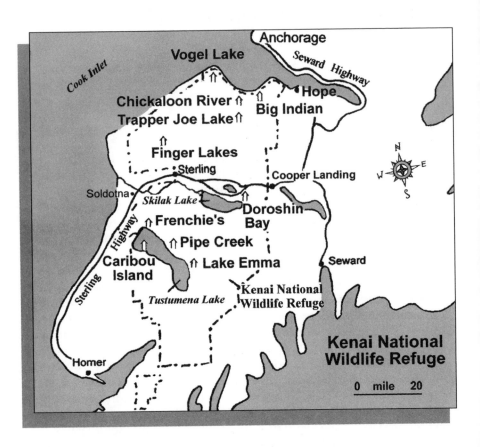

Kenai National
Wildlife Refuge

0   mile   20

The Secret Cabins
(Or, why there are 49 featured cabins in this book, instead of 50)

The Kenai National Wildlife Refuge volunteer in Soldotna had no firsthand knowledge of them. A young waiter at a Sterling cafe was a little more helpful.

"There aren't any signs," he told us on a chilly autumn morning as Brian, my children, and I filled our bellies in preparation for the search. "You almost have to go with someone who's been there first, or you could spend a day looking and still not find them. I've been to a few. They're kind of a secret. And locals want to keep them that way, I guess."

The waiter's warnings only encouraged us. We planned to spend the day visiting the Finger Lakes Cabin, the most popular and accessible of 10 no-fee, no-reservation Kenai National Wildlife Refuge cabins. We deduced that it was no more than one or two miles off the trail, according to an annoyingly, per-

Where there's a trail, you can follow it

haps intentionally vague fact sheet that gave only map coordinates instead of directions. How could we miss it?

Already, this "free" cabin had cost us plenty. Four dollars for a topo map, $20 for gas. We'd arrived in Sterling the night before at dusk. If we'd had better directions, we would have hiked to the cabin anyway. But in these unknown woods, we knew better than to head into the dark — especially since we had no way of knowing whether it was vacant. So, my family and I had spent a night in a motel off the highway. There went $50. And we spent some more money on dinner. (We did find a fantastic out-of-the-way restaurant called "Through the Seasons" in Soldotna, which only made us cocky about our orienteering skills.) And we spent some more on breakfast — well worth it for the waiter's advice. Our wallets were empty, but our spirits were still high.

Originally, I hadn't intended to include the Kenai refuge cabins in this guidebook. They're historical curiosities — old trappers' cabins, mostly, located away from prime backpacking, biking, canoeing, or kayaking routes. Since you can't reserve them, you can't count on using them even after (or rather, if) you find them. They're as close as you get to old-fashioned, backcountry emergency cabins — the type of crumbling structures you'd stumble upon in a storm. Some are in decent shape. Others have dirt floors and rotting logs.

Before there were state parks — heck, before there was an Alaska — the code of the bush allowed you to enter a backcountry cabin, even if it was private, to find temporary shelter. The refuge cabins maintain that tradition. Often, the line between past and present, public and private, is blurred. In addition to the 10 listed refuge cabins, there are others that are even more mysterious — older structures dating back to the 1920s, not mentioned on fact sheets for the public. Some refuge cabins have signs and visitor logs. Some don't. One angry old-timer keeps ripping down refuge signs at Pipe Creek Cabin. He thinks it belongs to him. But don't worry, I was told by a ranger — he only uses it once a year.

Gore-tex™ and Polartec™ may have replaced wool and flannel in some parts, but not on the sideroads of the two-million-acre Kenai National Wildlife Refuge. On the day of our Finger Lakes trip, we passed a horn and antler shop and turned down a long, gravel road. After about 20 minutes, we pulled off the road and parked the car, flipping through our maps yet again. Where we'd expected to find a trail, there was only a closed gravel road. Instead of a trail or cabin sign, we found a gas company sign and a gate. Dead end, we thought.

Just when we were going to drive away, a man heading toward a drill site on the refuge opened the gate. He didn't know about any cabin, but he said that the Finger Lakes were this way. We parked and followed the one-lane road on foot. The tall grass alongside the road was brittle with frost. We passed a family hunting for spruce grouse. They confirmed we were on the right track.

In another 10 or 20 minutes, we were sure we'd spot the cabin. But we couldn't find the right sidetrail, and we didn't pass any more hunters. Skinny game trails led off the closed road in all directions. Stomachs were grumbling. Our children were cold. I sensed a mutiny brewing.

Two more hours of walking deflated us. Had we gone too far? Not far enough? The blue glimmer of one of the Finger Lakes raised our spirits again briefly, but even after we'd detoured to the water's edge, we still couldn't see any sign of human habitation. I felt certain the cabin was close, yet we'd already spent the better part of a day looking, and we were due back in Anchorage, a three-hour drive away, that evening. So much for cabin #50.

"Maybe it's better this way," I said to my husband, Brian, who was pre-pared to head farther off-trail in pursuit of our elusive quarry. "They're secret cabins. Maybe they should stay secret."

After my unsuccessful Finger Lakes hike, I tracked down a refuge staff member who knew more about the cabins.

"We're not trying to hide them. But we're not trying to advertise them, either," refuge ranger pilot Rick Johnston told me. "You can't plan your vacation around them. But then again, a Soldotna person doesn't have to worry about someone in New York having a reservation." He said this a little gleefully. And hey, anyone can try to locate them, he added. "They're difficult even for a local person to find. They're for those who are a little more savvy, who know how to ask the right questions, who want a little more adventure."

It was a call to arms. I asked a few more questions and studied the map again. I think I've got it, now. And the next time I need a free place to crash after a $70 dinner in Soldotna, I'll know just where to go.

Waterlilies

About the Kenai National Wildlife Refuge Cabins

Cabins are first-come, first-served; no reservations required and no fees. Access is mostly by plane or motorized boat because of the distances involved. Only the Finger Lakes Cabin is anywhere close to a road. Maintenance of cabins is minimal. Since you may travel for hours without any guarantee that the cabin isn't already occupied or is in useable condition, it is imperative that you bring adequate supplies, including a tent. Remember, you'll need to do some local research and/or orienteering, since precise cabin locations aren't given, just general areas as defined by township, range, and section coordinates on USGS topographical maps. The maximum stay is two weeks.

In Brief:
Ten Refuge Cabins

BIG INDIAN CABIN

Map location: USGS Seward D8, Kenai T9N, R4W, Section 4, NW 1/4 (NW end of Big Indian Airstrip).
Access: Wheel aircraft on Big Indian Airstrip, ATV from September 1 to October 20, or snowmachine.
Sleeps: Four to six.
Recreation: Waterfowl hunting, fishing for salmon, and big-game hunting in Chickaloon estuary.
In brief: The 12x16-foot cabin is used mostly in September and October by hunters. It's in generally good condition with an operable stove and there's abundant firewood in the area.

In Brief:

CARIBOU ISLAND CABIN

Map location: USGS Kenai A3, T2N, R10W, Section 29, NW 1/4.
Access: Boat, floatplane, and snowmachine.
Sleeps: Four.
Recreation: Hunting and fishing in Nikolai Creek.
In brief: The log cabin, with loft, is the refuge's most popular Tustumena Lake public shelter. The shore of the lake is exposed to southerly winds. Large waves could swamp boats not pulled out on the beach. There is little beach area available during high water.

KENAI WILDLIFE REFUGE

In Brief:

CHICKALOON RIVER #1 CABIN

Map location: USGS Kenai D1, T9N, R7W, Section 8, SE 1/4.
Access: Float or wheel plane (requires skilled off-airport pilot; floatplane landing requires careful negotiation of Lower Chickaloon River's tides and waves), or boat from Hope or Chickaloon River.
Sleeps: Four.
Recreation: Waterfowl hunting.
In brief: The 12x16-foot cabin is built on stilts and has an oil stove (oil not included). There is no firewood in the area. Cabin is used during waterfowl season by hunters.

In Brief:

DOROSHIN BAY CABIN

Map location: USGS Kenai B1, T4N, R5W, Section 22, NW 1/4.
Access: Mostly by boat, with minimal floatplane access (use caution — there are large submerged rocks near shore).
Sleeps: Four.
Recreation: Fishing in nearby Kenai River, about two miles from the cabin, and big- and small-game hunting in the Skilak Flats area.
In brief: The cabin is constructed of unpeeled logs with a tarpaper batten roof and rough-cut plank floor. Recent improvements include enlarged windows and a new outhouse, but major work is still needed. The area is very buggy; firewood is limited.

In Brief:

FINGER LAKES CABIN

Map location: USGS Kenai C3, T7N, R9W, Section 33, SW 1/4.
Access: By foot from Swanson River Road along the Finger Lakes Trail (an unsigned, closed road), or by floatplane or snowmachine.
Sleeps: Four.
Recreation: Rainbow trout fishing in the lakes; hunting for moose, bear, and small game.
In brief: This is the most heavily used cabin in the refuge due to easy access from the road. The log cabin is in good condition and has a stove.

KENAI WILDLIFE REFUGE

In Brief:

FRENCHIE'S CABIN

Map location: USGS Kenai B3, T2N, R10W, Section 3, NW 1/4 (on Tustumena Lake).

Access: Boat, floatplane, snowmachine, or horse.

Sleeps: Four.

Recreation: Hunting and fishing.

In brief: The cabin is constructed of dovetail-connected logs with an enclosed loft, open front porch, and five large windows. Refuge staff may decide to deter future users due to the cabin condition, which is fair to poor.

In Brief:

LAKE EMMA CABIN

Map location: USGS Kenai A2, T1S, R7W, Section 6, NW 1/4.

Access: By boat on Tustumena Lake, then by foot on the Lake Emma Trail. Access by snowmachine is possible but difficult. Floatplanes are not allowed on Lake Emma.

Sleeps: Two.

Recreation: Hunting for moose, sheep, bear, and mountain goat in alpine terrain beyond the cabin.

In brief: This is one of the nicer log cabins in the refuge, with a large enclosed porch and a coal stove. It is used mainly in spring and fall by hunters. Trappers use the cabin intermittently.

In Brief:

PIPE CREEK CABIN

Map location: USGS Kenai A3, T1N, R9W, Section 23, NE 1/4 (2.5 miles south of Bear Creek off Tustumena Lake).

Access: Boat, floatplane, or snowmachine.

Sleeps: Two to three.

Recreation: Fishing for red salmon and Dolly Varden in Pipe Creek; hunting for brown bear.

In brief: The cabin is constructed of dovetail-connected logs, with a dirt floor. Public use is light.

In Brief:

TRAPPER JOE LAKE CABIN

Map location: USGS Kenai D1, T8N, R5W, Section 24, SE 1/4.
Access: Primarily floatplane; also snowmachine or four-wheel drive.
Sleeps: Two to four.
Recreation: Fishing for trout in the lake (rowboat available at cabin), and
hunting.
In brief: The cabin is next to a marsh; area is extremely buggy. Black and
brown bears are common in the area. The log cabin has a plank floor
and is poorly lit, with only two windows.

In Brief:

VOGEL LAKE CABIN

Map location: USGS Kenai D2, T10N, R7W, Section 1, NE 1/4.
Access: Primarily floatplane; also snowmachine.
Sleeps: Four to six.
Recreation: Fishing and boating in Vogel Lake, and hunting.
In brief: The log cabin has an enclosed porch with glass on three sides;
lighting is excellent.

KENAI WILDLIFE REFUGE

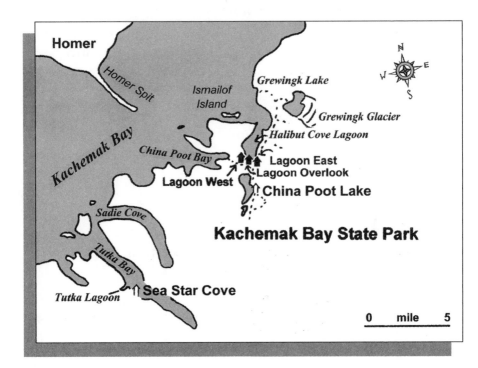

Prince Of Tides: Kids and Coastal Cabins

"You moved the stick," my 2-year-old son insisted, seeing that the branch we'd planted vertically in the sand before dinner was surrounded now by foaming water.

"I didn't," I assured him. "The sea moved."

This was our first lesson in the tides. Aryeh didn't believe me right away — a heresy, considering he was conceived in a tiny fishing village and now lives in a state with 33,904 miles of shoreline. Evidently, we'd logged too many urban, landlocked months since his birth. But now I had four days, a public cabin overlooking the ocean, and the critter-rich tidepools of Kachemak Bay State Park to help me reintroduce him to the mystery of the sea's daily waxings and wanings.

We'd repeat the tidal experiment again and again, using sticks, stones, and neat lines of shells — entire make-believe villages — that somehow "crept," over time, closer to or farther from the water's edge. By trip's end, he'd understand a bit of the ocean's rhythms and know, firsthand, some of its wonders: squirting sea cucumbers, blood-red sun stars, skittering crabs, and lurking sculpins. And we'd all be breathing a little easier, our frantic summertime tendencies calmed by the maritime cadences of this sheltered stretch of coast across the bay from Homer.

Our previous experiences with family vacations on the Alaska coast had proven a little daunting. The coast is a wondrous place for young, curious eyes and hands. But it can be cold. And it's nearly always wet. Not prime conditions when you have a usually sweet, occasionally uncivilized 2-year-old on your hands. On camping trips, it doesn't take too many tantrums out among the tidepools before you wish you were back home.

That's why the State Park cabins in Kachemak Bay, near Homer, and Resurrection Bay, near Seward, open up a whole new world for ocean-adventuring families. Even if you alternate camping with cabin-ing, as we did on one trip, there's nothing like a roof overhead to restore one's energy following a few days of sea kayaking, hiking muddy coastal trails, or just sloshing around in the wet sand with children.

All three areas offer combinations of sheltered coast for family paddling, beaches for combing, and tidepools for exploring. There's good salmon fishing (in season) close to all the cabins, too. When the sea turns rough or the fish won't bite, there's always hiking. Halibut Cove Lagoon, on the eastern shore of Kachemak Bay, is the hub of an extensive network of trails through the dark, enchanted forest of Kachemak Bay State Park. Derby Cove, on the western shore of Resurrection Bay, has its own trail system leading to Caines Head, site of World War II relics. Sea Star Cove in Tutka Bay is connected by a short ridge-line trail to a small inland lake and fish hatchery. The China Poot Lake Cabin is located inland, but within a short dayhike of China Poot Bay, one of the best areas for clamming and tidepooling.

The Halibut Cove Lagoon public cabins are tucked behind a screen of lichen-covered trees, overlooking an emerald-colored lagoon. While I curled up in the middle cabin with my son for an afternoon nap, my husband Brian paddled around the head of the glassy lagoon, towing a fishing line. (One nibble from a king salmon — enough to keep him hoping for days.) In the evening, we switched. I paddled, while Brian and Aryeh played on the small gravel beach near the docks, turning over sea stars and sea urchins.

The next morning we packed up our kayaks and left the most developed fringe of the park behind. We wanted to spend the day a few miles north, to trade the chatter of fellow anglers for the shriek of bald eagles. Aryeh sat in my kayak, comfortably wedged between my legs. As I paddled less than 10 feet offshore, he stared wide-eyed at the slowly changing panorama: gardens of moss and wild-flowers spilling down from steep bluffs, barnacle-encrusted boulders slipping under our bows, and east to views of the snow-covered Kenai Mountains. Frantic squadrons of puffins circled a rocky islet in the distance. Pigeon guillemots lift-

Aryeh tidepooling in Halibut Cove Lagoon

ed off from the water ahead of us, their orange feet and legs glowing like beacons against a blue/grey sky.

Our son had hit the age of "why," but as we traced the perimeter of the lagoon, his usual barrage of questions and typical toddler antsiness mellowed into an occasional sigh or a soft, whispered request. He asked to paddle. With his chubby fingers gripping the paddle between my hands, we muscled the blade through the water together. After a while, his fingers relaxed and his arms fell. I squinted toward the shape of a distant sea otter, and when next I peered around the wide curve of Aryeh's cheek to see his eyes, they were closed.

Getting Aryeh to sleep at home is an hour-long ritualized affair of stories, threats, and bribes. Here, rocked by the gentlest of waves and warmed by the sun, he had crashed without a peep. Our son would have been happier as an Aleut. In the days that followed, we used our kayaks as a wave-rocked bassinet whenever Aryeh neared his nap time. That gave us hours of silent paddling — bliss for two devoted kayakers who had been kept too long ashore by new parenthood. But when our son was active and ready to play, it was the tidepools that lured us back to land again.

We paddled from Halibut Cove to nearby Peterson Bay, site of the Center for Alaskan Coastal Studies, and tagged along on one of the center's tidepool tours. We made our own exploration of adjacent China Poot Bay, great parts of which empty at low tide, revealing a vast universe of crabs, clams, and sea stars. (We could have walked to China Poot Bay just as easily — a 1.25-mile hike along the Coalition Trail from the cabins at the head of Halibut Cove Lagoon.)

Eventually, we returned all the live critters we found to their homes under rocks and weeds, but the memory — and vocabulary — of our tidal hunts remained. Several days into our combination camping and cabin trip, and an equal number of days since my last shower, Aryeh noticed that my hair was starting to stick up at odd angles. "You look like a sea anemone," he said, grinning at his own pronunciation of the tricky word. And I did, indeed.

It was time to head back across Kachemak Bay — time to head home and wash the salt from our hair and the dark sand from our fingernails. But before the water taxi came to motor us back to Homer, Aryeh prepared to make one last dash down the beach. He'd noticed the foamy edge of the sea creeping down the sloping shore, revealing rocky crevices and trapped pools.

Four days older, and a salty world wiser, he implored us to go with him. "The tide's going out," he said, no longer skeptical. "I just know I'll find creatures down there."

About Kachemak Bay, near Homer

Traveling from the Homer Spit, on the developed western shore of Kachemak Bay, to the state park on the bay's eastern shore, you enter another world. The topography of the shore changes from merely bluff to mountainous. The water changes from deep, wind-ruffled blue to translucent green, the shoreline from straight to indented and protected. On the eastern side, day-glo sea stars cling to boulders, clouds of seabirds flap around rocky islets, and sea otters frolic in far greater numbers. Even if you've visited the "end of the road" in Homer, you haven't seen Kachemak Bay until you've gone where there are no roads — only trails, boardwalks, and beaches.

Halibut Cove Lagoon is the starting point for most Kachemak Bay State Park visits, and the location of three popular shoreside cabins, as well as a ranger station, dock, and network of hiking trails through lush old-growth forest. Access to the park is by private boat, water taxi, or floatplane. It's possible — but not as common — to paddle across Kachemak Bay from the Homer Spit in good weather, but most kayakers skip the risks and opt for a water taxi instead.

The 375,000-acre Kachemak Bay State Park and Wilderness Park (its unwieldy, complete title) is Alaska's oldest, and it's still evolving thanks to money from the Exxon Valdez oil-spill settlement. Outside of Halibut Cove, two more cabins — Sea Star Cove Cabin in Tutka Bay and China Poot Lake Cabin — opened in 1998. Contact the State Parks office for continuing developments.

Expect maritime weather, with summer temperatures from 45 to 70 degrees. The area averages 60 inches of rain annually — more than the Kenai interior, but considerably less than Prince William Sound.

HALIBUT COVE LAGOON CABINS

Kachemak Bay State Park (Alaska State Parks)

Snapshot: Lagoon luxuries: Three spacious cabins of varying designs, including a wheelchair-accessible cabin, perched on high bluffs over the water.

Location: On the southern shore of Halibut Cove Lagoon, 10 miles from the Homer Spit.

Elevation: 50 feet.

Map: Alaska State Parks brochures: *Kachemak Bay State Park & Wilderness Park*, and *Kachemak Bay State Park Trails Guide*. USGS Seldovia C4 or forthcoming Trails Illustrated™ map, *Kachemak Bay State Park*.

Access: By floatplane, water taxi, or private boat up to 26 feet long. Enter and exit the lagoon at high tide only. An 80-foot-long floating dock is in place during the summer season only. (A ramp to the bluffs is available the rest of the year.) The Lagoon East Cabin is wheelchair accessible, with assistance. The Lagoon West Cabin has its own mooring buoy, and a staircase leading to the beach.

Available: Year-round, but the dock and water pump are closed September 16 to May 14.

Best: May 15 through September 15.

Sleeps: Six in the Lagoon East or West cabins (four more comfortably). Or eight, comfortably, in the Lagoon Overlook Cabin.

Maximum stay: Seven nights per month.

Cost: $50.

Reservations: DNR Public Information Center (907) 269-8400, or any Alaska State Parks office. The closest office to the cabin is the Kenai/Prince William Sound Area Office, at mile 85 of the Sterling Highway, Soldotna (907) 262-5581. For best local information, contact the Homer Ranger Station (907) 235-7024. Info and cabin availability via Internet at https://nutmeg.state.ak.us/ixpress/dnr/parks/index.dml.

Misc.: See Appendix 2 or contact the Homer Ranger Station for an updated list of water-taxi operators.

For all Halibut Cove Lagoon cabins

Wildlife sightings: This is a great place for observing seabirds, sea mammals, and tidepools. Sea otters, seals, porpoises, salmon, sea stars, crabs, eagles, gyrfalcons, cormorants, pigeon guillemots, Steller's jays, and puffins are frequently spotted. Also in area: whales, moose, black bears, mountain goats, coyotes, and wolves.

Recreation: Fishing for king salmon in early June. Berries ripen July through August. Naturalists will find tidepools and lots of opportunities for birdwatching. The lagoon is a sheltered place to kayak and observe wildlife, or a gateway to campsites and the less-sheltered coastline north and west of the lagoon.

The tiny community of Halibut Cove, on Ismailof Island just outside the lagoon, has art galleries and a fine restaurant, the Saltry (907) 235-7847. Visitors arriving aboard the *Danny J* yacht get first dibs on lunch and dinner, but by calling ahead, you may be able to arrange a reservation for an assigned seating (1:30, 3:00, 6:00, or 7:30 P.M.) and paddle right up to restaurant's boat dock, returning to your cabin at sunset. (Diners may not be dropped off by water taxi.)

Hikers can explore an 85-mile network of easy-to-difficult trails that start just behind the cabins. A trail leads south to China Poot Lake, 2.5 miles away, and beyond, forking to become the South Poot Peak and Wosnesenski River trails. From China Poot Lake there is also a primitive trail around the north side of Poot Peak, to its 2,600-foot summit. The Coalition Trail heads 1.25 miles west to China Poot Bay — a great place for tidepooling and clamming for littleneck or butter clams.

Hikers desiring an overnight challenge can be dropped by water taxi at the Grewingk Glacier trailhead, near a campsite at Rusty's Lagoon, north of Halibut Cove Lagoon. From here, the Grewingk Glacier Trail leads 3.2 miles to Grewingk Lake, where you can camp on a lakeshore and watch icebergs float by. The challenging Saddle and Lagoon trails link Grewingk Glacier Trail to the head of Halibut Cove Lagoon. It's possible to hike all day, climbing a saddle between Halibut Cove and the glacier, crossing glacier-fed Halibut Creek, and ending up almost 8-tired-and-muddy miles later at one of the public cabins. Hopefully, you will have arranged a water-taxi pickup the following day to avoid hiking back the way you came. For this and other hiking opportunities on new Kachemak Bay State Park trails, do some homework before your trip.

Consult a hiking guidebook (see Appendix 3), check in at the ranger station at the head of the lagoon, or visit an Alaska State Parks office.

Getting there: By boat, use caution and enter and exit lagoon at high tide only. Shoals are present at the mouth of the lagoon and currents are fast. If you're a first-time visitor and have any questions about the hazards, rangers invite you to contact them about boating procedures. To reach the Lagoon West Cabin, it's recommended you use that cabin's mooring buoy and staircase, rather than the main dock.

LAGOON OVERLOOK CABIN

"What a lovely little stroll to the top of Poot's Peak and back. We are going to the hospital now."

Halibut Cove Lagoon Overlook Cabin log.

Facilities: This is the original Halibut Cove Lagoon Cabin, opened for rental in 1992 and now located between two newer log cabins. The 16x20-foot, light green, wood-frame building resembles a small dormitory more than a rustic cabin. Interior walls are painted white, the floor is plywood-paneled, and the decor is "college dorm." Still, you might choose this cabin over its more rustic neighbors if you're traveling with a larger group and want privacy. Unlike nearly all Alaska public cabins, this one has three rooms: two bedrooms and a common room, to sleep a total of eight people comfortably on bunks.

The main room has a counter and cooking area with a draining sink (though no running water), table and chairs, some old, stuffed lounge chairs, a coffee table, plus some wildlife posters tacked on the wall. The bedrooms are dark (a plus in the summer), while the main room is well-lit by picture windows facing north and west. An outhouse is just east of the cabin, toward the dock. A deck-sized porch with nautically decorative rope railings overlooks Halibut Cove Lagoon.

At present, the cabin is heated by a propane wall unit (propane is provided in summer), but rangers plan to refit the cabin with a wood stove in 1999. Water is available from the ranger station when the generator is operating (it must be treated). When the ranger station is closed, purify water from a stream next to the Lagoon West Cabin. You can purchase firewood at the ranger station or collect some. Because of the logging of beetle-infested spruce, dead-and-down wood is fairly abundant, but it may not be dry.

Condition: Good.

View and surroundings: The cabin's main picture window and railed deck overlook the lagoon from a height of about 50 feet. The view encompasses forested bluffs, rocky outcroppings, and the lagoon's transparent waters below, which in June are home to schools of king salmon, sometimes visible as they cruise near the surface. A few yards west of the cabin is a bench on the bluff, overlooking the lagoon. Behind the cabin is a shadowy forest of old spruces and hemlocks dripping moss, and a lush forest understory of ferns, moss, devil's club, and blueberry bushes. The cabin sits between the Lagoon West and Lagoon East cabins. All three are connected to the dock and ranger station by zigzagging boardwalks. Expect to carry your gear about 500 feet from the dock to the cabin.

The area is exceptionally scenic, but not necessarily secluded; you'll probably see some sportfishing boats in the lagoon below and other cabin-users and ranger-station visitors on the boardwalks. The dock and boardwalks are steep and slippery; children should be closely accompanied outside the cabins and should wear life jackets on the dock.

LAGOON EAST AND LAGOON WEST CABINS

Halibut Cove Lagoon East Cabin

Facilities: These natural log cabins, opened in 1997, are bright and beautiful. Both are 16x16 feet, not including the back decks. Inside each you'll find bunks to sleep six (with foam padding; bring your sleeping bag but leave your Thermarest™ at home), benches, counter, and a flat-topped wood stove. Removable, inlaid cutting boards lift from the center of the dining tables, with buckets to catch wastewater beneath. (Rangers are trying to discourage cabin-users from dumping waste onto the bluffs.) Outside you'll find decks overlooking the lagoon, with built-in counters for your camp stoves. Outhouses, fire rings, and benches are next to both cabins.

You can purchase firewood at the ranger station or collect some. Because of the logging of beetle-infested spruce, dead-and-down wood is fairly abundant, but it may not be dry. Water is available from the ranger station when the generator is operating (it must be treated). When the ranger station is closed, purify water from a stream next to the Lagoon West Cabin.

Condition: Excellent.

View and surroundings: The cabins are perched among trees on rocky bluffs over the lagoon, with views of the emerald water 50 feet below.

Staircase leading to Lagoon West Cabin

Behind the cabins is a shadowy forest of old spruces and hemlocks dripping moss, and a lush forest understory of ferns, moss, devil's club, and blueberry bushes.

All three cabins are connected to the dock and ranger station by zigzagging boardwalks. Lagoon East Cabin is 250 feet from the dock. It is designed to be wheelchair-accessible, although you will need assistance up the steep dock. Lagoon West is about 0.5 mile (a 20-minute walk) from the dock, and is the most secluded of the three cabins. It can be reached over the boardwalks, but rangers recommend that you access it directly via a long, steep staircase from a gravel beach at the lagoon's head. A mooring buoy is just offshore.

From Lagoon East Cabin, expect to see other cabin-users and ranger-station visitors. From Lagoon West Cabin, you'll see sportfishing boats in the lagoon and hikers on their way to a campground about 300 feet west. The dock and boardwalks are steep and slippery; children should be closely accompanied outside the cabins and should wear life jackets on the dock.

In Brief:

CHINA POOT LAKE CABIN

Kachemak Bay State Park (Alaska State Parks)

KACHEMAK BAY

Location: East shore of China Poot Lake, 2.4 miles from the Halibut Cove Lagoon trailhead.

Elevation: 100 feet.

Map: USGS Seldovia C4 or forthcoming Trails Illustrated™ map, *Kachemak Bay State Park.*

Access: By floatplane or water taxi to Halibut Cove Lagoon, then on foot for 2.4 miles along a moderately easy trail. Or by floatplane directly to China Poot Lake.

Available: Year-round.

Sleeps: Six (four would be more comfortable).

Maximum stay: Seven nights per month.

Cost: $50.

In brief: This 16x16-foot cabin, built in 1998, has a wood stove. Wildlife include moose, black bears, and nesting loons. You can fish for rainbow trout in the lake. The cabin is a good base for hikers, near the crossroads to the Poot Peak Trail and Wosnesenki River Trail. Winds on the lake can be strong. You'll share the area with tent-campers, about 0.2 mile south of the cabin.

Reservations: DNR Public Information Center (907) 269-8400, or any Alaska State Parks office. The closest to the cabin is the Kenai/Prince William Sound Area Office, (907) 262-5581. For best local information, contact the Homer Ranger Station (907) 235-7024. Info and cabin availability only via Internet at https://nutmeg.state.ak.us/ixpress/dnr/parks/index.dml.

Misc.: See Appendix 2 or contact the Homer Ranger Station for an updated list of water-taxi operators serving this cabin. If this cabin is booked, you may wish to inquire about the Moose Valley Cabin. Rangers plan to make the renovated, 8x10-foot trapper's cabin available in early 1999 (hike-in access only).

In Brief:

SEA STAR COVE CABIN

Location: South shore of Tutka Bay, 1.2 miles from entrance to Tutka Lagoon.

Elevation: 300 feet.

Map: USGS Seldovia B4 or forthcoming Trails Illustrated™ map, *Kachemak Bay State Park.*

Access: By boat, water taxi, or floatplane. There is a mooring buoy but no dock. A staircase and trail lead to the cabin's small knoll above the beach.

Available: Year-round.

Sleeps: Six (four would be more comfortable).

Maximum stay: Seven nights per month.

Cost: $50.

In brief: The new 16x16-foot cabin has a wood stove. Built on a knoll behind a screen of trees, the cabin was designed to be more secluded than the Halibut Cove Lagoon cabins and is popular with boaters and hikers. Tutka Bay and Sadie Cove are top kayaking destinations. A short trail leads from the cabin to the fish hatchery on Tutka Lagoon. A new trail (1998) starts across the bay and traverses Grace Ridge, the ridge separating Tutka Bay from Sadie Cove. True to its name, the cabin is located in excellent tidepooling territory. Low tides reveal many species of sea stars, clams, and mussels. The elevated cabin faces northwest, with great late-night sunset views in summer.

Reservations: DNR Public Information Center (907) 269-8400, or any Alaska State Parks office. The closest to the cabin is the Kenai/Prince William Sound Area Office, at mile 85 of the Sterling Highway, Soldotna (907) 262-5581. For best local information, contact the Homer Ranger Station (907) 235-7024. Info and cabin availability only via Internet at https://nutmeg.state.ak.us/ixpress/dnr/parks/index.dml.

Misc.: See Appendix 2 or contact the Homer Ranger Station for an updated list of water-taxi operators.

About Resurrection Bay, near Seward

Resurrection Bay is a stunning deepwater fjord, famous for silver salmon, abundant marine wildlife, and mid-afternoon chop. Reaching any of the four Resurrection Bay cabins requires careful planning: on the west side, because you need to plan your coastal hike around the tides; and on the east side, because access by small boat (especially kayak) is difficult when the weather isn't cooperating. The town's only water-taxi service comes in handy in both cases, and can be found at Miller's Landing, located on Lowell Point.

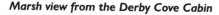

     Hikers and history buffs will prefer Callisto Canyon or Derby Cove cabins; kayakers will prefer Porcupine Glacier or Spruce Glacier cabins; and fishermen and wildlife-watchers will have a good time on either side of the bay. All of these State Park cabins are in great shape.

Marsh view from the Derby Cove Cabin

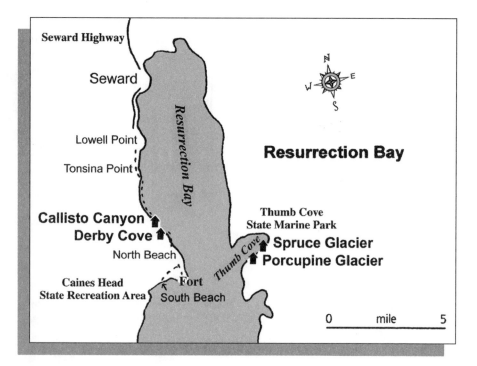

CALLISTO CANYON AND DERBY COVE CABINS

Caines Head State Recreation Area (Alaska State Parks)

Snapshot: Enchanted forest, tidal trails, historic relics, and wild coast. Two newer, secluded log cabins for hikers and boaters on Resurrection Bay.

Location: Both cabins are located in the Derby Cove area, on the western shore of Resurrection Bay, about 4 and 4.5 miles south of Lowell Point, near Seward.

Elevation: Sea level.

Map: Alaska State Parks brochure *Caines Head State Recreation Area* (shows hiking trails and historic sites but not cabins); USGS Seward A7 (Derby Cove and Callisto Canyon not labeled); or Trails Illustrated™, *Kenai Fjords National Park.*

Access: By kayak, motor boat, water taxi, or floatplane along a fairly unsheltered stretch of coast. By foot along a tidal trail that can be hiked only at a plus-5-foot low tide or lower.

Available: Year-round.

Best: Late April to early October.

Sleeps: Eight on bunks, the maximum allowed.

Maximum stay: Seven nights per month.

Cost: $50.

Reservations: DNR Public Information Center (907) 269-8400, or any Alaska State Parks office. For best info on local conditions, the closest State Parks office is the Kenai/Prince William Sound Area Office, at mile 85 of the Sterling Highway, Soldotna (907) 262-5581. Info and cabin availability only via Internet at https://nutmeg.state.ak.us/ixpress/dnr/parks/index.dml.

Misc.: Miller's Landing, a water-taxi operator at Lowell Point (907) 224-

5739, offers dropoffs and pickups to all the Resurrection Bay cabins (see Appendix 2).

Caution: Consult Cordova District tide tables before hiking to the cabins. When the tide rises above plus-5 feet, you could be stranded and swimming on a cliff-backed beach between Tonsina Point and Derby Cove.

For both Callisto Canyon and Derby Cove cabins

Recreation: Most coastal cabin-users have to content themselves with beach walks. These cabins provide the added opportunity for satisfying hikes on a well-developed trail system through coastal spruce forest littered with World War II-era structures and relics. A trail from Derby Cove heads 0.5 mile south to North Beach, site of a ranger station (not always staffed) and a campground. From here, old army roads lead to Fort McGilvray and South Beach (about 2 and 2.5 miles away, respectively). Fort McGilvray, built to protect Seward from anticipated Japanese attacks, was closed in 1944. The strategic command center, which perches on a 650-foot cliff with good views of the bay, is open for your exploration. (Bring a flashlight to walk through a maze of underground passages.)

South Beach, reached via a southwest fork in the trail north of Fort McGilvray, is a ghost town that was home to 500 soldiers stationed here from 1941 to 1943. The remaining structures are unsafe; do not walk on or disturb them. South Beach lies outside Resurrection Bay, with spectacular views of a rocky, wave-lashed coast. A third, very different kind

Small waterfall near Derby Cove Cabin

of trail also begins at North Beach. The 3-mile Alpine Trail climbs 1,600 feet into high, rolling tundra, with a fork heading off to South Beach at mile 2.

Kayakers and boaters can explore the coast using caution, since it is exposed and subject to wind and waves. Silver salmon runs in July and August attract fishermen to this area. Derby Cove, in particular, is known as a good spot for surf fishing.

Wildlife sightings: Sea lions, seals, sea otters, Dall porpoises, and occasionally, humpback whales, are visible from shore, as are numerous birds, including pigeon guillemots, cormorants, oystercatchers, and harlequin ducks. Black bears have been spotted near both cabins. Ghost trees (dead, standing trees killed by saltwater inundations) lining the beach are favorite perches for bald eagles. Peregrine falcons have been seen from the Callisto Canyon beach. Avid birders will spot many more species in the protected marshy area fronting Derby Cove Cabin. Mountain goats sometimes can be seen on the steep slopes behind the cabins. Also in area: brown bears, wolves, wolverines, marmots, coyotes, and porcupines.

History: Caines Head, a prominent headland south of the cabins, was a strategic defense site during World War II. Early in the war, the Aleutian Islands (part of what was then the territory of Alaska) were attacked and occupied by Japanese forces. Fort McGilvray and the nearby South Beach Garrison were completed at great expense to protect the Port of Seward, a critical gateway and supply line into Alaska, from subsequent attacks. Luckily, these never came, and the fort was abandoned in 1944 and dismantled three years later. (See "Recreation" above for more details and hiking notes.)

Getting there: Driving into Seward, follow Third Avenue south to the waterfront, where it curves west and then south, becoming a rough coastal road paralleling the bay. You'll cross three bridges and drive about 2 miles to Lowell Point. If you follow the road to its end, you'll arrive at Miller's Landing, a private campground and boat launch — your starting point if you're getting a lift to the cabins by water taxi or launching your boat or kayak from the campground. Paddlers should aim to launch early in the morning, since Resurrection Bay is usually choppy by midday.

If you're hiking to the cabins, turn right on Martin's Road, just before Miller's Landing, and follow the road and State Park signs to the Lowell Point Recreation Area trailhead and parking lot. Minding your tide tables, start hiking north about two hours before a low tide. The trail leads 1.75 miles through the woods from Lowell Point to Tonsina Point, a walk-in campground. From here, the tidal trail continues south along the beach for about 2.25 miles to Callisto Canyon Cabin (just behind the beach), or 2.75 miles to Derby Cove Cabin (located 500 feet back from the beach).

RESURRECTION BAY

CALLISTO CANYON CABIN

Facilities: The 16x16-foot, light-colored milled log cabin, constructed of beetle-killed spruce, is similar to the other Resurrection Bay cabins, but with extra decorative details. It has eight bunks (two full-sized doubles), a picnic table and benches, a flat-topped fireplace-style wood stove surrounded by attractive rockwork flooring, shelves, decorative driftwood hooks and shelf supports, and a firewood box. Outside, the covered, railed porch has a wide, bracketed corner shelf — just the place to set your cup of coffee — next to a rustic log bench. A carved eagle and the "Callisto Canyon" nameplate hang under the eaves of the porch. Two more rustic benches are arranged around a fire ring with grill. The outhouse, made of fitted logs with a green trim roof, perfectly matches the cabin.

Only dead-and-down wood can be gathered. (Do not use driftwood in the wood stove or cut the standing ghost trees on the beach.) Purify water from either of two sources near the cabin: a stream on the hillside directly southwest of the cabin, or a waterfall that empties on the beach about 400 yards south of the cabin.

Condition: Excellent.

View and surroundings: The cabin sits in a shady spruce grove, facing Resurrection Bay — visible through a thick screen of trees — to the northeast. Windows face the woods in all four directions. A slate trail links the cabin to a beach, about 75 feet away. Devil's club and alder surround the cabin.   From the wide, slate beach, which curves gently between here and Tonsina Point, you can see the town of Seward to the north and the steep, snowcapped peaks of Resurrection Bay east across the bay. The cabin is partially hidden from the water and there is no mooring buoy; if approaching the beach by boat, you may not spot it until you're practically onshore.

DERBY COVE CABIN

Facilities: The 14x18-foot light-colored, milled log cabin is a little darker inside than the Callisto Canyon Cabin, but with similar furnishings, including eight bunks (two full-sized doubles), a picnic table with benches, an older flat-topped wood stove, and shelves. The cabin and its covered, railed porch are elevated on pilings, about three feet off the ground. Windows face all four directions. This porch, too, has a wide, brack-eted corner shelf for your coffee cup. Outside, driftwood logs are arranged around a fire pit (no grill). An outhouse stands across the small creek next to the cabin.

RESURRECTION BAY

Only dead-and-down wood can be gathered. (Do not use drift-wood in the wood stove or cut the standing ghost trees on the beach.) Purify water from the creek next to the cabin.

Condition: Excellent.

View and surroundings: The northeast-facing cabin sits 500 feet back from the beach, in a shady glen behind a high berm and a wide tidal marsh. Just a few yards from the cabin are a sparkling creek and a tiny waterfall. The creek with a small, crystal-clear pool in front of the water-fall are lined with smooth slate rocks — the perfect place for a very secluded, freezing-cold dip. From the cabin's porch, the sea is visible as a distant glimmer behind a screen of spruce trees dripping with moss. Highbush cranberries, marsh grasses, and a slate-covered forest floor sur-round the cabin. Surf sounds, buffered by the marsh and woods, are replaced by the softer, melodious tinkling of the cabin-side falls. Altogether, an unexpectedly fairytale-like ambience.

From the wide, slate beach, which curves gently between here and Tonsina Point, you can see the town of Seward to the north; the steep, snowcapped peaks of Resurrection Bay across the bay to the east; and a rocky headland enclosing Derby Cove just to the south. The 500-foot access trail runs between the cabin, around the north side of the marsh, and out to the beach. There is no mooring buoy, but the trail and a cabin sign on the beach are visible from the water.

PORCUPINE GLACIER AND SPRUCE GLACIER CABINS

Thumb Cove State Marine Park (Alaska State Parks)

Snapshot: Blue water, dazzling ice. Two attractive, newer log cabins — one of them, wheelchair-accessible and both great for kayakers — in a glacier-ringed cove on Resurrection Bay.

Location: The cabins are about 0.5 mile apart, on the sheltered southern shore of Thumb Cove, on the east side of Resurrection Bay.

Elevation: Sea level.

Map: USGS Seward A7 (Thumb Cove is at the very bottom of the map, so you also might want to bring USGS Blying Sound D7 for kayaking forays to the south); or Trails Illustrated™, *Kenai Fjords National Park.*

Access: By kayak, motor boat, or sailboat (Thumb Cove is a popular anchorage), a trip of 8 to 11 miles depending on launching point, along a fairly unsheltered stretch of coast; by private water taxi from Lowell Point; or by floatplane.

Available: Year-round.

Best: Late April to early October.

Sleeps: Eight on bunks, the maximum allowed.

Maximum stay: Seven nights per month.

Cost: $50.

Reservations: DNR Public Information Center (907) 269-8400, or any Alaska State Parks office. For best info on local conditions, the closest State Parks office is the Kenai/Prince William Sound Area Office at mile 85 of the Sterling Highway, Soldotna (907) 262-5581. Info and cabin availability only via Internet at https://nutmeg.state.ak.us/ixpress/dnr/parks/index.dml.

Misc.: Miller's Landing, a water-taxi operator at Lowell Point (907) 224-5739, offers dropoffs and pickups to all the Resurrection Bay cabins (see

Appendix 2).

For both Porcupine Glacier and Spruce Glacier cabins

Recreation: The shoreline from Seward to just north of the cabins is straight and exposed, but from Thumb Cove south boaters have the best part of the bay to explore — Humpy Cove, and Fox Island, with two more state marine parks great for paddling or cruising: Sandspit Point and Sunny Cove. Thumb Cove is sheltered enough that kayakers can get some time on the water even when open Resurrection Bay is choppy (about eight or nine afternoons out of ten). Fishing is the second most popular pastime here, especially when Seward's famous silvers (salmon, that is) arrive in July. Berries ripen in July and August. Tidepooling is good on the cobble beaches fronting both cabins.

Wildlife sightings: Sea lions, seals, sea otters, Dall porpoises, and occasionally, humpback whales are visible from shore, as are numerous birds, including pigeon guillemots, cormorants, oystercatchers, harlequin ducks, grebes, and eagles. Bold black bears, porcupines, and river otters have been spotted near the cabins. Mountain goats sometimes can be seen on steep slopes behind the cabins.

Getting there: By motor boat or sailboat, launch from the downtown boat harbor (a trip of about 11 miles) or from Miller's Landing at Lowell Point (a trip of about 8 miles). Kayakers have a few additional options. Paddling directly from Lowell Point (where Miller's Landing offer kayaks for rent) is not popular because the 2.5-mile crossing can be difficult in all but glassy conditions, and because tour boat traffic is heavy in Resurrection Bay. One option is to get water-taxied to Fourth of July Creek beach, on the eastern shore of the bay (if not all the way to the cabins). You can also drive to the Fourth of July Creek beach and launch directly from there. Follow Nash Road (3 miles north of Seward) around the head of Resurrection Bay to the road's end at Fourth of July Creek. From there, you'll paddle south for about 9 miles to Thumb Cove. Look for a crude cabin sign on the beach in front of the Porcupine Glacier Cabin, or the large wheelchair-accessible boardwalk in front of the Spruce Glacier Cabin. The cabins are only 0.5 mile apart, but not visible from each other.

RESURRECTION BAY

PORCUPINE GLACIER CABIN

RESURRECTION BAY

Facilities: The 16x16-foot cabin is almost identical to Spruce Glacier Cabin, with eight bunks (two full-sized doubles), a picnic table with benches, a flat-topped wood stove, a counter, and an elevated, covered porch with railings. Outside is an outhouse, and a fire ring with grill, next to two wood-plank benches. Only dead-and-down firewood can be gathered. Purify water from a creek running off a hillside directly west of the cabin, about 150 feet away. To reach the creek you must walk along the shore, so plan on filling your water containers at anytime except the highest tide.

Condition: Excellent.

View and surroundings: This northwest-facing cabin is tucked behind a few trees, but close enough to the cove (about 70 feet) for dramatic, open-water views. It's also brighter than than the State Park cabins on Resurrection Bay's western shore. Older spruce trees dripping moss, and blueberry and highbush cranberry bushes surround the cabin. You can't get a good view of the glaciers from the cabin itself — for that, you have to paddle or motor to the middle of the cove. But when you do, the sight is astounding: glowing crevassed ice, trapped between pinnacles high up on the steep, fjord-shaped slopes.

SPRUCE GLACIER CABIN

Facilities: This 16x16-foot, wheelchair-accessible cabin in one of Alaska's most dramatic marine parks opens up fantastic possibilities for travelers with limited mobility. A well-constructed boardwalk leads about 100 feet from the beach berm, over a slough, to the cabin and extra-wide outhouse. A wheelchair-user will still require some muscular assistance to get up the steep, cobblestone beach itself (distance varies with the tide). Aside from the boardwalk, the cabin is almost identical to Porcupine Glacier Cabin, with eight bunks (two full-sized doubles), a picnic table with benches, a flat-topped wood stove, a counter, and an elevated, covered porch with railings. The large, clean outhouse is also wheelchair accessible.

RESURRECTION BAY

Only dead-and-down firewood can be gathered. Purify water from a creek running beside a large boulder beyond the farthest barge wreck east of the cabin. (Cabin-users with limited mobility should bring sufficient water for their stay.)

Condition: Excellent.

View and surroundings: This north-facing cabin is tucked behind a few trees, but close enough to the cove for dramatic, open-water views. It's also brighter than than the State Park cabins on Resurrection Bay's western shore. Even in fall, when the sun is low in the south, light filters through a wide gap in the peaks, burnishing the cove with light. The boardwalk to the cabin doubles as a lovely footbridge over a tidal slough, lush with tall grasses. As with the Porcupine Glacier Cabin, you can't get a good view of the glaciers unless you're out on the water — good reason to bring a boat with you, if possible. But from shore, the mountains themselves, which rise above 3,500 feet and are snowcapped even in summer, are majestic.

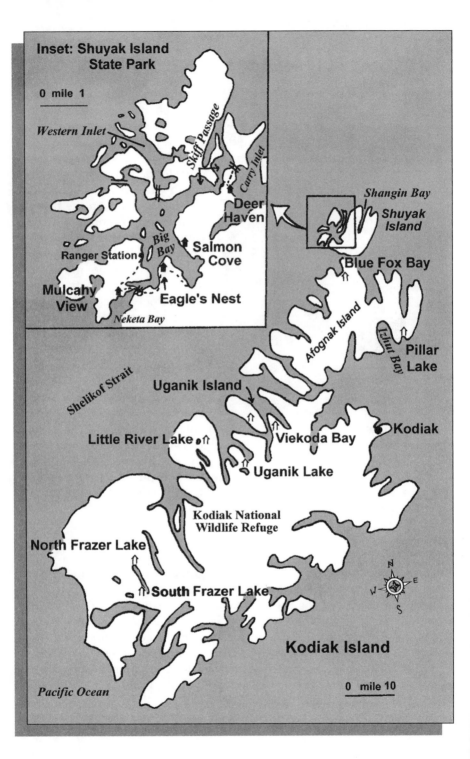

Inset: Shuyak Island State Park

0 mile 1

Western Inlet

Skiff Passage

Carry Inlet

Deer Haven

Big Bay

Ranger Station

Salmon Cove

Mulcahy View

Eagle's Nest

Neketa Bay

Shangin Bay

Shuyak Island

Blue Fox Bay

Afognak Island

Izhut Bay

Pillar Lake

Shelikof Strait

Uganik Island

Viekoda Bay

Kodiak

Little River Lake

Uganik Lake

Kodiak National Wildlife Refuge

North Frazer Lake

South Frazer Lake

N
W   E
S

Kodiak Island

Pacific Ocean

0   mile 10

Part III THE LONELY COAST

Remote Coastal Cabins From Kodiak To Cordova

Room For Bears: Shuyak Island

The airplane roared away, leaving the hunter alone on the shore of Neketa Bay. He watched it go, then turned toward the shadowy forest and hiked the short uphill trail to Mulcahy View Cabin. He planned to stay for five days, hunting deer beneath the snow-dusted spruce canopy of this remote island.

    His arrival at the cabin had a Goldilocks-like twist. "It was quite obvious that a bear had been inside the cabin," he wrote in the cabin visitor log, as he would write an entry conscientiously every day of his early December stay. "The entire door and jam had been pushed into the cabin. And the inside was a mess. First priority was to make a repair of the door. Had to scrounge for nails, but was able to secure cabin door. Will notify State Parks upon leaving."

    The unflappable hunter cleaned up the cabin. The bear had stomped all over the small building, pawing every shelf and window. Miraculously, little was broken. That same day, the hunter ventured into the woods and shot his first deer. Seeing no bear sign, he assumed that the limited damage had been done a while ago and the vandal would not return. He expected no other surprises during his stay at this "beautiful little cabin in paradise."

    I didn't know about the hunter's close call with a member of the continent's largest race of brown bears when I flew over Shuyak Island three years later, heading with my husband, Brian, and our double kayak to the same western corner of the state park. Good thing, too. I booked this once-in-a-lifetime trip believing — a little naively, as it turned out — that each of the island's four public cabins would be an unbroachable fortress, providing absolute protection from any wild visitors.

Like most Shuyak Island visitors, I felt some ambivalence about brown bears. On the Kodiak archipelago, which includes Shuyak, they can weigh up to 1,600 pounds. (Elsewhere in the Alaska Interior, 500- to 900-pound males are the norm.) Part of me wanted to see them. Why else would I have paid nearly $1,500 to kayak here? Another part of me wanted, quite desperately, not to see them.

I was like the German couple that asked Shuyak ranger Kevin Murphy, "Tell us where we can camp to stay away from bears. And then tell us where to go to see bears." As Murphy informed the German couple — and later, me — "Sorry. It's all the same place."

Hike, paddle, and camp where you will, but there's no guarantee that you won't come face-to-face with a bruin. On Shuyak, bear population density is somewhat less than on the Kodiak mainland, where one bear per square mile is the average. But the coastal brown bears still live densely on this mostly flat, forested island perforated by creeks and narrow waterways. However, there's no guarantee that you will come face-to-face with a Kodiak brown on Shuyak, either. Plenty of visitors don't. I'll be fair and cut to the chase: in five days on Shuyak Island, at the height of salmon and blueberry season, I did not see a single bear.

This doesn't mean they didn't see me, however. Even more certainly, every one of the island's 20 to 30 bears stalked me in my dreams.The bears framed my existence on Shuyak. Every day, I read about them in each cabin's visitor log. I read about them in guidebooks. I talked about them with the ranger. Some sources convinced me I had nothing to fear from the bears. Others convinced me that a little fear was perfectly rational.

As Brian and I kayaked across Shuyak Island, the dip of our paddlestrokes would create a daily rhythm echoed by my seesawing sentiment. I want to see the bears. I don't want to see the bears. I want to see the bears. I don't want to see the bears.

〰〰〰

Just before landing on Shuyak, I'd asked our pilot about the famous bruins. He said he hadn't seen them here. And he said he'd never heard of any ever coming within sight of a public cabin.

By the time we'd settled into Mulcahy View Cabin, as I sat reading the December hunter's first log entry, I knew the pilot had been wrong.

The entries continued. "12/7/95. Today was overcast with slight snowfall. While out hunting saw a large bear at very close range of approximately 20 yards yet I don't believe the bear ever saw me as he went right by."

The next day the hunter had another surprise. Maybe he'd started feeling a little lonely, or just wanted to tell someone about his cabin's damaged door and frame. He hiked to the ranger's cabin, one mile from Mulcahy View Cabin, and "found that it had been severely thrashed by a bear. Windows were broken out, and the bear must have pushed his way through the wall also. Looking inside the cabin, all contents were piled on the floor and around the cabin. The bear also hit every outbuilding at the ranger cabin, ripping open every building he found." Actually, the same bear had busted windows and attacked buildings all over the island.

The hunter's brave stoicism softened just a bit. "I hope he doesn't decide to return here," he wrote in the log, "as my door is barely hanging and he could be inside in no time."

No ranger. No other hunters around. Signs of a mad bear on the loose everywhere. None of it stopped the hunter from enjoying himself. Subsequent entries describe overcast days, light snow, cold nights, and peaceful forays around the island. He shot another deer. He saw a hawk, otters, eagles, and waterfowl.When the weather turned bad and his expected departure day came and went, and still a plane hadn't arrived to pick him up, he shrugged it off and wrote, "Looks like another night in paradise."

The following day, the hunter's plane still hadn't come. Now, he didn't feel comfortable leaving the cabin, just in case the overdue plane did arrive. Low clouds socked in the bay. No doubt, those four cedar walls started closing in a little, especially since midwinter days in these parts last barely five good hours.

"Can only hope weather improves," he wrote. "Food is running low on variety, but I have enough deer to last awhile. As for water, no problem, the warmer weather has freed the stream at least partially of ice, and it is once again flowing."

Reading the hunter's entries, I worried for him. First the bear, and now the weather. And most of all, being alone, in the dark cabin, with that damn door hanging loose on its hinges.

On December 13, he wrote, briefly, "No change in the weather, and can only hope it gets better." The entries end there, suddenly, as they so often end when a mechanical buzzing in the sky sends a cabin's occupant packing quickly, in preparation for pickup. The hunter made it out, evidently.

During his winter stay, which stretched from an intended five to at least eight days, he had confessed only the mildest trepidation. I was impressed, especially when I read the next entry, left four months later by the cabin's next occupants. They arrived in April and saw signs of the winter rampage: "big muddy grizzly paw prints on the inside of the windows."

Unlike the stoic hunter, who had evidently sat in that cabin for days on end, staring fearlessly at those muddy tracks, the April visitors were spooked. They confessed the need to clean the windows immediately.

~~~

But that was old news. We'd arrived, three years later, at a fully repaired Mulcahy View Cabin. That crabby bear could have died during the intervening time — or at least mellowed with age. Our second day dawned sunny and calm — perfect for paddling. During breakfast, we heard the sound *of a floatplane landing on the bay. Brian dashed out to meet the pilot. It was the same young man who'd dropped us off the day before. We'd forgotten some nonessential gear behind in Kodiak. Since he was on the island again today, picking up kayakers from Eagle's Nest Cabin, the pilot kindly decided to drop by and deliver it.*

He also delivered some news. The kayakers he'd just picked up reported that their inflatable boat had been shredded overnight. Inside the cabin, Brian conveyed the news to me.

"Shredded?"

"Shredded."

I pressed for more details. There weren't any. The pilot had chatted quickly and left, heading south with his passengers.

"Why," I asked Brian, "Would a bear shred a kayak?"

〰〰〰

We paddled that day to Eagle's Nest Cabin. Along the way, we kayaked close to shore, marveling at the translucent-green water of Neketa Bay and old-growth spruce trees thickly draped with velvety moss.

Neketa Bay is separated from Big Bay by a narrow gravel bar. We portaged over the hump with ease, and then continued our paddle, into a stiffening breeze. Even with wind, this was the easiest paddling we'd done in Alaska. Shuyak Island State Park's sheltered waterways and deluxe cabins are perfect for easy kayaking trips. Perhaps because of the excellent brochures and kayakers' maps created by local rangers, the number of paddlers now equals or surpasses the number of hunters visiting the island.

Pulling up to the Eagle's Nest Cabin, we discussed the one item rangers neglected to mention in brochures. Don't leave your kayak on the beach. *The girl and her father who had stayed at Eagle's Nest Cabin ahead of us guessed that a bear was attracted to the beach and raked its claws through their inflatable because the girl had spit toothpaste on the gravel nearby. They knew it was something larger than a porcupine, because the same creature headed up the hill and*

Brown bears' claw marks on Eagle's Nest exterior

slammed against their cabin at 4 A.M. that morning. "The whole place shook like there was an earthquake!" the girl wrote.

Sweet-smelling toothpaste probably wasn't to blame, ranger Kevin Murphy told me later. Bears are just curious. They ramble along the tideline, turning over shells and rocks, sticking their noses into anything interesting — and sometimes their claws and teeth, too. "That bear was just sampling with its mouth," Murphy said.

We hauled our 74-pound folding double kayak up the trail to Eagle's Nest Cabin and pushed it under the cabin's raised foundation. We didn't want to take any chances. The previous cabin occupants were using their kayak for fun, to poke along the coast on day trips. We were using our kayak for transportation. If the Shredder came after our Feathercraft™, we wouldn't make it to our next cabin, where our floatplane pilot expected to find us in two more days.

As it turns out, we weren't being paranoid. The shredding behavior wasn't an isolated occurrence. Two months earlier, a different group of kayakers at Deer Haven Cabin, several miles northeast, had left their boats on the beach overnight and found them destroyed the next day. The kayakers didn't hold a grudge, though. They left a note in the log mentioning the incident with a final "P.S. Please do not hurt Pete the Bear," written in a young child's loopy handwriting and signed by six names.

Our layover day at Eagle's Nest Cabin dawned rainy, gray, and gusty. After less than a day of sitting around, reading more visitor-log descriptions of bear sightings at nearby Twin, Little, and Big creeks, cabin fever seized us. While hiking inland, a friend was charged here in 1987 by a mother bear guarding her cubs. We balanced our memories of that story with our mounting claustrophobia. The claustrophobia won out.

Brian and I left our kayak stowed under the cabin and set out on foot, treading loudly and slowly into an enchanted forest, where giant trees blocked out the wind. We made our way past tea-colored creeks, vast carpets of moss, and still ponds covered with flowering lily pads. The air was gauzy. Fine mist covered every stone and leaf. A gravity-defying raindrop balanced on the end of each spruce needle.

Our slow, cautious hike slowed down even further. We crouched down on the trail, counting all the shades of the forest: lime-colored moss on the ground, olive moss on the trees, bright green devil's club, and banana-yellow flowers floating in a pond. We sat and breathed, silent for several minutes. Sleepiness washed over us. Then we realized that we'd been too quiet, and hopped to our feet once more. "Ho there! Hey bear!" we jabbered, hurrying back to the cabin on the coast, where the wind continued to blow.

That night, Big Bay calmed. We paddled through peach-colored sunset ripples to the ranger station, to visit with Kevin Murphy and his two volunteers. He made us hot tea and stood while we talked, yielding us his only comfortable chairs. In Murphy's presence, bear fear quickly dissipates. He downplays the damage bears have done, and laughs about the kayak shreddings. A Shuyak ranger for eight years, he patrols the island constantly and knows the bears not as charging blurs or cabin-rattling monsters, but as individuals. Occasionally mischievous individuals.

"There are triplets in your area," he cautioned me. "They're three to

four years old, and they've just left their mama. They don't know how to behave quite yet. They're still staking our their territories." If they get too close, he said, try throwing rocks at them.

Just by painting a behavioral portrait of the juvenile bears, Murphy made them seem a little less scary. At least for the moment. Then he reminded us that a 4-year-old bear in the Kodiak archipelago was as big as an Interior adult grizzly.

Outside the ranger station, Murphy showed us his skull collection. I studied the more massive of the two, an ivory brute, wide and fanged.

"Kodiak bear?" I asked.

"No, Steller sea lion," he said. "We don't find many of the bear skulls. It's a mystery where they go to die."

After visiting Murphy, we went for a final evening paddle. We saw no bears, but we paddled among rafts of seabirds and between curious sea otters as a salmon-colored twilight enveloped us. Pulling up to our cabin near dark, we knew we'd stayed out too long. Every boulder on the shore looked like a potential bear. And if there'd been any real bears, we wouldn't have known it.

Given my own fears, I was surprised we'd stayed out so late. But on this island, a serene enchantment tends to blot out anxiety (temporarily, at least), and even overwhelm caution. It had happened on our woodland walk. It happened again every evening near dusk.

Our next day's paddle was the best yet. We headed northeast, from Big Bay to a finger of saltwater called Skiff Passage, so narrow and sheltered it could be a tame creek. We timed the tides just right, arriving at the narrowest part of the passage just as the tide turned, and then riding out the far finger with the quick-flowing water. Seaweed curled and streamed around us as we rode the current, steering by rudder.

After a short portage, we paddled into Carry Inlet to the Deer Haven Cabin. Tired from the day's paddle, we still opted for another paddle that night. Our trip was nearing its end, and we desperately longed to stretch out its remaining hours.

Pink salmon (humpies) were flooding the inlet, with silver salmon on the way. As we paddled that evening, gleaming fish jumped everywhere. The salmon were gorgeous acrobats — sleek, fat, full of life. Brian towed a line, but they weren't biting. The salmon, lured by the scent of their birthplaces, fueled by the urge to spawn, struggled past us and up creeks that emptied into Carry Inlet. Every one of those creek mouths, we knew, would be prime, bear-feeding grounds. We paddled in the same direction as the salmon schools, entranced by the mass migration.

Kayaking into one lagoon, en route to Bear Creek, the outflowing tide swept so fast we could barely paddle forward. But we kept stroking. Our hearts were beating fast. The splashing of salmon migrating around and past us made our pulses thrum even faster. The old mantra kept hammering away at me. I want to see a bear. I don't want to see a bear. Bear Creek lured us onward. We knew we should turn back, but the tide made us contrary. We paddled even harder, trying to outride it.

Flailing against the current, we paddled into water so shallow that even the salmon's humps stuck halfway out of the water. We didn't speak. There wasn't time. We had to dig into the water, steering carefully, surrounded by schools of splashing, ragged-finned fish. On a bar directly opposite the creek mouth, we finally grounded out.

It was only then that the trance broke. For an hour, we'd been like the salmon — mindlessly tenacious, unable to resist the call of freshwater. But once we grounded out, panic replaced the desire to go any farther. Glancing around, I noticed that we were in the very center of a perfectly round, exceedingly shallow lagoon. A lagoon full of mussel-covered rocks and dying salmon. A bear could have loped from one side to the other without wetting the hair on its belly. A gooseflesh zing ran up my neck.

"You know what this is?" I said to Brian. "A great big dinner plate. We're sitting in the middle of a great big dinner plate."

I felt sick on adrenaline. My arms ached from flailing. Neither of us could rationalize having paddled this far — again, at such a late hour. We couldn't trust ourselves here.

We turned the boat, poled, and pushed into deeper water, and rode the tide back out of the lagoon, across Carry Inlet, back to the cabin.

〰〰〰

That night, for the last time, I read the Deer Haven Cabin log. There were many mentions of "Peter," a bear that had been named by a group of hunters in 1997. "Between the three of us we decided that he was bigger than the outhouse but smaller than a Peterbilt (truck). Thus the name comes Peter," one of the Deer Haven hunters wrote.

"Mike got to meet Peter last night," the hunter continued. "Up close and personal. 12 paces. After a false charge, Mike has developed some sort of stammer lately."

The hunters found the bear's bed about 100 yards south of the cabin. The bear came closer after catching a whiff of the four deer the hunters had shot and stored in the game shed. Peter "tried to move the woodshed and remove the siding," the men wrote. "Hope to get out today as knowing he shall return."

But they didn't get out. The weather turned bad and their floatplane was delayed. "Weathered in again," one of the hunters wrote later. "Two more nocturnal visits from Peter last night. 7 P.M. he showed up, we yelled at him and banged pots and pans together. Didn't do much good anymore. At 11:30 P.M. he tore the siding off the woodshed again and started unpacking firewood and stack-

Bill Sherwonit

Alaskan brown bear

ing it outside. Banging pots and pans no effect, fired two rounds in the air and he took off. That probably won't work next time. So far the best deterrent has been a radio outside on all night station."

Six months later, another pair of hunters came. This time, Peter wasn't an incidental nuisance. Peter was the quarry. The hunters stalked the bear for days, leaving a precise record of their efforts in the log. They studied his movements, his eating habits. They approached to within 30 yards of him once, and noted that upon spotting them, he walked away deliberately. He didn't flee, the hunters said.

Nothing scared me so much, on our last night on Shuyak Island, after five days of kayaking and portaging and hiking, as reading the hunter's meticulous description of their hunt for this single, particular bear. Throughout the hunt, the bear kept returning to the cabin area, circling its territory, which extended from Skiff Passage to trails just north and south of the cabin.

The hunters never did shoot Peter. But they left a final note in the log. "Visitors to Deer Haven should be aware of the bear's presence. Cabin seems to be in the middle of his range. He stays away from people, but he is not afraid of them."

That warning stayed with me all night as I tried to fall asleep. I needed to use the outhouse, but I refused to go out there, into the ebony forest behind the cabin. I kept seeing the cabin and its outbuildings as a map, with a sign pointing to the center, reading: Peter lives here. He is not afraid.

I fell asleep clutching my bladder, hoping that the weather would hold and our plane would come in the morning to pick us up.

〰〰〰

The next day, the sun shone. Light filtered through the spruce trees, bathing the cabin in a soft, cheery glow. Our pilot arrived only an hour or so late. Just enough to make us sweat.

Our plane revved across Carry Inlet, lifted and banked, circling the area of lagoon and creeks that had terrified me the night before. I searched one last time for any sign of bears far below, in the spruce forest that now looked like a shaggy putting green.

I thought about my reactions to the bears of Shuyak, how even from their hiding places, they had exhausted and obsessed me. A conservationist at heart, I recalled how many times — addled by my own fear — I'd half-wished the bears were gone from the island. Not all the bears, mind you — just Peter and the one or two others I was convinced wanted to claw me to bits.

Watching Shuyak Island fall away below, my thoughts swung in unpredictable circles. From a high altitude, the bears didn't seem scary at all. Next we flew over Afognak, a mostly unprotected island beyond the state park's borders. Afognak's mess of clearcuts had reduced the forest to rubble. From the air, all the fallen trees looked like toothpicks, stacked alongside winding roads. Where the toothpicks had already been carted away, there was just brown dirt. Just dust and death. No room for bears, to borrow the title of a classic book about the beleaguered coastal giants.

Meanwhile, on Shuyak Island, bear density on the island has actually increased in the last decade, ranger Murphy believes. From the air, I felt suddenly, ridiculously glad that Shuyak Island was not only protected, but thriving.

I felt happy to have seen it. Happy to have paddled it. And happy, oh so very happy, to be heading home.

About Shuyak Island State Park

Ask Alaska kayakers what their "dream trip" is, and many will name Shuyak State Park. It's a paddler's paradise, with more miles of sheltered intracoastal waterways than anywhere in the Kodiak archipelago. Novices can enjoy easy wilderness paddling and travel cabin-to-cabin without ever leaving the protected inner bays: Neketa Bay, Big Bay, Western Inlet, Carry Inlet, and Shangin Bay. Experienced kayakers can venture to the outer coast, an entirely different oceanscape of large swells and heavy surf. To explore both faces of the park, you may want to camp on the outer coast first, ending your trip in luxury at one or more of the public cabins.

The island is only 12 miles long by 11 miles wide, most of it flat. But the shoreline is convoluted enough — and the virgin Sitka spruce forest dense enough — that you probably won't explore more than a corner of it. In the most protected areas of the park, you may feel like you're paddling a calm river, until you spot unmistakably oceanic critters: whales, sea otters, harbor seals, and Dall porpoises. Land mammals are just as prolific: the 46,000-acre island is home to Sitka blacktailed deer and Kodiak brown bears.

Rainfall averages four to six inches per month in summer, with temperatures generally from the low 40s to the low 60s. The wet, cool climate is rendered easily sufferable — even enjoyable — by the deluxe state park cabins, possibly the finest and definitely the best-maintained in all of Alaska. The four cedar log cabins are identical, distinguished only by their surroundings (see "View and surroundings" below). All are located on low bluffs, just back from the water, and identified by bright orange buoys at the shoreline. You can rent a single cabin as a base camp, or paddle cabin-to-cabin to sample the whole area.

Shuyak Island State Park, which now encompasses practically the entire island, was expanded from its original 11,000 acres with proceeds from the Exxon Valdez oil-spill settlement. Changes are still taking place. In 1998, a new visitor center was being constructed next to the ranger station on Big Bay. Presently, hiking is limited, but construction of more trails is being considered.

Shuyak Island sits just north of Afognak Island, 250 miles southwest of Anchorage and 50 miles north of the city of Kodiak. Getting there is a logistical challenge. Access is by boat from Kodiak, or floatplane from Homer or Kodiak (see Appendix 2). If you're traveling directly from the Lower 48, the choice is simple: fly from Seattle to Kodiak directly, and then charter a small plane from Kodiak to Shuyak. But if you're starting your trip in Alaska, you have some options to weigh.

The roundtrip charter airfare to Shuyak from Kodiak — about $750 to $800 for two adults — is slightly less than the fare from Homer.

But when you add the cost of the state ferry, about $100 round-trip per person from Homer to Kodiak (plus ferry meals and your first night's accommodations in that city), or an even more expensive commercial air flight from Anchorage to Kodiak, then the direct flight from Homer to Shuyak may seem the better deal. Unless visiting Kodiak Island is part of your vacation plan, that is.

Some additional facts to consider: cabin-users are frequently "weathered in" on Shuyak. The odds may be even worse if your charter is coming from distant Homer. However, if you schedule a charter from Kodiak and storms or fog delay your pickup, you risk missing

Kayaking with map of Shuyak Island

SHUYAK, AFOGNAK and KODIAK ISLANDS

your flight or ferry trip back to the mainland — especially problematic in the the case of the ferry, since you will have to wait several days for the next one. To avoid the latter scenario, pad your vacation with two or three extra days after your paddling trip and before you head back to Homer or Anchorage. If you don't get stuck on Shuyak, you can spend that time in the city of Kodiak, visiting the small but excellent Alutiiq Museum and Archaeological Repository, and other local attractions.

Now for Trip Logistics, Part Two. If you own a folding kayak that you can carry as luggage on a charter plane, you're set. Or you can rent a folding boat outside of Kodiak. Seattle-based Folding Kayak Adventures (800) 586-9318 will ship you a folding single, double, or even triple at better rates than most Alaska outfitters (see Appendix 2). Wavetamer, a company that once stored hardshell rental kayaks on the island, is leaving the business, but you may want to ask the State Parks Kodiak District Office if any company has taken its place.

SHUYAK ISLAND CABINS

Shuyak Island State Park (Alaska State Parks)

Snapshot: Paddler's paradise or heaven for hunters. Four roomy, deluxe cedar cabins on the inner Shuyak coast.

Location: Neketa Bay (Mulcahy View Cabin), Big Bay (Eagle's Nest and Salmon Cove cabins), and Carry Inlet (Deer Haven Cabin).

Elevation: 50 feet.

Map: Alaska State Parks brochures, *Shuyak Island State Park Public Use Cabins and Sea Kayaking in Shuyak Island State Park* (available on waterproof plastic from the Kodiak District Office). USGS Afognak C2, C3. Or NOAA chart #16604, Shuyak and Afognak. Also bring the Seldovia tide table.

Access: By boat from Kodiak, or floatplane from Kodiak or Homer (see discussion above).

Available: Year-round.

Best: Late May through July for secluded paddling, mid-August to mid-September for silver salmon fishing, late fall for hunting.

Sleeps: Six on bunks, comfortably. Maximum of eight allowed.

Maximum stay: Seven nights.

Cost: $50.

Reservations: DNR Public Information Center (907) 269-8400, or any Alaska State Parks office. For best local information, contact the Kodiak District Office (907) 486-6339. Info and cabin availability only via Internet at https://nutmeg.state.ak.us/ixpress/dnr/parks/index.dml.

For all cabins

Facilities: Each 12x20-foot cedar log cabin has six bunks (two sets of bunks that each sleep double on bottom, single on top), with foam pads provided. You'll also find a picnic table and benches, a wood stove, shelves and counter, a draining sink with gravity-fed water system, and a basic set of cookware, dishes, and utensils for four to six people. Bottled propane is provided for each cabin's two-burner stove and for mounted propane lights. Propane is limited to 25 lbs. per party; bring some if you'll need more. Large picture windows let in lots of light. Each cabin has a deck-sized, railed porch.

Outside are a fully stocked wood shed (tools are available for splitting logs), game shed, outhouse, and cedar shower/wash-basin building with a gravity-fed water system. Jugs are provided for filling the shower with heated water. To make water collection easier, spring boxes (submerged boxes that form a deep, clear pool) are located in streams located 50 to 500 feet from each cabin. Purify all water.

Condition: Excellent; maintained by the resident State Park ranger in summer.

Wildlife sightings: Brown bears spend spring and early summer on the outer coast, where they eat vegetation and bird eggs. In midsummer they move inland to the creeks to prey on salmon and explore protected tidal areas. Sitka blacktailed deer inhabit the spruce forests; look for them around ponds, like those flanking the Deer Haven Cabin. Birds include puffins, black oystercatchers, cormorants, common and red-throated loons, mergansers, harlequin ducks, and bald eagles. On the water you may spot sea otters, harbor seals, sea lions, Dall porpoises, and whales. In July and early August, pink salmon leap acrobatically as they migrate from the bays to the creeks.

Recreation: See the excellent Alaska State Park brochure, *Sea Kayaking in Shuyak Island State Park*, for five recommended day trips. All but one are loops that combine sheltered and open-coast paddling. Big Bay is a good, protected area to paddle while watching for wildlife. The trip from Big Bay through narrow Skiff Passage, when paddled north just at the turn of the high tide, is a scenic and fun ride with the current. You can

Shower house and woodshed at Eagle's Nest

SHUYAK, AFOGNAK and KODIAK ISLANDS

Laying out all of the components

get a peek at the outer coast without paddling rough water by kayaking to the northwest arm of Big Bay and then hiking through rye grass along a short, unmarked portage trail to Dead Bird Beach, facing open Shelikof Strait and the distant Katmai coast.

Hiking on the island is limited, with most of the short trails clustered on the peninsula bordered by Big Bay and Neketa Bay. More trails are planned. A trail leads from the Mulcahy View Cabin to the ranger station, about 1 mile, and west to Eagle Cape. From the Eagle's Nest Cabin, a trail leads west over the Neketa Hump (the narrow isthmus that divides Neketa Bay from Big Bay) to the ranger station, and east to an unnamed 508-foot peak.

In fall, hunters pursue deer or brown bear. Especially in Big Bay and Carry Inlet, there is fishing for Dolly Varden (June and July) and rainbow trout (mid-June through September). Salmon anglers can try their luck with sockeyes (June and July), pinks (July to early August) and silvers (mid-August to mid-September). Halibut are fished from the outside waters. Shuyak's bays are periodically open to commercial seining. Up to three commercial openers may occur between August 1 and September 15, generally lasting between 24 and 48 hours. Immediately after the openings, sportfishing is slow, but it rebounds within a few days.

Kodiak, Afognak, and Shuyak islands, home to the Alutiiq peoples, are rich in archaeological sites. Enjoy them but do not disturb or remove anything you find.

Assembling folding kayak frame

Assembly almost complete

SHUYAK, AFOGNAK and KODIAK ISLANDS

MULCAHY VIEW CABIN

View and surroundings: The cabin sits on a bluff over Neketa Bay, facing southeast, about 150 feet from the water. It is surrounded by old-growth spruce forest, spongy moss understory, and abundant blueberry plants. A trail runs uphill from the slate beach — one of the lovelier and more secluded beaches fronting any of the cabins — and over a small boardwalk, across a narrow stream, to the cabin. Tidepools are just off the beach. Neketa Bay, facing open water to the west, offers beautiful sunset paddles with views of the distant Katmai coast.

Commercial fishing is prohibited in Neketa Bay. There's only one cabin on this side of Neketa Hump (the easily portaged gravel bar to the northeast), so you're not as likely to see other cabin-users in this corner of the park. Paddling and angling options are fewer than at the Big Bay cabins, but connecting trails to the outer coast and the seclusion of this narrow, quiet bay, make it a good choice if you're renting only one cabin in the park. Surprisingly, it's the least rented of the four cabins.

EAGLE'S NEST CABIN

"These water drops are tears. I've asked Jami to marry me — and she said yes. We're going to be married! This is a magical place."
Eagle's Nest Cabin log.

View and surroundings: The cabin sits on a bluff facing west, about 150 feet from the water, in one of the five fingers of sea star-shaped Big Bay. It is surrounded by old-growth spruce forest and spongy moss understory. The ranger station's buoy is visible across the bay. Trails head south and over the Neketa Hump to the ranger station (sections of the trail flood at high tide, so plan accordingly) and east, to a 508-foot peak. Little and Big creeks, east of the cabin, are good spots for salmon fishing and bear-watching. This cabin, like Salmon Cove Cabin, offers many opportunities for short, easy day-paddles and birdwatching around the five arms and small islands of Big Bay. It is the most frequently rented of the four cabins.

SALMON COVE CABIN

View and surroundings: The cabin sits on a bluff facing west, about 150 feet from the water, in another of the five fingers of sea star-shaped Big Bay. It is surrounded by old-growth spruce forest and spongy moss understory. The cabin is not visible from Eagle's Nest Cabin. Sunset views to the west, over a wide stretch of Big Bay, are spectacular. There are no maintained trails around the cabin. Little and Big creeks, south of the cabin, are good spots for salmon fishing and bear-watching. This cabin, like Eagle's Nest Cabin, offers many opportunities for short, easy day-paddles and birdwatching around the five arms and small islands of Big Bay.

DEER HAVEN CABIN

View and surroundings: The cabin sits on a high bluff facing northeast, connected to a wide slate beach by a long, steep gangplank. This is the most secluded and lushly forested of the four cabin areas. A tranquil pond, dotted with water lilies, is just beside the cabin's front porch. Deer, river otters, and "Peter" the bear have been spotted nearby. A hiking trail north of the cabin leads northwest to Skiff Passage, where there is a shorter, established portage (between 1000 and 1500 feet, depending on tides) linking Carry Inlet and Skiff Passage. Good paddling and fishing opportunities abound in Carry Inlet, with access at high tide to a creek-fed lagoon to the south.

In Brief:

PILLAR LAKE CABIN

Afognak State Park (Alaska State Parks)

Location: On the south shore of Pillar Lake, near Izhut Bay.
Elevation: 700 feet.
Map: USGS Afognak A1.
Access: By floatplane, 20 minutes from Kodiak. Pillar Lake may freeze as early as November 1; it is possible to make a wheel-landing on Izhut Bay beach, if necessary.
Available: Year-round.
Sleeps: Six, the maximum allowed.
Maximum stay: Seven consecutive nights per month.
Cost: $25.
In brief: The 12x14-foot cabin has a wood stove and limited eating and cooking utensils (frying pans, dish pans, and a large tea kettle). Recreation includes hunting, fishing, or hiking either in the spruce forest surrounding the cabin or alpine areas about one to two hours inland. A three-hour hike (experienced wilderness hikers only) to the lake directly south of Big Tonki Bay provides access to salmon fishing.
Reservations: DNR Public Information Center (907) 269-8400, or any Alaska State Parks office. For best local information, contact the Kodiak District Office, (907) 486-6339. Info and cabin availability only via Internet at https://nutmeg.state.ak.us/ixpress/dnr/parks/index.dml.

About Kodiak National Wildlife Refuge: Luck of the Draw in Bear Country

Kodiak National Wildlife Refuge was established in 1941 to protect habitat for the world-famous Kodiak brown bear and other wildlife. At nearly 1.9 million acres, the refuge covers about two-thirds of Kodiak Island — all of it undeveloped, with no roads or maintained trails. No place on the refuge is more than 15 miles from the ocean, and lakes, rivers, marshes, and vast wildflower-filled meadows abound. The weather is mild by Alaska standards. Covered by spruce forests in the north and moist tundra in the south, Kodiak touts itself as "Alaska's emerald isle."

Kodiak is the ultimate destination for bear hunters, but refuge staff are helping wildlife-watchers and photographers discover the island, too. Many people who visit the island book special wildlife-viewing day trips, some of which guarantee bear spottings. For more adventurous travelers, there's another option: do-it-yourself bear-habitat immersions from a refuge cabin. There are no guarantees, but the thrill of discovery is yours alone. Seclusion, with abundant fish and berries are part of the package. Brown bears may be spotted from any of the refuge's seven public cabins, but the Uganik Lake, Little River Lake, and South Frazer Lake cabins offer particularly good chances in late summer, when salmon are spawning in nearby streams.

Information on bear viewing in the listings below comes directly from the excellent refuge newsletter, "Bear Country: Wildlife Viewing on Kodiak Island," which also includes monthly summaries of animal migrations and brief nature notes on fish, birds, marine mammals, and intertidal animals. Birders should also request a refuge bird-list brochure, which names 220 species and the seasons when they may be spotted.

Maximum length of stay at the cabins is 30 nights from January 1 through March 31; 15 nights from April 1 through May 15; and 7 nights from May 16 through December 31. Cabin reservations are scheduled by lottery, with drawings made in January, April, July, and October for periods beginning three months later (see "How to reserve a cabin," page 14).

All of the cabins have heaters, but kerosene is not included. Bring one to three gallons per day. Do not substitute any other kind of fuel. All of the cabins must be reached by boat or floatplane. Refuge staff will provide an updated list of charter operators on request.

In Brief:
Seven Refuge cabins

BLUE FOX BAY

Kodiak National Wildlife Refuge (KNWR)

Location: On Blue Fox Bay, on the northernmost part of Afognak Island (just south of Shuyak Island).
Map: USGS Afognak B3.
Access: Boat or floatplane, 20 minutes by air from Kodiak.
Sleeps: Four.
Recreation: Fair hunting for bear; good hunting for deer and elk. Fair fishing for pink salmon in late July and August; good fishing for silver salmon in August and September.
Maximum stay: See above.
Cost: $20.
In brief: The 12x20-foot cabin has a kerosene heater and a meat cache.
Reservations: Kodiak National Wildlife Refuge, 1390 Buskin River Road, Kodiak, AK 99615; (907) 487-2600.

In Brief:

VIEKODA BAY CABIN

Kodiak National Wildlife Refuge (KNWR)

Location: On Viekoda Bay, western Kodiak Island.
Map: USGS Kodiak D4.
Access: Boat or floatplane, 10 minutes by air from Kodiak.
Sleeps: Four.
Recreation: Fishing for pink salmon and Dolly Varden from beaches in July and August. Good deer hunting from fall to early winter; fair bear hunting; fair duck hunting.
Maximum stay: See above.
Cost: $20.
In brief: The 10x12-foot cabin has a kerosene heater and a meat cache.
Reservations: Kodiak National Wildlife Refuge, 1390 Buskin River Road, Kodiak, AK 99615; (907) 487-2600.

In Brief:

UGANIK ISLAND CABIN

Kodiak National Wildlife Refuge (KNWR)

Location: On the southern shore of Uganik Island, facing Kodiak Island across Uganik Passage.
Map: USGS Kodiak D4.
Access: Boat or floatplane, 15 minutes by air from Kodiak.
Sleeps: Four.
Recreation: Fishing for pink salmon and Dolly Varden from beaches in July and August. Fair bear hunting in spring and fall; good deer hunting October through December; fair waterfowl hunting. From September through November, bear viewing is possible, but definitely requires some hiking and can be irregular. By mid-fall, vegetation has died back and it becomes easier to walk the surrounding valleys and peaks.
Maximum stay: See above.
Cost: $20.
In brief: The 10x12-foot cabin has a kerosene heater and a meat cache.
Reservations: Kodiak National Wildlife Refuge, 1390 Buskin River Road, Kodiak, AK 99615; (907) 487-2600.

SHUYAK, AFOGNAK and KODIAK ISLANDS

In Brief:

UGANIK LAKE CABIN

Kodiak National Wildlife Refuge (KNWR)

Location: On the north shore of Uganik Lake, on Kodiak Island.
Map: USGS Kodiak C4.
Access: Floatplane only, 15 minutes by air from Kodiak. Because of the possibility of freezeup, cabin use is discouraged from November 1 to March 31.
Sleeps: Four.
Recreation: Good fishing for pink salmon (August), coho salmon (August to October), sockeye salmon (June to August); fair fishing for rainbow trout (June to November) and excellent fishing for Dolly Varden (April to November). Good bear and deer hunting.
   From August through October, there are fair to good chances for viewing bears. The cabin sits next to the main river supplying the lake, so cabin-users commonly observe bears traveling to and from upstream spawning areas.
Maximum stay: See above.
Cost: $20.
In brief: The 12x14-foot wheelchair-accessible cabin has a kerosene heater and a meat cache.
Reservations: Kodiak National Wildlife Refuge, 1390 Buskin River Road, Kodiak, AK 99615; (907) 487-2600.

In Brief:

LITTLE RIVER LAKE CABIN

Kodiak National Wildlife Refuge (KNWR)

Location: Near Little River Lake, west of Uganik Bay, on Kodiak Island.
Map: USGS Kodiak D5
Access: Floatplane only, 20 minutes from Kodiak. Because of the possibility of freezeup, cabin use is discouraged from November 1 to March 31.
Sleeps: Four.
Recreation: Good fishing for sockeye salmon (July) and Dolly Varden (April to November); fair fishing for coho salmon (September to November) and rainbow trout (June to November). Good bear hunting;

excellent-to-good deer hunting early in season. From mid-June through mid-September, there are good chances for viewing bears. In July and August, a strong red salmon run attracts bears to Little River. Cabin-users have a reasonably good chance to observe bears right from the cabin deck, but viewing is better if you hike the river corridor below the cabin. Activity along Little River is sharply reduced after early August when salmon have moved through the river and into the lake. From mid-July through most of September a motorized raft (not included with cabin rental) will provide good viewing at the south end of the lake where three streams are regularly visited by bears feeding on spawning fish. Also, large congregations of eagles are often seen at this site.

Maximum stay: See above.

Cost: $20.

In brief: The 12x20-foot cabin has a kerosene heater and a meat cache.

Reservations: Kodiak National Wildlife Refuge, 1390 Buskin River Road, Kodiak, AK 99615; (907) 487-2600.

In Brief:

SOUTH FRAZER LAKE CABIN

Kodiak National Wildlife Refuge (KNWR)

Location: On the south end of Frazer Lake, on Kodiak Island.

Map: USGS Karluk A1.

Access: Floatplane only, 40 minutes by air from Kodiak. Because of the possibility of freezeup, cabin use is discouraged from November 1 to March 31.

Sleeps: Five.

Recreation: Good bear and deer hunting. Excellent fishing for coho salmon (August and September) and sockeye salmon (July and August) in Dog Salmon Creek. Excellent lake fishing for Dolly Varden from April to November. Good lake fishing for steelhead (September to November) and rainbow trout (June to November). This cabin offers excellent chances for viewing bears in July and August, with fair-to-good chances in September and October. A kayak or motorized raft (not included with cabin rental) is required to travel across the lake to the area's best bear viewing along the Dog Salmon Creek, the upper mile of which is heavily used by bears beginning in July. The fish ladder, one mile down the creek, is a favorite gathering place.

Maximum stay: See above.

Cost: $20.

In brief: The 12x20-foot cabin has a kerosene heater and a meat cache.

Reservations: Kodiak National Wildlife Refuge, 1390 Buskin River Road, Kodiak, AK 99615; (907) 487-2600.

In Brief:
NORTH FRAZER LAKE CABIN

Kodiak National Wildlife Refuge (KNWR)

Location: On the north end of Frazer Lake, on Kodiak Island.

Map: USGS Karluk B1.

Access: Floatplane only, 40 minutes from Kodiak. Because of the possibility of freezeup, cabin use is discouraged from November 1 to March 31.

Sleeps: Four.

Recreation: Good bear hunting and fair deer hunting. Dabbling ducks and shorebirds frequent this area. Excellent fishing for Dolly Varden (April to November) and sockeye salmon (July and August); fair fishing for rainbow trout (June to November). This cabin offers fair-to-good chances for viewing bears. Although there is no single gathering place near the cabin, there are individual bears and small groups throughout the area. Hike the high country surrounding the cabin for better viewing opportunities.

Maximum stay: See above.

Cost: $20.

In brief: The 10x12-foot cabin has a kerosene heater and a meat cache.

Reservations: Kodiak National Wildlife Refuge, 1390 Buskin River Road, Kodiak, AK 99615; (907) 487-2600.

SHUYAK, AFOGNAK and
KODIAK ISLANDS

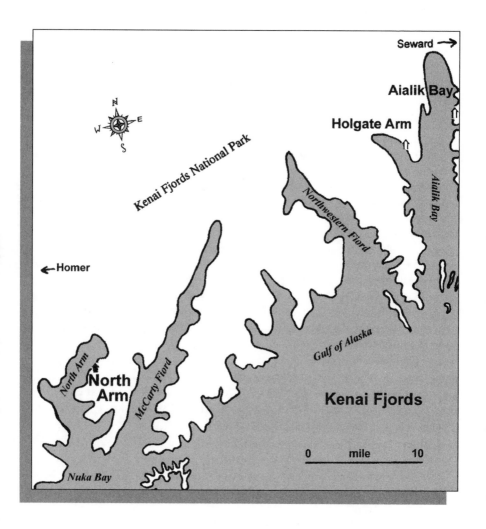

Seward →

Aialik Bay

Holgate Arm

Aialik Bay

Kenai Fjords National Park

N
W E
S

Northwestern Fjord

←Homer

Gulf of Alaska

North Arm

North Arm

McCarty Fjord

Kenai Fjords

Nuka Bay

0   mile   10

Solitude For Two: Kenai Fjords' North Arm

By Bill Sherwonit

The Kenai Peninsula's outer coast is notorious for its wet, overcast, and often stormy weather. So it's no surprise when we awaken, our first morning along the coast, to discover the sun has vanished behind thick gray clouds. At least the skies are dry and the air still. North Arm, a remote, fingerlike bay at the extreme western end of Kenai Fjords National Park, is glassy smooth. Perfect for coastal kayaking.

Trailed by swarms of white sox, those small but vicious white-legged biting flies, my brother Dave and I take our double Klepper™ for a short exploratory paddle along the arm's eastern edge. We turn into a small embayment, where seals and otters play hide-and-seek with us and a low-flying eagle spooks a large flock of mallards into flight. Then we watch as three dozen crows leave their roosts in old-growth hemlock and chase, in Keystone Cops fashion, a sharp-shinned hawk. Ducking into the forest, the hawk finally escapes its tormentors and the crows, with raucous caws, return to their beach-front perches.

Continuing to the arm's northern headwaters, we approach a small creek that's drawn a mix of fish-eaters: gulls, mergansers, crows, eagles, and two belted kingfishers. Handsome, loquacious birds with big, shaggy heads, the kingfishers scoot across the water, grab a seat in an old spruce, and speak in their raspy, rattling way. Still several hundred feet away, Dave spots a black bear browsing in salmonberry bushes; perhaps sensing our presence, it retreats into the forest shadows.

Our final stop is a large glacial river. Walking across sandbars, we find many sets of tracks: gull, duck, coyote, and black bear. The bear tracks are fresh; looking up from them, Dave sees two black bears in the distance, fishing for salmon in a smaller, clearwater stream that cascades down from the steep, lush mountains. One soon leaves; the other grabs a fish and moves to a clearing where it sits down to eat. A couple salmon later, it too slowly ambles into the forest. We stay a few minutes more, then return to the cabin for dinner. Our planned two-hour paddle has become a seven-hour journey.

~~~

    This is my fifth trip into Alaska's 580,000-acre Kenai Fjords National Park, known for its abundant marine wildlife, tidewater glaciers and, of course, the coastal fjords: long and steep-sided glacially carved valleys now filled with seawater. I've done the wildlife boat tours out of Seward, listened to the booming echoes of calving glaciers in Aialik Bay and Holgate Arm, mingled with tour-bus crowds at road-accessible Exit Glacier, and hiked to the Harding Icefield overlook. But never before have I explored the park's remote and largely unpeopled southern fringes. Of the 231,000 people who visited Kenai Fjords in 1996, less than 100 came to North Arm, which is easily accessible only by air.

    The solitude is one reason I've come here with Dave. That and the coastal scenery and the wildlife. A resident of upper New York state, Dave, like me, has always loved wild places and wild creatures. Here he'll discover an ecosystem different than any he's known, one with glaciers and old-growth coastal rain forest, puffins and sea otters and harbor porpoises. I'm excited to share it with him.

    A small town on the shores of Resurrection Bay, Seward is the primary gateway to Kenai Fjords, but North Arm lies much closer to another Kenai Peninsula coastal community, Homer. On a straight line, it's only 35 miles away. After our half-hour flight we quickly settled into our temporary home: North Arm Cabin, one of the park's three coastal cabins (a fourth is located inland, at Exit Glacier). North Arm is the least popular of Kenai Fjords' coastal cabins. It's also the most isolated and difficult to reach.

    "North Arm tends to attract loner types who are comfortable in remote wilderness settings," says park superintendent Anne Castellina. "In fact we try

Paddler and kayak, North Arm

Bill Sherwonit

to discourage inexperienced people from going there." Because it gets so little use, North Arm Cabin can be reserved for up to nine days; the others have three-day limits.

Built to blend with their surroundings, the cabins have a minimal negative impact on either the environment or the aesthetic sensibilities of backcountry travelers. They also provide dependable protection from the park's often stormy weather. It makes all the difference to spend the day paddling or hiking in wet, raw, windy weather, and then return to a roomy, dry, heated shelter. Ours is a 16x20-foot cedar-sided cabin with front porch, dining table, chairs, bunkbeds, and oil-fueled stove. It's connected to the beach by a gravel trail and has an outhouse that smells of cedar: wonderful surprise.

Outside the cabin in mid-August are berry patches rich with ripe blueberries and salmonberries; sweet and easy pickings for snacks and pancake breakfasts. Equally bountiful is the wildlife. In our first few hours we meet several local residents: black-capped chickadees and golden-crowned kinglets sing brightly in the trees, gulls screech along the shoreline, bald eagles do fly-bys, a splashing sea otter dives for its dinner and black oystercatchers — strange-looking, crow-sized shorebirds with long red bills, pink legs, yellowish eyes, and all-black bodies — peck for food along the gravel beach. A stone's throw from the cabin's path is a small, shallow, clearwater creek, source of our drinking water and home to a small run of pinks, the only salmon species to spawn nearby.

At noon on our third day, Dave and I revel in midday heat as we share lunch on a black-sand beach. A plane passes somewhere far overhead; ten seconds of motorized humming and it's gone. In five days we'll see or hear a half-dozen aircraft, all of them distant, and meet only two other people, rangers on patrol. Yes, we've picked the right spot.

The air had been still, the sky overcast, and the paddling easy when we left the cabin three hours earlier. Now the sun has appeared. And as it heats the land, it sets in motion a current of air; a steady southeast wind begins blowing up the bay.

Lunch finished, Dave grabs his camera gear and heads toward the glacial Nuka River. I linger, content to intermittently daydream and study our surroundings. Across Beauty Bay is one of the area's few named peaks: Mount Diablo, topping out at 2,451 feet. Its lower slopes are cloaked in dense spruce forest and subalpine brush, so it must be a devil of a peak to climb; maybe that's what prompted its naming. If so, then just about every mountain around here is similarly devilish.

My thoughts don't stay in high places for long. There's too much going on down here, by the water. At the head of the bay hundreds of gulls talk noisily among themselves, while in the saltwater two seals hunt salmon. It's been another good day for wildlife; paddling here, we'd seen two harbor porpoises off in the distance, their dark gray backs and dorsal fins gracefully rolling in and out of the water. And we'd crossed paths with eight horned puffins — the first Dave has seen — *their squat bodies skimming the water, wings beating furiously.*

Dave and I rendezvous at 3 P.M. and prepare for our return voyage. The wind is now blowing 15 or 20 mph, right into our faces, and the water is churned into white-capped swells. Progress is slow as we angle into the wind, across 3- and 4-foot waves. "Are we moving?" Dave finally asks. "Sometimes it seems like we're going backward."

"We're doing OK," I assure him. "We just need to keep at it, keep paddling."

We're soaked by waves that crash against the bow and occasionally midship, but we're not in any danger. The double Klepper™ is a sturdy, stable, seaworthy boat; we won't capsize as long as we don't take unnecessary chances. If conditions worsen we can retreat, wait out the wind.

Paddling hard and steady, we move out of Beauty Bay and into the arm. Twenty minutes more and the worst is over; the wind eases, the swells diminish. For the first time in an hour, we can rest. We sit in silence for several minutes, content to dry out, warm up in the late afternoon sun, relax.

〰〰〰

We've brought a single Klepper™ as well as the double and on our fourth day, Dave and I go on separate adventures. He follows the east shore, while I head west toward a 900-foot waterfall. It's a gray, still, foggy day and an almost invisible mist settles upon me. The arm has a peaceful, surreal feel to it. Even the birds are quiet.

I'm nearly halfway across when I notice the fall's deep, throbbing song. It reminds me of the rhythmic rumblings of a distant freight train or faraway thunderstorm. Looking through binoculars I see whitewater sheets cascading through a narrow slot in the bedrock. They bounce along dark gray canyon walls before dropping hundreds of feet in a free-fall. Elegantly powerful, the waterfall is a dazzling, musical pendant strung across the mountainside's dark body. Attuned to the fall's deep voice, I will later hear it from our cabin's waterfront, singing bass to our nearby creek's higher-pitched gurgling.

While I'm chasing waterfalls, Dave is again stalking wildlife. By day's end he'll paddle among sea otters and porpoises and watch a black bear mom with two cubs fish for salmon. But his most memorable encounter will come another time, when he meets a clan of river otters.

We'd first seen the otters in the saltwater shallows near our creek. Six of them swam 30 to 40 yards offshore, diving, splashing, chasing each other. With binoculars we could see they were fishing — and having great success. Time and again they surfaced with silvery, minnow-sized fish in their mouths. After 15 or 20 minutes of unabashed gorging, they moved on up the arm single file, heads and tails dipping rhythmically in and out of the water.

Two days after that first sighting, Dave hikes to a rocky point of land and discovers several small piles of bone and shell fragments. Guessing it to be an otter dining spot, he stakes it out; 90 minutes later, the otter family arrives. The two adults are chocolate brown; their four offspring almost black. The otters soon sense there's a stranger in their midst. But instead of retreating, they curiously approach to within 15 feet. Reaching a bed of kelp, the otters lose interest in Dave and instead roll around in the seaweed; a couple pee on the kelp, marking it with their scent. After several minutes of ritualized rolling and peeing, the otters return to the saltwater. Dave sits in silent wonder, amazed at his good fortune.

Our last morning at North Arm, Dave and I go for a final beachwalk. Standing on the otter's rock, we watch a hundred pinks that have schooled up in the water below. Unlike the frenetic, struggling salmon we've seen in the shallow creeks, these swim placidly in circles, to form a submarine, slow-motion pinwheel of fish. Every now and then one of the salmon — usually a male — launches into the air, landing with a loud splash. We watch silently, mesmerized by this mass of swirling, jumping fish, by their mix of grace and zest.

Our pilot arrives right on time, shortly after noon. But before we leave, Dave returns to the empty cabin and writes in its log book: "Another memorable trip. First time in a floatplane, first time to a wilderness area on the coast, first time in a kayak. I have a hard time putting into words the beauty and wildness this area has given me . . .

"I hope to come back here sometime, but if I don't, I'll always have the memories within me. And when I'm back in New York State, on some cold winter day, I can sit by my wood stove and daydream about the great trip to Kenai Fjord's North Arm."

Bill Sherwonit is a nature writer and photographer who has lived in Anchorage since 1982. He is the author of five books on Alaska and has edited an anthology of Alaska mountaineering stories.

About Kenai Fjords National Park

Spend a night in the Ice Age. It's not the motto of Kenai Fjords National Park, but it could be. Dominated by the Harding Ice Field, one of four major ice fields remaining in the United States, the national park has changed little since the Pleistocene. The park's narrow coastal margins are the exception, however. There, where ice has scoured and waves have swept, flora and fauna now take hold. Glaciers retreat; the land submerges. Yesterday's cirques have become today's crescent-shaped bays. Within this evolving landscape, three coastal cabins provide base camps for observing wildlife, kayaking a remote coast, and marveling at the beauty and power of ice, water, and time.

Kenai Fjords National Park is one of the best-rated national parks in the country, just two and a half hours south of Anchorage. Over 200,000 cruiseship passengers enjoy a passing glimpse of the park's coastal edge. Commercial fishing boats motor by, and floatplanes bring day-trippers into the fjords. But surprisingly few people actually travel deeply enough — or stay long enough — to explore this unique wilderness.

Except for Exit Glacier, north of Seward, there is no road access into Kenai Fjords National Park. Access into the fjords — deep, high-walled bays carved by retreating tidewater glaciers — is by boat or floatplane only. You can camp in the park, but cabins provide more reliable shelter from wet weather and bugs, which can be thick. The National Park Service recommends you bring headnets in July and August.

En route to and within the fjords you may see humpback whales, orcas, Dall porpoises, sea otters, puffins, storm petrels, common murres, black-legged kittiwakes, and more. From Holgate Arm Cabin, you'll wake to the rumble and splash of ice calving from Holgate Glacier, less than four miles away.

Holgate Arm and Aialik Bay cabins are most easily reached by boat charter from Seward. A typical fare is $250 to $270 per person round-trip. A ranger station is located near both cabins, in Coleman Bay, at the head of Aialik Bay. North Arm Cabin, farther west, can be reached by floatplane from Moose Pass, Seward, or Homer for about $300 to $375 per person round-trip. (Note: the Delight Spit Cabin is no longer available for rental at this writing.)

Your chances of being weathered in for several days at any of the cabins is good, so bring plenty of food, plenty of extra reading, and prepare to think of time in geologic, instead of digital, terms. In these surroundings, that isn't hard to do.

NORTH ARM CABIN

Kenai Fjords National Park (National Park Service)

KENAI FJORDS

Snapshot: Remote retreat: The farthest west and most secluded of three attractive coastal cabins in the fjords.

Location: Eastern shore of North Arm, south of Pilot Harbor.

Elevation: Near sea level.

Map: USGS Seldovia C2 or Trails Illustrated™, *Kenai Fjords National Park.*

Access: By boat or floatplane (40 minutes by air from Homer, 60 minutes by air from Seward). Anchoring can be difficult at low tides.

Available: About May 23 to September 2 (season can be longer, weather depending).

Sleeps: Six on bunks, the maximum allowed (four would be more comfortable).

Maximum stay: Nine nights per calendar year.

Cost: $35.

Reservations: Kenai Fjords National Park Office in downtown Seward, 1212 Fourth Ave., (907) 224-3175. Reservations are accepted beginning January 2 for the summer season.

Facilities: The 16x20-foot wooden-frame cabin has a light wood exterior, a green roof, and white interior walls. Inside the high-ceilinged cabin are six bunks, counter, kitchen table with chairs, informational bulletin board, and diesel oil stove. (Oil has been provided in the past, but this may change; confirm with the Park Service before you go.) Outside is a covered porch and an outhouse. Purify water from the creek next to the cabin.

Condition: Excellent.

View and surroundings: The cabin sits back from the water, tucked behind a screen of trees, with views across the arm of the 900-foot Kvasnikoff Falls, recently named for a well-loved, local Native Alaskan. Extensive tidal flats in front of the cabin are exposed at low tide. The narrow fjord is forested with old-growth spruce. Much of the area surrounding the cabin is owned by the English Bay Corporation. A map inside the cabin shows nearby trail and site easements. Corporation lands may be accessed only by permit.

Wildlife sightings: Eagles, black bear, salmon, seals, sea otters, river otters, seabirds, and shorebirds.

Recreation: Hiking is limited, except along the beach. There is good kayaking and boating in the arm, and fishing by boat for halibut, rockfish, and salmon. Salmonberries and blueberries ripen late July through August. No hunting is allowed.

In Brief:

AIALIK BAY CABIN

Kenai Fjords National Park (National Park Service)

Location: Northeast shore of Aialik Bay, opposite Pederson Glacier.
Elevation: Near sea level.
Map: USGS Blying Sound D8 (D7 optional); or Trails Illustrated™, *Kenai Fjords National Park.*
Access: By boat, four hours from Seward; by air, 30 minutes from Seward.
Available: About May 23 to September 2 (weather depending).
Sleeps: Four on bunks.
Maximum stay: Three nights per calendar year.
Cost: $35.
In brief: The 16x20-foot cabin has two twin-sized bunks, counter, table and chairs, couch, diesel oil stove (oil has been included in past, but confirm this with the Park Service before you go), informational bulletin board, porch, and outhouse. It's located in one of the few cabin areas you can explore extensively on foot. At low tide, you can walk, explore tide pools, and watch for whales over a one-mile stretch of sandy beach. This is a popular location for viewing eagles and other seabirds. Expect to see tour boats daily. Good kayaking destinations include Pederson Lagoon and Pederson Glacier, across the bay, but wakes from passing tour boats can disrupt kayaking, to some extent, and make landings difficult.

Reservations: Kenai Fjords National Park office in downtown Seward, 1212 Fourth Ave., (907) 224-3175. Reservations are accepted beginning January 2 for the summer season.

In Brief:

HOLGATE ARM CABIN

Kenai Fjords National Park (National Park Service)

Location: Northeastern shore of Holgate Arm, on west side of Aialik Bay, about 4 miles from Holgate Glacier.

Elevation: Near sea level.

Map: USGS Blying Sound D8 or Trails Illustrated™, *Kenai Fjords National Park.*

Access: By boat, four hours from Seward; by air, 35 minutes from Seward. Heavy pack ice can make boating and landing by floatplane in Holgate Arm difficult; some charters prefer not to travel here.

Available: About May 23 to September 2 (weather depending).

Sleeps: Six on bunks.

Maximum stay: Three nights per calendar year.

Cost: $35.

In brief: The 16x20-foot cabin has six bunks, counter, table and chairs, diesel oil stove (oil has been included in past; confirm this with the Park Service before you go), informational bulletin board, porch, and outhouse. There are spectacular views and sounds of calving ice from Holgate Glacier. You can fish by boat for halibut and rockfish, and along beaches at Pederson Lagoon for sockeye salmon (late June to Late July), silver salmon (late August to late September), and Dolly Varden. Humpback whales are spotted occasionally. Heavy pack ice can make boating, kayaking, and beach landings difficult. Expect to see tour boats daily. Wakes from passing tour boats can disrupt kayaking and boating, to some extent, and make landings difficult.

Reservations: Kenai Fjords National Park office in downtown Seward, 1212 Fourth Ave., (907) 224-3175. Reservations are accepted beginning January 2 for the summer season.

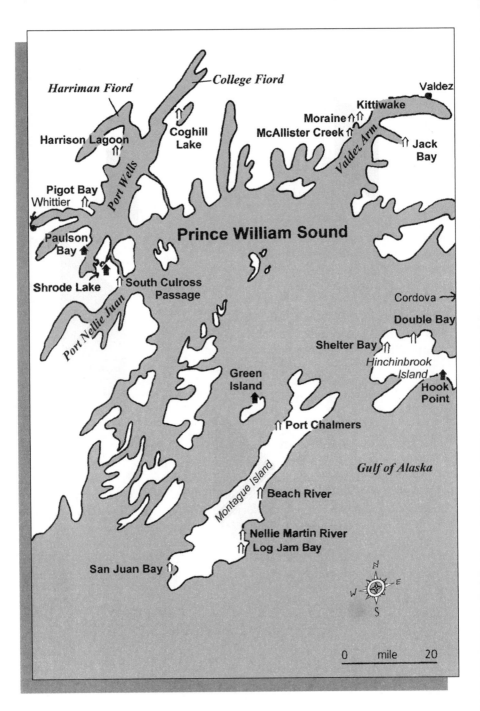

Harriman Fiord

College Fiord

Valdez

Kittiwake

Moraine

McAllister Creek

Harrison Lagoon

Coghill Lake

Valdez Arm

Jack Bay

Pigot Bay
Whittier

Port Wells

Prince William Sound

Paulson Bay

Shrode Lake

South Culross Passage

Port Nellie Juan

Cordova →

Double Bay

Shelter Bay

Hinchinbrook Island

Hook Point

Green Island

Port Chalmers

Gulf of Alaska

Montague Island

Beach River

Nellie Martin River

Log Jam Bay

San Juan Bay

N
W · E
S

0   mile   20

In This Light: Reflections From Green Island

by Marybeth Holleman

It is bigger, brighter. Its tail streaks farther across the night sky. When I look at it through binoculars, I have to move them slowly, steadily, panning like a photographer at a race, to see it all, to see the sunburst head and the tail that arches and fans like a single wide brush stroke. This comet seems so different from here than from my porch at home, but it is the same comet, Hale Bopp, I have come to expect on a clear night—as I expect to see Orion's Belt and the Big Dipper—even though I know that in a few weeks it will disappear, not to return in my lifetime.

In the west I see the quarter moon, filled out with earth shine and so brilliant that through binoculars I can see its craters. Turning east, I find the red beacon that is Mars. All this shines above me from the porch of a cabin on Green Island in Prince William Sound, Alaska, in mid-March. Within a week this comet will reach its zenith, and this place will have eight years between it and the Exxon Valdez oil spill that coated the beaches before me and killed throngs of seabirds, sea otters, and fish in the waters beyond me.

Green Island. I've never been here before, but I've heard of it. In April 1989, a month after the tanker hit Bligh Reef, birds started arriving by the thousands, some to stay and some just passing through on their spring migrations to northern nesting grounds. People awaited them, firing gunshot into the air to keep the tired birds from landing, for instead of respite the birds would find only deadly oil. Now, eight years later, I stand here watching a giant comet within a few million miles of Earth, Mars in direct opposition with the sun, and the moon on its way to a near total eclipse. What does this mean, this brilliant celestial event and this dark anniversary converging?

The oil spill has profoundly affected me, as it has irrevocably harmed the Sound. Memories of those dark years haunt me, as does the knowledge that it isn't over yet: oil still underlies the rock: animals are still suffering from it. I cannot separate this place from that event. At times their entanglement tightens into a near obsession. Yet, underlying this bedrock despair, is love. Prince William Sound is dearer to me than anywhere else on earth, and I crave time in it. I have wanted to visit Green Island for years. Though I've spent time in the Sound for over a decade, this is farther out than I have yet been able to travel.

We are staying in a cabin that sits on a bight of land, sandwiched between two beaches, on the western edge of the island. The front beach faces Montague Strait, with Naked Island in the distance; the back beach faces a wide, quiet finger of water flanked by the main body of the island and a narrow spit. Green Island lacks the towering peaks of Knight and Montague islands to either side of it; instead, true to its name, it remains green year-round with a dense forest of spruce. It is low-lying, marshy, dotted with ponds, perfect for migrating birds. And it is lovely.

The morning after our arrival, the beach facing Montague Strait rumbles with waves thumping against long rows of tangled kelp, sea grass, and driftwood washed up in winter's storms. Wind roars through the trees around us. The seas, though, lay low enough for us to venture out in our canoe. We push off into the wind—Rick, my son Jamie, and I—hoping to paddle around the point to see Montague Island. Montague is the largest island in the Sound, and protects the Sound from Gulf of Alaska storms. Montague, Green, and Knight Island to the north caught most of the oil in their fjords. I am anxious to lay eyes on Montague, having only seen it from the air. The choppy seas make for slow going, though, and Jamie complains of cold. While the spring equinox falls in March, here it is still winter—snow crusts the shoreline, ice covers fresh water, and the slightest breeze sends a chill. Then my dog Keira, who is following us on shore, disappears into the woods. Things seem rougher than the water's surface.

A Prince William Sound cabin view

We are almost to the point, so close I can imagine rounding that steep headland and coming into full view of that magnificent island of snow-capped peaks, forty miles long and wild with brown bears and deer. But Rick worries about Keira—who is notorious for not returning from her wanderings—and Jamie whimpers with cold. We turn our backs to Montague and head to the cabin. After beaching the boat, Rick heads off in search of the dog. Disappointed at not making it to the point, I follow Jamie down the beach to the headland nearest the cabin.

It is low tide, and every crevice, every cirque in the rock, holds saltwater filled with life. Jamie and I climb from one tide pool to the next, peering to discover what lives within. Once our eyes adjust, we can see rockfish, anemones, star fish, sea urchins, barnacles, limpets, and snails among forests of sea lettuce, kelp, and eel grass. We find one long narrow pool packed with starfish—orange, burgundy, and yellow stars—among bright green, waving eel grass. I use a long yellow float that Jamie found and pry one up, turning it over so that its pale belly shows.

"Watch and it will turn itself back over," I whisper to him. A few pale tentacles wave around, reaching out for a firm footing. Gradually more and more tentacles reach, rippling across the thick arm like ocean swells. Almost imperceptibly the legs stretch and turn, and the body of the starfish slowly begins to right itself.

"C'mon, let's go," says Jamie after a few minutes. "I want to climb up to there." He points to a rock face and the forest above it.

"We have to wait. The starfish is vulnerable this way. I don't want anything to happen to it because we turned it over," I tell him.

"What could happen?" he says, interested again.

We continue to stare into the tide pool as the tentacles wave and reach. The change is slow but certain. Except for two feet, it has almost turned over, squeezing itself back in among the other stars, when we start climbing the cliff.

My hand presses against smooth gray rock. My fingers reach for a small hold that juts out, where rain has eroded a dimple, a crack. My eyes focus on patterns of granite inches away.

"Put your foot here, and then put your hand here," my 5-year-old son tells me. He leads, watching me closely as I follow him up the cliff.

"Go the same way I do," he reminds me. I do. He finds the best route.

We crouch on top, feet on soft moss, shoulders touching, and look out from the headland to the waters of Prince William Sound. The morning waves flatten to ripples on the surface. The rock that contains our tide pool is now washed by the incoming tide. I point to it.

"Look," I say, "see how that rock is becoming an island? See how the lay of the land changes with the tide?"

We climb down from the headland, pick our way across rocks not yet submerged by the tide, and return to the sandy beach. Jamie grabs a wave-washed spruce branch and prods the kelp berm at the high-tide line, digging for treasure among the storm debris. I find a stone slab half-buried in sand, smooth, gently sloping, facing the sun. Leaning against it, I close my eyes and feel the heat emanating from black sand and rock. My head and back are cradled in the curve of rock; my feet—free of boots and socks—dig into warm sand. I drift in place.

"Mom, come look at this," Jamie says. I get up, too quickly, and see stars, lost for a moment in a universe of my own. Jamie points to a dead sun star.

Its bright orange color is fading, bleaching away, and its skin peels off in strips, eaten by the spring tails and beetles hidden in the kelp berm. We turn it over and see the skeleton beneath, white cartilage radiating out in twelve thin lines, each with matching patterns of thinner strips across, the whole thing like a snowflake magnified. When we check on the sun star the next day, I am surprised at how quickly it has become something new: just white filaments strewn starlike upon black sand: a skeleton.

Standing up, I see Rick trudging down the beach toward us, head down, without Keira.

"Don't worry," I tell him when I see his face, trying to sound more certain than I am. "It's an island, and we're the only people on it. She'll come back."

As spruce shadows lengthen over the beach, we walk over to the quiet lagoon on the other side of the cabin. Jamie plays at the water's edge, throwing in rocks and singing. I start to read from a book I'd brought, but the words on the page can't draw me away from this place, so I join Jamie and stand at the water's edge, staring down into it.

Something moves in the clear water, something small and translucent. A feather? An embryonic stage of a marine animal? It wiggles back and forth, propelling itself slowly through still water. Its body is soft and oval-shaped, with flaps on either side and a row of three, fin-like appendages. It is ethereal. I show it to Rick and Jamie.

"I think it's a nudibranch, a sea slug," Rick says.

"I thought about that," I say, "but I've only seen nudibranchs in photographs of tropical waters. I didn't know they lived this far north." I now remember seeing something in the water when we were paddling in this lagoon the day before. We were rushing to get back, and I didn't stop to look longer or mention it to anyone.

I had never seen the water so clear, in all the times I've been in the Sound. I could stare deeply into it, as if I were looking through a telescope, no surface movement to distort the image. Long, thick stands of kelp waved up from the bottom, dark green palms arising from burgundy stalks. Attached to and floating among them drifted tiny, translucent pink wisps. My eyes focused on one, and then I saw more than I could count: underwater flowers blowing in currents instead of breeze: blossoms blown off their branches floating through the kelp forest.

By evening, clouds obscure the cosmic display. Yet, as I set our dinner on the table, I look out the window to something no less remarkable, however mundane: Keira returning on her own. She trots up the path, tongue lolling, ears back, satisfied grin on her wild, husky face.

The next morning, we paddle out from the front beach again, this time heading toward the western point, hoping to paddle around it and to some islets on the other side. Keira is off on another adventure, but we no longer worry for her return. At the point, we paddle through some sea stacks, coming right up on a couple of sea otters and a raft of seabirds. Among them are cormorants and guillemots, but what are the ducklike birds with the striking, silver, white, and burgundy markings? I have never before seen harlequin ducks, but I have heard about them just as I have heard about this island. Harlequins are still suffering from the oil spill. They haven't been able to breed successfully for eight years. That familiar, confusing mix of sadness and pleasure comes back—sadness over the loss, pleasure at seeing them here nonetheless, seeing their brilliance like the comet, like the tide pools.

At the headland, we pull the canoe up on some boulders covered with pop weed and walk up to the high-tide beach. Strong, thick blades of beach rye-grass are just starting to push new leaves through the layer of snow and last year's grass. I sit in the sun, basking like a seal on a rock, and then open my eyes quickly as I hear a sound at once strange, familiar, and unfortunate.

An outboard engine. A small aluminum skiff carrying three people in bright orange, float coats zooms toward us. The person in front holds a clipboard, so I know they are scientists studying these creatures, seeing what happens in the aftermath of an oil spill. Perhaps they are counting the harlequins, or maybe sea otters or scoters.

I do not want them here. They intrude into our solitude. Even more, they intrude into my thoughts, the roar of their engine like nature itself raging over what happened and what continues to happen. It is as if their boat rushing toward me carries all my memories of the spill. Carries, too, my anger that now, because of the oil spill, dozens of humans zip around out here counting, captur-ing, and prodding these animals, which have already suffered so much. I watch as they motor through slowly, staying far out from land. I watch as the otters dive and seabirds fly at their passage. I watch as they pick up speed and disap-pear in a rush of noise and wake into the horizon.

When the boat's wake dissipates, we climb back in the canoe, paddling in the same direction as its passing. We come into view of the islets, a beautiful maze of cliffs, trees, and beaches. We stop and eat lunch on a rocky beach. Harbor seals are all around, eyeing us curiously and playing hide and seek, though they do all the hiding. From the canoe it is so clear that we can see the bottom where the seals were moments before. How wonderful it would be to see them swim underwater, where their rounded bodies, so awkward on land, must slip like sun-light through cloud cover.

All day long we paddle in the equinoctial sun, our faces, hands, and forearms reddening. All day long we look down into water, out over water, up into sky. Paddling through narrow passageways, we talk quietly, briefly, our voices as calm as the water's surface. Puffins ahead of us flap out of the water, then land again behind us, settling on the surface. Every now and then, a salmon leaps through glass. My senses vibrate with the life around us.

We round the last headland and come back into view of the quiet lagoon that leads to the cabin. To my left I see another sea otter perched on a rock. He stretches up, looks our way, then slips into the water, leaving a small splash. I consider paddling over quickly in hopes of seeing him underwater, but I do not suggest it. This day has already given so much. I watch to see where the otter will resurface, hoping at least to see him again.

Look. The sea otter is underwater beside me. He is sliding around the front of the canoe, with bubbles streaming from fur and nostrils as he swims. With hair finer and fur denser than any other animal, the otter's escaping air pours off him in long waves. Beside the canoe he moves like a comet in the night sky. He zigzags back, rolls, and stops in mid-roll, curled into a half-moon. For a moment sea otter looks up calmly through clear water. Then, rolling, he shimmers and is gone. And I am saying, over and over, "Look! Look! Look!"

〰〰〰

The next day, a few hours before the floatplane returns to pick us up, we walk on the front beach again. The sun star skeleton is nowhere to be found, washed away in the night's high tide. I imagine its fragile bones scattered along the shore like sunlight.

Past the smooth rock I leaned against, Rick begins turning over stones, finding oil. He shows me the signs on boulders that look like splattered asphalt. Removing one big, flat rock reveals a puddle whose surface rainbows when exposed to light. Eight years later, oil slicks the beach.

"I've got to bring some of this back," he says. "People all over the U.S. need to see this. They need to see that Exxon's lying about how clean the Sound is." He collects some crud in a trash bag, wiping his hands on his coat as he works. These stains are forever. I know. We both have oil-streaked pants from eight years ago. I don't want to see them again. I bring him a towel to use, but it's too late.

The question I asked our first night here resurfaces in that pool of oil. What does this mean, all this beauty and horror mixed together? I pick up an oiled pebble and start to put it in Rick's collection bag, but then I stop. I drop it, straighten up, and look out at the water. All the moments of absolute being— Jamie's boulder, the nudibranch blossoms, the sea otter under water —wash over my grief as freshwater washes saltwater, diluting pain, drawing it out like the moon draws the tide.

For a moment I shed questions. For a moment everything fits and I feel only peace. Look. All this is changing. The comet will be gone in a few weeks, not to return for thousands of years. The Sound was harmed by the oil spill; it continues to suffer and to heal. As do I. As do we all. Look now. All I have is this moment, in this place, at this time. All I know is what I see: moon, water, comet, trees, starfish, otter, light.

Marybeth Holleman teaches creative writing at the University of Alaska Anchorage and is the author of a forthcoming pocket guidebook to Prince William Sound.

About Prince William Sound

One hundred gorgeous ways to get wet: that's one way to think of Prince William Sound, a rainy, snowy, maritime wilderness. The coastline of this mostly sheltered body of water extends for 3,500 sinuous miles. Waterfalls plunge into the sea from steep, forested slopes. One hundred and fifty glaciers hang like a frozen mantle over the surrounding mountains. Inland are pristine blue lakes — sometimes frozen well into June — and countless creeks. There's water, water everywhere — plenty to play on *and* plenty to drink. And that's even before the rain begins to fall — a redundancy in this wet, wet, wet place. Whether you hike, kayak, or sail here, you're bound to end the day soggy. Thank goodness for the public cabins.

Most of the Sound is encompassed by the Chugach National Forest, a 3-million-acre wooded wilderness. The Forest Service maintains 13 cabins in northern and western Prince William Sound. (See the Cordova section for cabins in the Sound's southeastern corner.) A popular handful are easily reached from Whittier, the gateway town that's only a 1-hour drive from Anchorage to Portage, followed by a short train trip (and soon, a planned road) under the mountains. In the Sound's northwest corner, boaters can choose between four coastal cabins, with two more located just inland. Across the Sound, in its northeast corner, a seventh cabin is located outside Valdez. (Three more Valdez-area cabins are managed by Alaska State Parks.) Other Forest Service cabins are located in the remote southern Sound: one at Green Island (subject of the essay in this chapter), and five, used mainly by deer hunters and some anglers, on Montague Island.

Unless you have your own transportation, the southern Sound cab-

Landscape with Schrode Lake Cabin

PRINCE Wm. SOUND-
Whittier to Valdez

ins can be very expensive to reach. Access is usually by plane, because of the distance and because several of the cabins are located on the open Gulf of Alaska. A 45- to 60-minute chartered airplane trip from Seward can cost $700 to $1,000 (two adults, including dropoff and pickup).

The northwest Sound is a much better deal, especially when you travel by boat. Charter fares vary considerably, but to reach the northwest Sound cabins by boat you will probably pay about $6 per nautical mile, or between $175 and $300 each way (for up to six adults). The more kayakers in your party, the more you can save. Especially to the nearer cabins, like Pigot Bay, paddlers often opt for a one-way charter and then paddle back to Whittier.

Three cabins are clustered closely enough for a cabin-to-cabin paddle, albeit a challenging one: Paulson Bay, Shrode Lake, and South Culross Passage. Shrode Lake, the middle cabin, is located on an inland lake, with long portage routes linking the lake to saltwater to the west and north. You can be dropped off at Paulson Bay and picked up at South Culross Passage — or vice versa — but grant yourself plenty of time to complete the trip so you don't miss your pickup.

A more popular option is to choose one cabin and simply use it as a base for exploration. Harrison Lagoon, Paulson Bay, and South Culross Passage all make fantastic base camps, with great paddling and wildlife-watching in several directions.

Reaching the northwest Sound cabins by floatplane is pricier than by boat, since most charters originate in Anchorage. Expect to pay about $1000 round-trip for two or three adults to reach the landlocked Coghill Lake or Shrode Lake cabins — two favorite spots for anglers. Below, you'll get a closer look at three featured cabins in very different environments.

PRINCE Wm. SOUND-
Whittier to Valdez

GREEN ISLAND CABIN

Chugach National Forest, (U.S. Forest Service)

Snapshot: Center of the Sound: a new wheelchair-accessible cabin offering seclusion, superb wildlife-watching, boating, and angling.

Location: Northeast end of Green Island in a protected bay in Gibbon Anchorage.

Elevation: Near sea level.

Map: USGS Seward B2 (some features on map are inaccurate due to island uplift).

Access: By boat (75 miles from Cordova, 70 miles from Whittier, 100 miles from Seward) or by floatplane (40 minutes from Cordova). Boaters should use caution; uncharted rocks are in the area.

Available: Year-round.

Best: May through August.

Sleeps: Six on bunks (the maximum capacity is eight).

Maximum stay: Seven consecutive nights.

Cost: $35.

Reservations: Forest Service toll-free reservation center, (877) 444-6777 or via Internet at http://www.reserveusa.com. For info on trail and cabin specifics, call the Cordova Ranger District Office (907) 424-7661.

Facilities: The 16x20-foot cabin was built in the 1990s, replacing an older Forest Service cabin at this location. It has six bunks, table, wood stove, oil stove with oven (#1 stove oil not included), rainwater catchment system, wraparound deck, and outhouse. Improvements for disabled visitors include wide doors, lowered and enlarged windows, boardwalk, and interior furnishings (bunks, table, and shelves) designed for accessibility. A 200-foot saltwater ramp is accessible from middle to high tide. Some

PRINCE Wm. SOUND-
Whittier to Valdez

users may still require assistance since the boardwalk has a 10 percent grade.

Condition: Excellent.

View and surroundings: The cabin is on a protected shore, surrounded by rolling muskeg and dense spruce/hemlock forest. The island was uplifted by the 1964 earthquake. Lakes in the area are slowly drying up and the muskeg is gradually converting to forest.

Wildlife sightings: Sea otters, harbor seals, and waterfowl. Also in area: Steller sea lions, whales, brown bears, and Sitka blacktailed deer.

Recreation: Pink salmon (mid-July to early August) and silver salmon (mid- to late August) are best fished from saltwater, though some can be caught in streams by the cabin. You can fish for Dolly Varden in a stream one mile north of the cabin. By boat offshore, halibut and bottom fishing are also good. There is good tidepooling on shore. Hiking on muskeg is possible with rubber boots. Bring a kayak or small boat to explore Gibbon Anchorage and small offshore islands, and to maximize your chances of catching fish and spotting wildlife.

Getting there: Use caution boating in the area: weather and sea changes can be extreme, and some rocks are uncharted.

PRINCE Wm. SOUND-
Whittier to Valdez

PAULSON BAY CABIN

Chugach National Forest (U.S. Forest Service)

Snapshot: Shimmering ice, blue mirror: A paddler's and angler's cabin on a sheltered island-dotted bay, with spectacular views of distant Harvard Glacier.

Location: At the head of Paulson Bay, on the western shore of the larger Cochrane Bay.

Elevation: 30 feet.

Map: USGS Seward C4 or Trails Illustrated™, *Prince William Sound — West*.

Access: By boat, 18 miles from Whittier; by floatplane, 40 minutes from Anchorage or 60 minutes from Cordova.

Available: Year-round.

Best: June through August.

Sleeps: Six on bunks (four would be more comfortable). The maximum allowed is eight.

Maximum stay: Seven nights.

Cost: $35.

Reservations: Forest Service toll-free reservation center, (877) 444-6777 or via Internet at http://www.reserveusa.com. For info on trail and cabin specifics, call the Glacier Ranger District Office, (907) 783-3242.

Facilities: The 12x14-foot dark brown, Pan Abode log cabin has bunks for six, with the lower bunks doubling as benches on either side of a table. It also has a flat-topped wood stove, counter, and propane lantern. (It was present during a recent visit, but shouldn't be relied upon; bring a lantern or lots of candles, since the cabin is fairly dark inside.) Outside are a wood shed, new outhouse, and small front stoop.

Condition: Excellent.

View and surroundings: The cabin is set just back from a steep bluff, facing north with open views of Port Wells and College Fiord. On a clear day, Harvard Glacier, 50 miles away, is visible across the water. A rustic log ladder and short, steep trail links the cabin with a slate beach at the head of the bay. Creeks flank the cabin directly to the left and right, carving narrow canyons on either side. A long staircase leads up from the cabin's west creek, near a small waterfall. Large flat boulders and tidepools where the creek meet the sea make the area perfect for sunning and exploring. Behind the cabin, rolling spruce forest gives way to more rugged, mountainous countryside. Salmonberries and blueberries abound.

The mouth of Paulson Bay is partly blocked by five, small wooded islands. Just to the northwest, a large lagoon winds inland, connecting to a broad marshy area and creek. From late July to mid-August, the lagoon is flooded with salmon. The area — accessible by kayak — is a great place to watch the salmon migration, one of the world's natural wonders. It's also a good place to look for eagles, black bears, and any other creatures arriving to take advantage of the raucous feast.

Wildlife sightings: Sea otters, seals, salmon, eagles, harlequin ducks, murrelets, mergansers, and other waterfowl. Also in area: Fin, orca, and humpback whales are sometimes spotted in Cochrane Bay. Black bears and Sitka blacktailed deer roam the forests behind the cabin.

PRINCE Wm. SOUND- Whittier to Valdez

Recreation: Fishing for chum salmon and pink salmon in the creek and bay (late July through early August); and for rockfish, shrimp, and halibut in the deeper waters of Cochrane Bay. Abundant salmonberries ripen from late July through August. Good kayaking day trips include paddling to Surprise Cove State Marine Park, 5 miles north — also a good place to camp overnight if you're paddling to or from Whittier. Kayakers can also explore each finger of Threefingers Cove, about 4 miles southeast. See Shrode Lake Cabin for information on hiking inland from Threefingers Cove.

Getting there: The entrance to Paulson Bay is not obvious. Its mouth is partly obscured by five small islands. Enter the bay from the north, staying well to the right of the center (western edge of the bay). Beware of submerged rock ledges around the islands and coastal points.

SHRODE LAKE CABIN

Chugach National Forest (U.S. Forest Service)

PRINCE Wm. SOUND-Whittier to Valdez

> *"Highlight of trip — the driving torrential rain and gale force winds were particularly breathtaking. Bummer of trip — lake frozen and fishless. Trip proverb — many are cold but few are frozen."*
>
> *Shrode Lake Cabin log, June 15.*

Snapshot: Fresh to saltwater, and everything in between. A secluded, lakeside A-frame cabin with access to fishing on a lake, creek, lagoon, and ocean.

Location: On the northeast side of Shrode Lake, a small subalpine lake on the peninsula between Cochrane Bay and Culross Passage.

Elevation: 50 feet.

Map: USGS Seward C4 or Trails Illustrated™, *Prince William Sound — West.*

Access: By floatplane, 45 minutes from Anchorage or 55 minutes from Cordova. By boat, 25 miles from Whittier into Long Bay and then a 1-mile hike; or 22 miles into the middle finger of Threefingers Cove, and then a 3-mile hike. Only shallow-draft vessels can proceed during high tide as far as the lagoon at the head of Long Bay. Sea kayakers must portage in and out from Long Bay to the cabin, since the creek connecting them drops quickly from Shrode Lake, creating some short stretches of mostly Class I whitewater. Numerous rock hazards are in the channel and lagoon.

Available: Year-round, though difficult to access until snow and ice have melted, usually in mid-June but sometimes as late as July.

Best: July and August.

Sleeps: Five on bunks, comfortably, with plenty of extra space in the loft. Maximum capacity is eight.

Maximum stay: Seven nights.

Cost: $35.

Reservations: Forest Service toll-free reservation center, (877) 444-6777 or via Internet at http://www.reserveusa.com. For info on trail and cabin specifics, Glacier Ranger District Office (907) 783-3242.

Facilities: The 16x16-foot dark brown, A-frame cabin has bunks for five (two wide platforms and one narrow one) and a loft. It also has a picnic table, benches, a poorly maintained oil stove, counter, and dutch door. Outside are a boat shelter and rowboat (life jackets not included), outhouse, and narrow porch. Weathered, ceiling-high plexiglass windows face east and west, but the cabin's interior is still quite dark. Bring a lantern or lots of candles.

Condition: Poor (worn floor, weathered surfaces, and just plain dirty).

View and surroundings: The cabin faces west across Shrode Lake, surrounded by open shrubby muskeg, backed by scattered spruce trees. Located near treeline, the cabin has sweeping views of tundra-covered mountain slopes rising from the lake. Abundant blueberries and salmonberries grow in the woods just beyond the outhouse, and on the trail to Long Bay, behind the cabin. Be prepared for bugs.

Wildlife sightings: Loons, black bears (especially at the lake outlet), and salmon. Also in area: Sitka blacktailed deer, and other waterfowl.

Recreation: The opportunity to fish in diverse environments and away from summer crowds are the best reasons to come here. A small run of sockeye salmon passes through in mid-July, followed by abundant pink salmon through mid-August, and silver salmon in late August. Salmon fishing takes place in Shrode Lake, in the lake outlet and the creek it feeds, in the lagoon beyond that, and in Long Bay, beyond the lagoon. There's also fishing for Dolly Varden in Shrode Lake. Berries ripen in August.

A recently improved 1-mile hiking trail leads from the cabin to Long Bay. There's no bridge across the creek draining Shrode Lake, but once you've waded across at a ford site marked with posts, you can hike 3 miles to Threefingers Cove along a new hiking trail. You can also hike east along a more primitive trail to Jack Lake, about 0.5 mile away. Sea kayakers can portage to saltwater west or north, but it's a hard, long haul. Access via the Long Bay trail is the shorter, better route.

Getting there: From the lagoon at the head of Long Bay, hike 1 mile along the trail that follows the eastern side of the creek to the cabin. (Your hike will be longer and more difficult if you're dropped off at low tide.) Alternately, from Threefingers Cove, follow the trail from the middle finger of the cove toward the lake. (It is possible to cross the creek at the lake outlet, but the water can be thigh-high and swift.) The boardwalked trail takes a detour to parallel the creek, heading north (away from the lake) to a shallower ford site, marked by posts. Once you've crossed, you'll follow a recently improved trail along the creek's east shore, back to Shrode Lake and the cabin. Note: From the middle finger of Threefingers Cove, you may also notice a shorter, primitive trail that leads past two ponds and more directly to the lake. Avoid it if possible, since the vegetation is fragile, and there is some bushwhacking required (not fun, especially with a kayak).

Prince William Sound Cheesecake

Highbush cranberry

Ingredients: no-bake cheesecake mix (Royal brand will do)
2 cups fresh mixed berries, available near most cabins
in July and August
a pinch of desperation

You're at a cabin perched on the edge of a subalpine lake, framed on all sides by lush green mountains. You haven't seen another human being in two days, maybe three. Then, last night, the sky fell. Clouds rolled in. The rain started — never strong, just a moody, irregular spatter. "That old Prince William Sound spit," as a friend described it.

You can't see much of the mountains anymore. Even the far end of the lake is hidden in a bank of pewter-colored fog. The entire world has turned monochromatic, a century-old silver-gelatin print. The only color visible is directly behind the cabin, where plump blueberries grow on glistening bushes, and where salmonberries hang in fluorescent clusters.

You know, deep down in your heart, that the floatplane you chartered to pick you up won't be coming anytime soon. Here is what you do. After you've read your last book, and the book your partner brought, too, and played several games of cards, and explained to your confused children twelve times that no, you're not going home today, go outside and pick berries. Forget about trying to keep dry — even with a rain jacket, you'll come back soaked from ankles to ear-lobes just from rubbing against the bushes and slipping onto the muddy ground. But that's why you're in a heated cabin, not a tent. Fill two camping mugs full of forest jewels: yellow and orange and red salmonberries, blueberries, some crowberries if you don't mind the tiny seeds, and whatever else you can find. Nothing's wrong, you tell your children, answering their questions one more time. In fact, you're the only one worrying — which is why you need to watch them now, laughing, slipping, filling their hands and mouths with berries. You are reminded, as both children and Alaska weather remind you often, to live in the moment.

Whip up the instant no-bake cheesecake mix you hid in your backpack for just this occasion. (You knew well enough not to tell your children, girlfriend, or whoever you brought along on this trip, or they would have eaten it yesterday, when the sun was shining.) One cake will divide nicely into two camping plates with raised sides. Sprinkle the berries on top. Now set the camping tins outside on the front stoop. The box says set them in the refrigerator, but don't worry — on a gray day in Alaska, even in summer, the outdoors is a refrigerator. If your kids are convinced that bears or wolverines will come to steal the cheesecake, send them up to the loft where they can look down over the porch and scream and holler when any marauders come near. Now, while the kids are distracted, count your tins of tuna and your packets of ramen noodles, just to quell any anxieties about imminent starvation. The plane may not arrive for another day, or another two, or another three. But at least you have cake. In an hour (shorter if it's really cold out) it will be ready. Relax and enjoy.

In Brief:
Eight Northwest Prince William Sound cabins

PIGOT BAY CABIN

Chugach National Forest (U.S. Forest Service)

Location: On the southwest shore near the head of Pigot Bay — the closest cabin to the gateway town of Whittier, 18 miles away.

Elevation: Near sea level.

Map: USGS Seward D4 or Trails Illustrated™, *Prince William Sound — West*.

Access: By boat, or by floatplane (40 minutes from Anchorage or 60 minutes from Cordova).

Available: Year-round.

Sleeps: Eight, the maximum allowed.

Maximum stay: Seven consecutive nights.

Cost: $35.

In brief: The 16x16-foot A-frame cabin with loft has a wood stove. It is located on a 12-foot-high bluff over a wide outwash valley at the head of the bay, with mountains rising steeply farther along the shore. Stairs lead up the bluff to the cabin. The area is a favorite with kayakers, since it is close to Whittier and makes a good base for exploring north into Port Wells. Hiking is limited. Wildlife include black bears, eagles, geese, sea otters, harbor seals, sea lions, and Dall and harbor porpoises. Fishing is fair for pink salmon (late July to early August) in the bay and nearby streams. Butter clams may be dug on the few gravel beaches at the head of the bay.

Reservations: Forest Service toll-free reservation center, (877) 444-6777 or via Internet at http://www.reserveusa.com. For info on trail and cabin specifics, call the Glacier Ranger District Office, (907) 783-3242.

In Brief:

HARRISON LAGOON CABIN

Chugach National Forest (U.S. Forest Service)

Location: On the west side of Port Wells, 34 miles from Whittier.

Elevation: Sea level.

Map: USGS Seward D4 or Trails Illustrated™, *Prince William Sound — West*.

Access: By boat, or by floatplane (40 minutes from Anchorage, 60 minutes from Cordova).

Available: Year-round.

Sleeps: Six (the maximum is eight).

Maximum stay: Seven consecutive nights.

Cost: $35.

In brief: This extra roomy, 16x20-foot wooden-frame cabin is a favorite among kayakers and families looking for a wilderness base camp. Even those who stay ashore will enjoy hiking the lagoon at low tide, exploring a barge wreck, and picking abundant salmonberries and blueberries. Wildlife include black bears, Sitka blacktailed deer, eagles, seabirds, harbor seals, sea otters, sea lions, Dall and harbor porpoises, and occasionally, whales. Fishing is fair for pink salmon (August) either in Lagoon Creek or in the lagoon itself. The lagoon drains at low tide and should be used by skiffs or kayaks only. The glacial coast wilderness of Barry Arm, Harriman Fiord, and College Fiord lure boaters north. Improvements for disabled visitors include extra floor space, wide doors, ramps and boardwalk, and a modified outhouse.

Reservations: Forest Service toll-free reservation center, (877) 444-6777 or via Internet at http://www.reserveusa.com. For info on trail and cabin specifics, call the Glacier Ranger District Office, (907) 783-3242.

In Brief:

COGHILL LAKE CABIN

Chugach National Forest (U.S. Forest Service)

Location: On a lagoon on the southwest shore of Coghill Lake, 3 miles inland from College Fiord.

Elevation: Near sea level.

Map: USGS Anchorage A3 or Trails Illustrated™, *Prince William Sound — West.*

Access: By floatplane (50 minutes from Anchorage or 60 minutes from Cordova). It is also possible, though not recommended, to hike/bushwhack 3 miles along a primitive trail from saltwater. (The trail has been improved for the first mile, starting from the lake, and future work may improve access. Contact the Forest Service for an update.)

Available: Year-round.

Sleeps: Eight, the maximum allowed.

Maximum stay: Seven consecutive nights.

Cost: $35.

In brief: The 16x16-foot A-frame cabin has a loft, wood stove, and woodshed. This cabin is an angler's favorite, offering seclusion, awesome scenery, and access to four species of salmon. It is located in rolling hills, backed by glacier-capped mountains. Salmonberries and blueberries are abundant. Wildlife include black bears, eagles, river otters, and waterfowl. There is excellent fishing from the lakeshore, stream, and lagoon for sockeye salmon (mid-June through July), pink and chum salmon (July and August), and silver salmon (August and September). There is no rowboat provided, so bring an inflatable for best fishing access.

Reservations: Forest Service toll-free reservation center, (877) 444-6777 or via Internet at http://www.reserveusa.com. For info on trail and cabin specifics, call the Glacier Ranger District Office, (907) 783-3242.

In Brief:

SOUTH CULROSS PASSAGE CABIN

Chugach National Forest (U.S. Forest Service)

Location: On the northwest side of Picturesque Cove, on the western shore of Culross Passage, 1.5 miles north of the south entrance point to the passage.

Elevation: Near sea level.

Map: USGS Seward C4 or Trails Illustrated™, *Prince William Sound — West.*

Access: By boat (27 miles from Whittier) or floatplane (45 minutes from Anchorage or 55 minutes from Cordova).

Available: Year-round.

Sleeps: Six (the maximum capacity is eight).

Maximum stay: Seven consecutive nights.

Cost: $35.

In brief: The 12x14-foot cabin has a wood stove. Culross Passage and Port Nellie Juan are favorite areas for kayakers, boaters, and wildlife-watchers. Orcas may be observed feeding in south Culross Passage. A lagoon near the cabin is a good place to spot eagles and black bears fishing for pink salmon (July to mid-August). Other wildlife include Sitka blacktailed deer, foxes, and waterfowl. Steamer clams may be dug on the few gravel beaches in the area. A waterfall spills into a deep pool in Picturesque Cove (not visible from the cabin but accessible by kayaking or hiking the beach at low tide).

Reservations: Forest Service toll-free reservation center, (877) 444-6777 or via Internet at http://www.reserveusa.com. For info on trail and cabin specifics, call the Glacier Ranger District Office, (907) 783-3242.

PRINCE Wm. SOUND-
Whittier to Valdez

In Brief:

KITTIWAKE, McALLISTER CREEK AND MORAINE CABINS

Shoup Bay State Marine Park (Alaska State Parks)

Location: On Shoup Bay, off Port Valdez, in northeast Prince William Sound.

Elevation: Near sea level.

Map: USGS Valdez A7 or Trails Illustrated™, *Prince William Sound — East.*

Access: By boat (8.5 miles from Valdez) or floatplane. By planned trail from Valdez in 1999.

Available: Year-round. A third cabin, Moraine Cabin, is leased to the U.S. Fish and Wildlife Service in summer but can be rented off-season. Call for information.

Sleeps: Eight, the maximum allowed.

Maximum stay: Seven nights per month.

Cost: $50.

In brief: Kittiwake and McAllister Creek cabins, both 16x16-feet, are two of Alaska State Parks' newest cabins. The McAllister Creek Cabin is located on the west side of outer Shoup Bay. Kittiwake Cabin is located on the inner lagoon, accessible by boat with shallow draft at high tide, or (starting in 1999) by a compacted-gravel, wheelchair-accessible trail that will begin outside the bay, toward Valdez. Kittiwake Cabin is wheelchair accessible. Both cabins have oil stoves. A third cabin, Moraine Cabin, is used by bird researchers in summer and may be available to the public off-season. A colony of black-legged kittiwakes nest on an island in Shoup Lake, a tide-influenced lake dotted with ice from the calving Shoup Glacier. In May, when snow still blankets the trails, the avian din is surprisingly loud. Contact Alaska State Parks for more details on boating hazards, access, and overland trail development.

Reservations: DNR Public Information Center (907) 269-8400, or any Alaska State Parks office. The closest to the cabins is the Kenai/Prince William Sound Area Office, (907) 262-5581. Please note, information and cabin availability only via Internet at https://nutmeg.state.ak.us/ixpress/dnr/parks/index.dml.

PRINCE Wm. SOUND-
Whittier to Valdez

In Brief:

JACK BAY CABIN

Chugach National Forest (U.S. Forest Service)

Location: Near the head of Jack Bay, off Valdez Narrows, 10 miles southwest of Valdez.

Elevation: Near sea level.

Map: USGS Valdez A7 and Cordova D7; or Trails Illustrated™, *Prince William Sound — East.*

Access: By floatplane (15 minutes from Valdez, 40 minutes from Cordova) or boat (20 miles from Valdez).

Available: Year-round, but Jack Bay is recommended as a summer, fair-weather anchorage only.

Sleeps: Six (the maximum capacity is eight).

Maximum stay: Seven consecutive nights.

Cost: $35.

In brief: The 12x14-foot log cabin sits on the beach, backed by steep mountains. Wildlife include brown and black bears, mountain goats, river otters, harbor seals, and sea otters. Fish for pink salmon (July and August) in saltwater, or a limited run of silver salmon (late August through September) in the bay and mouth of the streams.

Reservations: Forest Service toll-free reservation center, (877) 444-6777 or via Internet at http://www.reserveusa.com. For info on trail and cabin specifics, call the Cordova Ranger District Office, (907) 424-7661.

PRINCE Wm. SOUND- Whittier to Valdez

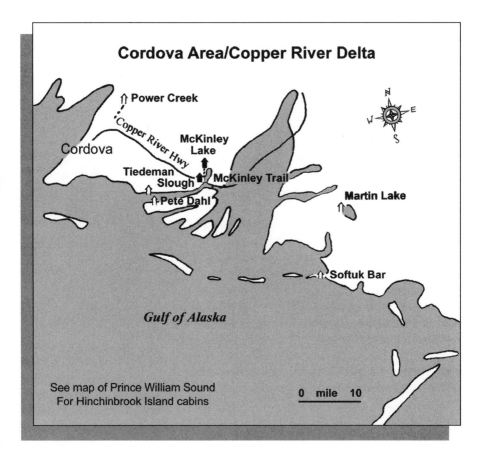

Cordova Area/Copper River Delta

Power Creek

Copper River Hwy

Cordova

McKinley Lake

Tiedeman Slough

McKinley Trail

Pete Dahl

Martin Lake

Softuk Bar

Gulf of Alaska

See map of Prince William Sound
For Hinchinbrook Island cabins

0   mile   10

About Cordova/Copper River Delta

Cordova, a fishing town of about 3,000 in southeast Prince William Sound is unconnected by road to the rest of the state. Visitors come here for a taste of authentic, small-town Alaska: hard-working and friendly people, history, wildlife, and wilderness. Access is by air, or an all-day, scenic ferry ride from Whittier that is a worthwhile trip in itself.

Just beyond town is the vast Copper River Delta, a 700,000-acre wetland wilderness that is one of the world's most productive bird habitats, as well as a nursery for the red salmon that is Cordova's lifeblood. Viewed from the air, the delta is a seeminglessly endless arc of blue, green, and milky gray sediment-swollen capillaries, fed by six glacial rivers. It fans out toward the ocean, its margins as fluid as the tide.

Birders flock here in late April and May to view some of the 20 million (yes, million) shorebirds and waterfowl that pause at the delta to rest and feed. Up to 200,000 birds can pass overhead in a single hour. The fall return migration lasts from July to September. The entire world population of dusky Canada geese and ten percent of the world's trumpeters swans spend their summer in the delta's maze of shallow, fertile channels.

Cordova is also the gateway to 10 Forest Service cabins, several of them located in prime birdwatching and hunting territory on the sloughs and sand bars of the Copper River Flats. Three cabins, including the road-accessible, family-friendly McKinley Trail Cabin, are near town. Another three are located on remote Hinchinbrook Island, one of two

Hook Point beach view

**PRINCE Wm. SOUND-
Cordova to Montague Is.**

large islands that divide Prince William Sound from the rough, open Gulf of Alaska. With such a selection, you can easily plan an entire vacation in this area, alternating days spent enjoying the small-town atmosphere of Cordova, then hiking, boating, and/or flying to public cabins hidden in rainforest, perched on mile-wide beaches, or nestled on the shores of small lakes.

As an added plus, you'll find Cordova to be one of Southcentral Alaska's best cabin-vacation bargains. Some of the Forest Service cabins here cost only $25 a night (compared to $45 for high-use Kenai Peninsula cabins). Floatplane rates are more reasonable here than on the Kenai. There's no need to rent a car. You can be shuttled by van cheaply and efficiently to trailheads on the 49-mile-long Copper River Highway, Cordova's scenic, dead-end thoroughfare. In town, hotel and B&B rates may be steep, but you can chow down on reasonably priced local seafood, including delicious salmon chili and salmon tacos.

Finally, most of these Cordova area cabins aren't as heavily booked as many Kenai Peninsula cabins. You'll still need to plan ahead — especially to coordinate your cabin stays with the ferry schedule, and even more so if you're hoping to visit during the bird migrations. But if you're flexible, you can assemble a satisfying summer adventure that combines some of the best wildlife-watching, beachcombing and berry-picking you'll find anywhere in the state. Don't forget to bring your raingear, though. The area receives 160 inches of precipitation each year.

PRINCE Wm. SOUND-
Cordova to Montague Is.

McKINLEY TRAIL CABIN
Chugach National Forest (U.S. Forest Service)

Snapshot: Seeing Red: A road-accessible, family-friendly rustic cabin, perfect for salmonberry picking, sockeye salmon fishing, and easy rainforest hiking.

Location: Just off Mile 21 of the partially unpaved Copper River Highway.

Elevation: 50 feet.

Map: USGS Cordova B4 or Trails Illustrated™, *Prince William Sound — East.*

Access: By car, van shuttle, or mountain bike along the highway.

Available: Year-round.

Best: May for birdwatching, late June through September for salmon fishing, July for unbelievable berry-picking.

Sleeps: Six on bunks (four would be more comfortable). The maximum is eight.

Maximum stay: Seven consecutive nights.

Cost: $35.

Reservations: Forest Service toll-free reservation center, (877) 444-6777 or via Internet at http://www.reserveusa.com. For info on trail and cabin specifics, call the Cordova Ranger District Office, (907) 424-7661.

Note: It's quite possible (trust me) to confuse the McKinley *Trail* Cabin, just off the road, with the McKinley *Lake* Cabin, 2.2 miles up the trail. Make sure you're heading to the right one.

Facilities: The 12x14-foot cabin is a rustic original, constructed of round logs chinked with moss. A high ceiling, large picture windows on two sides, and skylight panel make this well-lit cabin seem larger than it is —

the perfect family base camp, with a low claustrophobia factor. The decor is a step up, too: the wood stove has an attractive screen, and the outhouse is painted inside with a wildflower motif. The cabin bunks six, with the lower bunks doubling as benches on either side of a dining table. Outside is a large salmonberry-fringed clearing with a picnic table and a fire ring with grill. The large and attractive covered porch, with a bench, provides shelter from the rain. Unlike some Cordova-area cabins, there is no catchment system. Purify water from streams just up the trail, or from the pond downhill of the cabin. Gather dead-and-down wood only; it will be very wet, so consider bringing at least a starter supply, if not all your wood.

Condition: Good to fair (some exterior logs are rotting, with gaps opening).

View and surroundings: The cabin is 250 feet off, and just visible from, the highway. Luckily, this is a "highway" in name only; traffic is not heavy, although the sounds of passing cars are audible from the cabin. The surrounding spruce/hemlock forest is mature, with thick carpets of glowing green moss, ferns, blueberries, and salmonberries every shade of yellow, orange, and red. Skunk cabbage grows to Jurassic proportions next to the tiny streams that trickle across the McKinley Trail, uphill of the

Alaganik Slough

cabin. The vegetation is so thick that my son had no trouble imagining we'd been transported back to "dinosaur time." A tranquil fishing hole (pond) fringed by fireweed and cow parsnip is just across the highway. Alaganik Slough, a turbulent glacial stream, and some interpretive panels are also on the south side of the highway, a 5-minute walk east.

Wildlife sightings: Trumpeter swans, Canada geese, beaver, and black bear. Brown bears are present, especially during peak salmon and berry time; use caution.

Recreation: Hike the McKinley Trail, an easy 2.2 miles to McKinley Lake (site of a second

PRINCE Wm. SOUND-
Cordova to Montague Is.

cabin) or beyond to the abandoned Lucky Strike Mine. Midway along the McKinley Trail, a sharp left fork leads to the more primitive, 1.8 mile-long Pipeline Lakes Trail, a soggy route that passes several good fishing ponds and loops back to the highway, about 0.3 mile west of the McKinley Trail Cabin. Fish for silver salmon (August through September), sockeye salmon (late June through July), and trout in McKinley Lake and its outlet stream, Alaganik Slough. Fish for grayling and cutthroat trout in the Pipeline lakes and roadside ponds.

If you enjoy riding gravel roads, pedal to the cabin from town. (There's no shoulder, but the traffic is fairly light except for tour buses.) From the cabin, you can spend a second day biking along the flat Copper River Highway, watching for wildlife. The highway ends, 28 miles east of the cabin, at the Million Dollar Bridge near Childs Glacier. The buckled bridge, which you can still cross on foot, was closed to cars after the 1964 Earthquake. Childs Glacier is one of Cordova's top attractions — a 300-foot-high wall of ice that calves noisily into the Copper River.

Getting there: Drive or mountain bike to mile 21 of the Copper River Highway. The cabin is just uphill of the parking lot, at the start of the McKinley Lake Trail.

McKINLEY LAKE CABIN

Chugach National Forest (U.S. Forest Service)

Snapshot: Seeing Red, Part II: A roomy lakeside cabin, perfect for salmonberry picking, sockeye salmon fishing, and easy rainforest hiking.

Location: On the western shore of McKinley Lake, north if Mile 21 of the Copper River Highway.

Elevation: 60 feet.

Map: USGS Cordova B4 or Trails Illustrated™, *Prince William Sound — East.*

Access: By foot, along the 2.2-mile McKinley Trail. By boat or canoe up Alaganik Slough (mile 22 of the Copper River Highway) to McKinley Lake; access is limited to high-water periods from mid-June to September. By floatplane, a 10-minute trip from Cordova.

Available: Year-round.

Best: May for birdwatching; late June through September for salmon fishing; July for unbelievable berry-picking.

Sleeps: Eight on bunks, comfortably.

Maximum stay: Seven consecutive nights.

Cost: $35.

Reservations: Forest Service toll-free reservation center, (877) 444-6777 or via Internet at http://www.reserveusa.com. For info on trail and cabin specifics, call the Cordova Ranger District Office, (907) 424-7661.

Note: It's quite possible (believe me) to confuse the McKinley *Lake* Cabin, 2.2 miles up the trail, with the McKinley *Trail* Cabin, just off the road. Make sure you're heading to the right one.

Facilities: The 16x20-foot, insulated, wooden-frame cabin has a cheerful red roof and wraparound porch, overlooking the lake. Inside are bunks to sleep eight, a picnic table and benches, wood stove, counter, and plenty of open floor space. The outhouse is about 80 slippery feet away. A rainwater catchment system on the porch provides easy access to water, and a standing barbecue grill provides incentive to cast your fishing line a few more times. Gather dead-and-down wood only; it will be very wet, so consider bringing at least a starter supply.

Condition: Good.

View and surroundings: The cabin overlooks McKinley Lake, with great views of the water from the wraparound porch and wall of large picture windows facing east. The surrounding spruce/hemlock forest is mature, with thick carpets of glowing green moss, ferns, blueberries, and salmonberries every shade of yellow, orange, and red. Skunk cabbage grows to Jurassic proportions along the tiny streams that trickle across the McKinley Trail. Hiking traffic is heavy. The grass-rimmed lake, backed by mountains, is a natural spot for a break, so it's likely that you will see passersby.

Wildlife sightings: Trumpeter swans, Canada geese, nesting loons on the lake, beaver, and black bear. Brown bears are present, especially during peak salmon and berry time; use caution.

Recreation: Hiking opportunities include continuing north of the McKinley Lake Cabin to the abandoned Lucky Strike mine, or detouring midway along the McKinley Trail (your access trail to the cabin) to the Pipeline Lakes Trail, a soggy, 1.8-mile loop that ends at the Copper River Highway about 0.3 mile west of the McKinley Trail Cabin. You can fish for silver salmon (August through September), sockeye salmon (late June through July), and trout in McKinley Lake and its outlet stream, Alaganik Slough. Fish for grayling and cutthroat trout in the Pipeline lakes. Unfortunately, there's no Forest Service boat at the McKinley Lake Cabin. It's hard to gaze at the lake without wishing you'd brought a canoe. Access by canoe via the Alaganik Slough is possible, but challenging.

Getting there: Drive to mile 21 of the Copper River Highway. The McKinley Lake Trail starts just uphill of the parking lot. You'll immediately pass the McKinley Trail Cabin, and continue for 2.2 gently rolling miles. The first mile or so is gravel, then the trail becomes increasingly muddy and slippery. It's an easy hike along a well-maintained trail, with planks and bridges over stream crossings, but it can be wet. The McKinley Lake Cabin is on the northwest corner of the lake.

To travel by boat or canoe, drive to mile 22 of the Copper River Highway and put in at the Alaganik Slough. Travel upstream to McKinley Lake. Boat access is limited to high-water periods from mid-June to September; the water is swift and cold and it's a challenging trip by canoe against the current.

PRINCE Wm. SOUND-
Cordova to Montague Is.

HOOK POINT CABIN

Chugach National Forest (U.S. Forest Service)

> *"Two great sunny days spent adventuring on the beach — building forts from flotsam, rafts from salvaged buoys, and attempting to 'sail off to the sea'."*
>
> *Hook Point Cabin log.*

Snapshot: Playful seclusion: A remote, A-frame, beachfront cabin on Hinchinbrook Island, facing the open Gulf of Alaska.

Location: On the southern coast of Hinchinbrook Island, just west of Hook Point.

Elevation: Sea level.

Map: USGS Cordova B7 or Trails Illustrated™, *Prince William Sound — East.* Bring tide table.

Access: By wheel plane only, landing on the beach at low tide (15 minutes from Cordova).

Available: Year-round.

Best: May through August for beachcombers and daring surf-waders; fall for hunters.

Sleeps: Two, comfortably, on bunks; two or three more would be comfortable in the loft. A maximum of eight are allowed.

Maximum stay: Seven consecutive nights.

Cost: $35.

Reservations: Forest Service toll-free reservation center, (877) 444-6777 or via Internet at http://www.reserveusa.com. For info on trail and cabin specifics, call the Cordova Ranger District Office, (907) 424-7661.

Facilities: The 16x16-foot cabin has two bunk platforms (double size, but since the walls of the cabin are sloping, it's hard to squeeze more than one adult on each bunk) and a loft. A new wood stove was installed in 1997. There's also an oil stove with oven (#1 stove oil not included), picnic table with benches and a chair, shelves, and counter. A small selection of pans and old blankets have been left behind by cabin-users (not quite enough to be relied upon, however, so bring what you need). Even with plexiglass windows facing north and south, the cabin is dark inside, so bring a lantern or lots of candles.

Outside are a wood shed, narrow porch, rainwater catchment system, and an outhouse affixed with a ship's porthole — perfect for these surroundings. The playful touches don't stop there, though. Many cabin-users have played Robinson Crusoe here over the years, finding objects along the beach and putting them to good use around the cabin. A hammock was constructed of old green netting and driftwood sticks. A large buoy was transformed into a swing near the bluff. More thick rope became a welcome mat. Buoys of all colors and shapes hang from the trees, and a climbing platform and rope wall are next to the cabin. Random bones, skulls, floats, and other flotsam and jetsam are every-

Outhouse at Hook Point Cabin

where. The ambience is nautically rustic and alternately, merry or enjoyably spooky, depending on how hard the wind is blowing.

There is a good supply of dead-and-down wood that can be gathered. If you're lucky, the folks ahead of you will have left you a dry supply in the wood shed. Don't use driftwood in the stove.

Condition: Fair.

View and surroundings: The cabin sits at the edge of a low bluff backed by mossy spruce/hemlock forest and facing a mile-wide sandy beach. A narrow slough ox-bows between the sea and the bluff just in front of the cabin, fed by a tiny stream running parallel to the bluff from the east. The slough swells at high tide and can be difficult to cross without getting wet. A bowler-hat-shaped offshore rock frames the cabin's view to the east. Sea cliffs rise to the west. Surf breaks on the distant horizon, and beyond that is seemingly endless sky. Gulf of Alaska storms pound the shore, delivering driftwood logs by the hundreds and mystery objects ranging from plastic bottles to bits of netting.

Wildlife sightings: Brown bears, Sitka blacktailed deer, river otters, and shorebirds. Also in area: sea otters and seals.

Recreation: Beach hiking here usually turns to beachcombing. The coarse sand seems to extend forever in all directions, especially when the tide is out. Few folks find glass balls from Japan, the ultimate prize, but everyone looks. A wrecked ship is east of Hook Point, according to the visitor log. I was delayed by beachcombing along the way and never made it far enough to check out.

Wading in the ocean or swimming in the slough is possible — it's not as cold as it looks. When the rain is pouring, the forest provides more sheltered meanderings. Limited primitive trails run behind the cabin, but there are plenty of blueberries (July and August) to pick in the area. Wild strawberries no bigger than a pinkie fingernail grow on the sandy bluff. There is fair fishing for pink salmon (early July through August) and silver salmon (late August) in the stream just west of the cabin and in another stream 1 mile east.

Getting there: After you're dropped on the beach by airplane, stay east of the slough as you walk up the beach to the cabin, about 0.5 mile. The cabin itself is hidden among the trees, but a buoy over the bluff marks the spot.You'll cross a very small stream and work your way behind the slough to the bluff in front of the cabin. If in doubt, have your pilot point you in the right direction.

In Brief:
Twelve Southeast Prince William Sound cabins

POWER CREEK CABIN

Chugach National Forest (U.S. Forest Service)

PRINCE Wm. SOUND-Cordova to Montague Is.

Location: 11 miles northeast of Cordova, in Power Creek Valley.
Elevation: 500 feet.

Map: USGS Cordova C5 or Trails Illustrated™, *Prince William Sound — East.*

Access: By foot along a moderately challenging 4.2-mile trail.

Available: Year-round, but hazardous in winter due to avalanches. (According to a Forest Service fact sheet, the cabin can be used in winter if reached from east of the trail.)

Sleeps: Ten, the maximum allowed.

Maximum stay: Seven consecutive nights.

Cost: $25.

In brief: Considering the proximity of this hike-in cabin to Cordova, and its deluxe design, you'd think the Power Creek Cabin would be booked every night in summer. It's not, so take advantage. Built in 1991, the 12x16-foot wooden-frame cabin has a loft (with windows), wood stove, rainwater catchment system, and 8x12-foot covered porch. That's not the typical Pan Abode design, and this isn't a typical setting, either. The cabin is located on a knoll about 100 feet above Power Creek Valley, with views of the basin, surrounding mountains, waterfalls, a hanging glacier, and snow-capped peaks. On the hike in, you'll pass the thundering Ohman Falls at mile 1 of the trail, and all along the way you'll be able to munch salmonberries and blueberries, in season. From the cabin, you can continue hiking on the more challenging Crater Lake Trail, along Mount Eyak Ridge. Wildlife include brown bear (lots of them — use caution), black bear, mountain goat, trumpeter swan, and beaver.

Reservations: Forest Service toll-free reservation center, (877) 444-6777 or via Internet at http://www.reserveusa.com. For info on trail and cabin specifics, call the Cordova Ranger District Office, (907) 424-7661.

Misc.: Shuttle vans in town will transport you to the trailhead, 7 miles north of town. See Appendix 2 or contact the Cordova Chamber of Commerce.

In Brief:

TIEDEMAN SLOUGH AND PETE DAHL CABINS

Chugach National Forest (U.S. Forest Service)

Location: On the south bank of Tiedeman Slough, and on the south bank of Pete Dahl Cutoff Slough, respectively, off Alaganik Slough, southeast of Cordova.

Elevation: Near sea level.

Map: USGS Cordova B4 or Trails Illustrated™, *Prince William Sound — East.*

Access: At high tide only by floatplane (10 minutes from Cordova) or jet-

PRINCE Wm. SOUND-
Cordova to Montague Is.

boat. Smaller motorized boats or canoes may have difficulty maneuvering in the swift currents and shallow depths of Alaganik Slough. The boat launch is located at the end of Alaganik Road, off mile 17 of the Copper River Highway.

Available: Year-round for both cabins, except about April through August, when the Pete Dahl Cabin is used by bird researchers.

Sleeps: Six (the maximum is eight).

Maximum stay: Seven consecutive nights.

Cost: $25.

In brief: Both secluded, 12x14-foot cabins have oil stoves with ovens (#1 stove oil not included) and rainwater catchment systems. They're located across Alaganik Slough from each other, in flat, delta wetlands, surrounded by high grasses, alders, and ponds. This is prime birdwatching territory, so much so that researchers use the Pete Dahl Cabin in late spring and summer, when millions of birds pass through the Copper River Delta. Bring hip waders and/or a boat to access mile-long stretches of mudflats along the edge of the delta, where birds congregate. Waterfowl in the area include dusky Canada geese, mallard, pintail, green-winged teal, gadwall, widgeon, and shoveler. Other wildlife include brown bears, beavers, moose, coyotes, and river otters.

Reservations: Forest Service toll-free reservation center, (877) 444-6777 or via Internet at http://www.reserveusa.com. For info on trail and cabin specifics, call the Cordova Ranger District Office, (907) 424-7661.

In Brief:

MARTIN LAKE CABIN

Chugach National Forest (U.S. Forest Service)

Location: On the west shore of Martin Lake, 42 miles southeast of Cordova.

Elevation: 70 feet.

Map: USGS Cordova B2 or Trails Illustrated™, *Prince William Sound — East.*

Access: By floatplane, 30 minutes from Cordova.

Available: Year-round, but lake is frozen from late November to early May.

Sleeps: Six (the maximum is eight).

Maximum stay: Seven consecutive nights. During the high-use period from late August through late September, only one reservation per person is accepted.

Cost: $35.

In brief: The 12x14-foot log cabin has an oil stove with oven (#1 stove oil not included), covered meat rack, and rowboat. The cabin is 150 feet from the lake with mountains rising sharply behind it, with views of the Martin River Valley. Wildlife include black and brown bears, moose, mountain goats, wolves, coyotes, and river otters. Fishing is good for lake trout, Dolly Varden, sockeye salmon (mid-June through July), and silver salmon (August and September) in Martin Lake and Martin River.

Reservations: Forest Service toll-free reservation center, (877) 444-6777 or via Internet at http://www.reserveusa.com. For info on trail and cabin specifics, call the Cordova Ranger District Office, (907) 424-7661.

In Brief:
SOFTUK BAR CABIN
Chugach National Forest (U.S. Forest Service)

Location: On the outside beach of Softuk Bar, on the Gulf of Alaska, 55 miles southeast of Cordova.

Elevation: Sea level.

Map: USGS Cordova A2 or Trails Illustrated™, *Prince William Sound — East.*

Access: By wheel plane at low tide only (25 minutes from Cordova).

Available: Year-round.

Sleeps: Six (the maximum is eight).

Maximum stay: Seven consecutive nights.

Cost: $25.

In brief: The 12x14-foot cabin has a wood stove and oil stove with oven (#1 stove oil not included), and a rainwater catchment system. It sits 120 feet from the sandy beach, backed by alder and spruce, with good views of the ocean. The area offers clamming for razor clams at low tide, hiking along an old road to the abandoned townsite of Katalla, and strawberry picking in late June. Wildlife-watchers may spot gray whales in April, hugging the shoreline en route to their summer grounds, as well as sea otters, harbor seals, and Steller sea lions. This is another good base camp for watching the Copper River Delta bird migrations in spring.

Reservations: Forest Service toll-free reservation center, (877) 444-6777 or via Internet at http://www.reserveusa.com. For info on trail and cabin specifics, call the Cordova Ranger District Office, (907) 424-7661.

PRINCE Wm. SOUND-
Cordova to Montague Is.

In Brief:

SHELTER BAY CABIN

Chugach National Forest (U.S. Forest Service)

Location: On the southwest shore of Shelter Bay on Hinchinbrook Island, southwest of Cordova.

Elevation: Near sea level.

Map: USGS Cordova B8 or Trails Illustrated™, *Prince William Sound — East.*

Access: By boat at high tide (11 feet or higher; boat must have a draft of no more than 4 feet); or by floatplane (best access at high tide); or by wheel plane on landing strip 0.2 mile north of cabin.

Available: Year-round, but use caution in winter when access is by floatplane; surface ice may form on bay.

Sleeps: Six (the maximum is eight).

Maximum stay: Seven consecutive nights. Three consecutive days during the high-use period in August.

Cost: $35.

In brief: The rustic and attractive 12x20-foot cabin has a 8x12-foot, covered front porch, wood stove and oil stove (#1 stove oil not included), and a rainwater catchment system. It overlooks the bay, surrounded by scattered trees, shrubs, grasses, and wildflowers. The area offers beachcombing and hiking along the shore, and fishing for pink and silver salmon. Bring a kayak or dinghy to explore Shelter Bay. High winds are common. Wildlife include brown bears, Sitka blacktailed deer, sea otters, seals, and waterfowl.

Reservations: Forest Service toll-free reservation center, (877) 444-6777 or via Internet at http://www.reserveusa.com. For info on trail and cabin specifics, call the Cordova Ranger District Office, (907) 424-7661.

PRINCE Wm. SOUND-
Cordova to Montague Is.

In Brief:

DOUBLE BAY CABIN

Chugach National Forest (U.S. Forest Service)

Location: On east side of Double Bay, on north shore of Hinchinbrook Island, southwest of Cordova.
Elevation: 25 feet.
Map: USGS Cordova B7 or Trails Illustrated™, *Prince William Sound — East.*
Access: At high tide by boat (35 miles from Cordova) or floatplane (20 minutes from Cordova). The bay goes dry at low tide. At high tide anchor in the entrance between the point on the west and large island on the east.
Available: Year-round.
Sleeps: Six (the maximum is eight).
Maximum stay: Seven consecutive nights.
Cost: $35.
In brief: The 12x14-foot log cabin has a wood stove and oil stove with oven (#1 stove oil not included), a covered meat rack, and rainwater catchment system. It is located on muskeg, surrounded by wet terrain that can be hiked with rubber boots. Bring a kayak or dinghy to explore the shallow waters and convoluted shorelines of Double and Anderson bays. Fish for abundant pink salmon (July through mid-August) or a small run of silver salmon (early to mid-August). Wildlife include brown bears and Sitka blacktailed deer.
Reservations: Forest Service toll-free reservation center, (877) 444-6777 or via Internet at http://www.reserveusa.com. For info on trail and cabin specifics, call the Cordova Ranger District Office, (907) 424-7661.

In Brief:

PORT CHALMERS CABIN

Chugach National Forest (U.S. Forest Service)

Location: On southern end of Port Chalmers, on the northwest side of Montague Island.
Elevation: Near sea level.
Map: USGS Seward A1 or Trails Illustrated™, *Prince William Sound —*

PRINCE Wm. SOUND-
Cordova to Montague Is.

East.

Access: By floatplane (best at high tide), 40 minutes from Cordova or 60 minutes from Seward.

Available: Year-round.

Sleeps: Six (the maximum is eight).

Maximum stay: Seven consecutive nights.

Cost: $35.

In brief: The 12x14-foot cabin has a wood stove and oil stove (#1 stove oil not included), and a rainwater catchment system. It sits on the beach with a good view across Port Chalmers to the mountains of Montague Island, surrounded by spruce/hemlock forest. At low tide, a hiker can walk around the bay. This is a good cabin for wildlife-watching. Sea life include whales, porpoises, sea lions, and sea otters in Montague Strait. Breeding colonies of black-legged kittiwakes and sea lions inhabit The Needle, located 15 miles southwest of Port Chalmers and accessible by larger boats only. Sitka blacktailed deer and brown bears are found inland. Anglers can fish for Dolly Varden and cutthroat trout in the Chalmers River, and silver salmon (August to early September) and more abundant pink salmon (August) in the bay or in Chalmers River.

Reservations: Forest Service toll-free reservation center, (877) 444-6777 or via Internet at http://www.reserveusa.com. For info on trail and cabin specifics, call the Cordova Ranger District Office, (907) 424-7661.

In Brief:

LOG JAM BAY AND NELLIE MARTIN RIVER CABINS

Chugach National Forest (U.S. Forest Service)

Location: Log Jam Bay Cabin is on the northeast end of Stump Lake. Nellie Martin River Cabin is at the mouth of Nellie Martin River, on the south shore of Patton Bay. Both cabins sit on the southern end of Montague Island facing the Gulf of Alaska, about 5 air miles apart.

Elevation: Near sea level.

Map: USGS Blying Sound D1 and D2; or Trails Illustrated™, *Prince William Sound — East.*

Access: By air, 45 minutes from Cordova; 45 minutes from Seward; 80 minutes from Anchorage. To reach Log Jam Bay Cabin, floatplanes land on Stump Lake. (Use caution; logs and stumps may be near the surface and the lake is frozen from mid-November to mid-April.) Wheel-plane

PRINCE Wm. SOUND- Cordova to Montague Is.

access is on the beach at low tide. To reach Nellie Martin River Cabin, wheel planes land on the beach at low tide, 0.5 mile from the cabin. There is no boat access to either cabin due to high surf and unprotected anchorages.

Available: Year-round.

Sleeps: Six (the maximum is eight).

Maximum stay: Seven consecutive nights.

Cost: $35.

In brief: The 12x14-foot log cabins have wood stoves and oil stoves with ovens (#1 stove oil not included), and rainwater catchment systems. Both are used primarily by deer hunters and anglers, although beach-combers and wildlife-watchers can come here for a unique Gulf of Alaska, island experience. The Log Jam Bay Cabin sits 0.5 mile inland from the ocean, on the shore of Stump Lake, surrounded by muskeg and spruce/hemlock forest. A short, wet hike (bring rubber boots) leads to open beaches, where miles of hiking and beachcombing are possible. Fishing is fair for cutthroat trout, Dolly Varden, and some silver salmon in the lake. Pink salmon (mid-August) are best fished at the lake outlet or between the ocean and the lake.

The more popular Nellie Martin River Cabin sits in a clearing near the bank of the river, an area frequently congested with silver salmon anglers. Fishing in the river is best for silvers (mid-August through mid-September) though Dolly Varden and pink salmon (mid-August) can also be caught.

Wildlife in both cabin areas include sea otters, Steller sea lions, harbor seals, waterfowl, and Sitka blacktailed deer. Montague Island has been closed to brown bear hunting and the local population has become bolder in the last few years, a ranger reports. Bears have broken into the Log Jam and Nellie Martin River cabins repeatedly. Use caution, close the shutters at the end of your stay, and leave no food or deer carcasses in or near the cabin.

Reservations: Forest Service toll-free reservation center, (877) 444-6777 or via Internet at http://www.reserveusa.com. For info on trail and cabin specifics, call the Cordova Ranger District Office, (907) 424-7661.

PRINCE Wm. SOUND-
Cordova to Montague Is.

In Brief:

SAN JUAN BAY CABIN

Chugach National Forest (U.S. Forest Service)

Location: On San Juan Bay, on the southwest end of Montague Island.
Elevation: Near sea level.
Map: USGS Blying Sound D3 or Trails Illustrated™, *Prince William Sound — East.*
Access: By wheel plane, landing on the beach at low tide (60 minutes from Cordova, 40 minutes from Seward). Expect to walk 0.25 mile from the landing site and ford a stream that may be difficult to cross after heavy rains or at high tide. No landing in the bay by boat or floatplane due to high surf.
Available: Year-round.
Sleeps: Six (the maximum is eight).
Maximum stay: Seven consecutive nights.
Cost: $35.
In brief: The 14x16-foot log cabin has a wood stove and oil stove with oven (#1 stove oil not included). The cabin faces east, overlooking a meadow. Views of the ocean to the west are impeded by a spruce and rock berm. There are numerous dayhikes from the cabin, offering chances to see diverse habitats and wildlife. From the beach, you may spot whales, porpoises, harbor seals, Steller sea lions, and sea lions. A waterfall is an easy 0.25-mile walk south from the cabin. A hike along the ridgeline to the east leads to spectacular views of Montague Island, Prince William Sound, and the Gulf of Alaska. Fishing is good for silver salmon (mid-August through September) in the San Juan River north of the cabin. Brown bear activity has been heavy on south Montague Island. Use caution and do not leave any food or deer carcasses in or near the cabin. A logging haul road is 450 feet behind the cabin. Logging activity on Montague Island is winding down, but you may want to contact the Forest Service for a logging update if you're seeking a secluded cabin experience.
Reservations: Forest Service toll-free reservation center, (877) 444-6777 or via Internet at http://www.reserveusa.com. For info on trail and cabin specifics, call the Cordova Ranger District Office, (907) 424-7661.

PRINCE Wm. SOUND-
Cordova to Montague Is.

In Brief:

BEACH RIVER CABIN

Chugach National Forest (U.S. Forest Service)

Location: 0.2 mile south of Beach River, north of Patton Bay, on Montague Island facing the Gulf of Alaska.

Elevation: Near sea level.

Map: USGS Blying Sound D2 or Trails Illustrated™, *Prince William Sound — East.*

Access: By wheel plane, landing on the beach at low tide only, 0.25 mile from the cabin (40 minutes from Cordova, 45 minutes from Seward). A gravel landing strip 300 feet from the cabin is not maintained and should be attempted by experienced pilots only. Boat access is not possible due to high surf and unprotected anchorages.

Available: Year-round.

Sleeps: Six (the maximum is eight).

Maximum stay: Seven consecutive nights.

Cost: $25.

In brief: The 12x20-foot wooden-frame cabin has a wood stove and oil stove with oven (#1 stove oil not included), and a rainwater catchment system. Long stretches of open beach facing the Gulf of Alaska offer dayhikes and beachcombing. Wildlife include brown bears, Sitka black-tailed deer, Steller sea lions, and sea otters. There is good fishing for silver salmon (mid-August), Dolly Varden (late July to mid-September), and pink salmon (mid-July through August).

Reservations: Forest Service toll-free reservation center, (877) 444-6777 or via Internet at http://www.reserveusa.com. For info on trail and cabin specifics, call the Cordova Ranger District Office, (907) 424-7661.

PRINCE Wm. SOUND-
Cordova to Montague Is.

APPENDIX 1

PUBLIC LAND AGENCIES
AND OTHER PUBLIC CABIN/HUT ORGANIZATIONS

UNITED STATES FOREST SERVICE

Forest Service Reservation Center (through Park-Net, a private contractor)
Toll-free at (877) 444-6777

Chugach National Forest
3301 C. Street, Suite 300
Anchorage, AK 99503
(907) 271-2500

Seward Ranger District
334 Fourth Avenue
Box 390
Seward, AK 99664
(907) 224-3374

Glacier Ranger District
Mile 0.3 Alyeska Highway
Box 129
Girdwood, AK 99587
(907) 783-3242

Cordova Ranger District
612 Second Street
Box 280
Cordova, AK 99574
(907) 424-7661

Another place to obtain fact sheets for Forest Service cabins, plus other public land information:

Alaska Public Lands Information Center (APLIC)
605 West 4th Ave., Suite 105
Anchorage, AK 99501
(907) 271-2737

ALASKA STATE PARKS
(Department of Natural Resources, Division of Parks and Outdoor Recreation)

Department of Natural Resources Public Information Center
3601 C Street, Suite 200
Anchorage, AK 99503
(907) 269-8400

Alaska State Parks Mat-Su Area Office
Finger Lake State Recreation Area
Mile 0.7 Bogard Road
HC 32 Box 6706
Wasilla, AK 99687
(907) 745-3975

Alaska State Parks Kenai Peninsula Area Office
Morgan's Landing, Mile 85 Sterling Highway
Box 1247
Soldotna, AK 99669
(907) 262-5581

Alaska State Parks Kodiak District Office
Ft. Abercrombie SHP
SR Box 3800
Kodiak, AK 99615
(907) 486-6339

Homer Ranger Station — (information, latest conditions only)
Mile 168.5 Sterling Highway
Box 3248
Homer, AK 99603
(907) 235-7024
(Sometimes closed in winter; call the Kenai Peninsula Area Office)

Nancy Lake State Recreation Area Ranger Office
Mile 1.3 Nancy Lake Parkway
Box 10
Willow, AK 99688
(907) 495-6273

Kenai Fjords National Park (National Park Service)

1212 Fourth Avenue
Box 1727
Seward, AK 99664
(907) 224-3175

Kenai National Wildlife Refuge (U.S. Fish and Wildlife Service)

Mile 58 Sterling Highway Visitor Contact Station
Box 2139
Soldotna, AK 99840
(907) 262-7021

Kodiak National Wildlife Refuge (U.S. Fish and Wildlife Service)

1390 Buskin River Road
Kodiak, AK 99615
(907) 487-2600

Eagle River Nature Center

Mile 12, Eagle River Road
32750 Eagle River Road
Eagle River, AK 99577
(907) 694-2108

Mountaineering Club of Alaska

Box 102037
Anchorage, AK 99510
Phone number changes with rotating presidency; best phone
contact is the Alaska Mountaineering and Hiking store at
(907) 272-1811.

APPENDIX 2

TRANSPORTATION

"Today, horizontal rain — playing in the cabin and packing up. Will the plane come? Our kids hope not."

Hook Point Cabin log.

Alaska State Parks provides extensive, regularly updated lists of charters authorized to serve their areas, especially for cabins in Kachemak Bay State Park (contact the Homer Ranger Station) and Shuyak Island State Park (contact the State Parks Kodiak District Office). The National Park Service (Kenai Fjords National Park) provides an abbreviated list. The Forest Service doesn't provide an updated list. You may also contact local chambers of commerce for gateway towns closest to the cabin you're visiting; check the yellow pages (especially for Anchorage air charters); or start your research by contacting some of the charters listed below.

AIR AND BOAT CHARTERS

Anchorage
Air Charters:
Trail Ridge Air
(907) 248-0838

Rust's Flying Service
(907) 243-1595

Cooper Landing
Kenai Lake Air Service
(907) 595-1363

Cordova
Air Charters:
Fishing & Flying
(907) 424-3324

Cordova Air Service
(907) 424-3289

Boat Charters:

Auklet Charter Services
(907) 424-3428

Orca Bay Charters
(907) 424-5777

Other:

Cordova Coastal Outfitters (boat charter, ground transport; boat, canoe, kayak, and mountain-bike rentals)
(907) 424-7424, (800) 357-5145

Northern Nights Inn (shuttle van to trailheads/ airport)
(907) 424-5356

Homer (contact Homer Ranger Station for updated list with prices)

Air Charters:

Bald Mountain Air
(907) 235-7969

Beluga Floatplane Service
(907) 235-8256

Kachemak Air Service
(907) 235-8924

Hughes Floatplane Service
(907) 235-4229

North Wind Aviation
(907) 235-8724

Boat Charters:

St. Augustine Charters
(907) 235-7847

Bay Excursions
(907) 235-7525

Mako's Taxi
(907) 235-9055, 399-4133

Tutka Bay Boats
(907) 235-7166

Tutka Bay Charters
(907) 235-7272

Homer Ocean Charters
(907) 235-6212

Jackolof Ferry Service
(907) 235-2376

Chief's Charters
(907) 235-8983

Kachemak Recreation Services
(907) 235-5464

Smoke Wagon Taxi/ Charter
(907) 399-3455

Bare Bones Charters
(907) 235-4133, 399-4369

Kodiak (note: see also Homer air charters; and contact State Parks Kodiak District Office for an updated list with prices)

Air Charters:

Andrew Airways
(907) 487-2566

Cub Air
(907) 486-5851

Highline Air
(907) 486-5155

Kodiak Air Service
(907) 486-4446

Peninsula Airways
(907) 487-4014

Sea Hawk Air
(907) 486-8282

Uyak Air
(907) 486-3407

Moose Pass (near Seward)

Scenic Mountain Air (air charter)
(907) 224-7277

Palmer

Meekin's Air Service (air charter — Supercub [1 passenger] only)
(907) 745-1626.

Seward

Miller's Landing (boat charter)
(907) 224-5739
The only water taxi/ boat charter for Resurrection Bay cabins. They also rent kayaks and motor boats, and run a campground. One person round-trip shuttle to Derby Cove or Callisto Canyon is $35; to Porcupine or Spruce Glacier is $50. Children under 10 are half-price. Kayaks are $25 extra each (1998 prices). Group rates available. Miller's Landing usually operates during summer season only, but off-season services can be arranged at the captain's discretion.

Air Charters:

Bear Lake Air & Guide Service
(907) 224-5985 or (800) 224-5985

FS Air
(907) 224-5920 or (800) 478-9595

Kenai Air Alaska
(907) 224-3778 or (800) 284-7561

Whittier

Boat Charters:
Sound Eco Adventures
March through November operation; ramp for easier off-loading; sliding scale for smaller parties and greater distances into Prince William Sound.
(907) 472-2312

Lazy Otter Charters   Honey Charters
(907) 345-3775   (907) 472-2493

FERRY (including Whittier to Valdez, Cordova; Homer to Kodiak):

Alaska Marine Highway
(800) 642-0066

TRAIN (including portage to Whittier):

Alaska Railroad
(800) 544-0552

EQUIPMENT RENTAL (canoes, kayaks, & bicycles)

Folding Boat Adventures
Specializes in Feathercraft™ kayak rentals and sales. Will ship folding kayak (single, double, or triple) and accessories anywhere in the country; the longer your trip, the better the daily rate. You pay shipping charges from Seattle, but the overall cost is often less than for Alaska folding-kayak rentals.
(800) 586-9318
http://www.foldingkayak.com

Cordova Coastal Outfitters (boat, canoe, kayak, and mountain-bike rentals)
(907) 424-7424, (800) 357-5145

Miller's Landing in Seward (boat and kayak rentals)
(907) 224-5739

Mountain Bike Alaska
Daily bike rentals and classes at the Hope trailhead of the Resurrection Pass Trail
(907) 230-2203

Tippecanoe (on-site canoe rentals for Nancy Lake State Recreation Area)
(907) 495-6688

Other Helpful Phone Numbers

ALASKA DEPARTMENT OF FISH AND GAME

(Information on fishing and hunting licenses, and regulations, which change yearly.)
(907) 267-2898
http://www.adfg.state.ak.us

WEATHER INFORMATION

Anchorage weather recorded forecast (907) 936-2525
National Weather Service (907) 266-5105

CHAMBERS OF COMMERCE / VISITOR CENTERS

Anchorage Chamber of Commerce
(907) 272-7588
Anchorage Convention and Visitor Center
(907) 274-3531

Cordova
(907) 424-7260

Homer
(907) 235-5300

Kodiak
(907) 486-5557

Seward
(907) 224-3094, 224-8051

COMMERCIAL MAP COMPANIES

Trails Illustrated™
Box 4357
Evergreen, CO 80437-4357
(303) 670-3457 or (800) 962-1643

APPENDIX 3

RECOMMENDED READING

I've already made recommendations for entertaining reading in the introduction pages to this guidebook. Additionally, here are two guidebooks every Alaska hiker should own:

Littlepage, Dean. *Hiking Alaska*. Falcon Press, 1997.

Nienhueser, Helen and John Wolfe, Jr. *55 Ways to the Wilderness in Southcentral Alaska*. Mountaineers, 1994.

INDEX

Author note

Brian Lax

Andromeda Romano-Lax is the author of *Walking Southeast Alaska* and *Sea Kayaking in Baja*, both published by Wilderness Press. She lives in Anchorage, Alaska, with her husband, Brian, and children, Aryeh and Tziporah. An avid sea kayaker, hiker, and cabin-user, Andromeda still can't split wood properly, though she intends to learn.

"Come Aboard"
to explore southeast Alaska

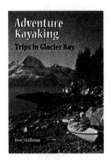

Adventure Kayaking: Trips in Glacier Bay
DON SKILLMAN

Enjoy the deep blue glacial waters of Southeast Alaska by paddle! This book covers more than 300 miles of trips in and around Glacier Bay and Glacier Bay National Park.

$12.95
176 pages, 6 x 9
ISBN 0-89997-225-X

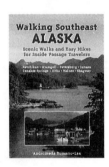

Walking Southeast Alaska
Scenic Walks & Easy Hikes for Inside Passage Travelers

ANDROMEDA ROMANO-LAX

Explore the Alaskan panhandle, a land of small, pedestrian-friendly ports along the "Inside Passage." Forty walks and hikes are described, as well as historical, cultural and natural points of interest.

$13.95
192 pages, 6 x 9
ISBN 0-89997-208-X

"Real" Estate –
from "cabins" to "fire lookouts"

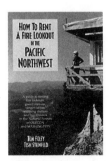

How to Rent a Fire Lookout in the Pacific Northwest
TOM FOLEY & TISH STEINFELD

You can now rent many of the fire lookouts, ranger cabins, guard stations and bunkhouses in the magnificent national forests of the Pacific Northwest. Some of these structures rent for as little as $20 per night, and many are surrounded by the wonderful wilderness areas of Oregon and Washington.

$12.95
224 pages, 5 1/2 x 8 1/2
ISBN 0-89997-195-4